Library
Davidson College

An Artillery Officer in The Mexican War

1846-7

GENERAL ROBERT ANDERSON
From a miniature

An Artillery Officer in The Mexican War

1846-7

Letters of Robert Anderson
Captain 3rd Artillery, U. S. A.

With a Prefatory Word by His Daughter
Eba Anderson Lawton

With 21 Illustrations

 BOOKS FOR LIBRARIES PRESS
FREEPORT, NEW YORK

First Published 1911
Reprinted 1971

INTERNATIONAL STANDARD BOOK NUMBER:
0-8369-5642-7

LIBRARY OF CONGRESS CATALOG CARD NUMBER:
74-148870

PRINTED IN THE UNITED STATES OF AMERICA

IN MEMORY OF

MY MOTHER

TO WHOM THESE LETTERS WERE WRITTEN

INTRODUCTION

THE story of the war which was carried on between the United States and Mexico during the years 1846, 1847, and 1848 constitutes an interesting and brilliant chapter in the history of the nation. The record of the campaigns of the little American army makes also a distinctive contribution to the history of war. Since this war was brought to a close, more than half a century has passed. Two generations have come and gone, and the scenes and events of these campaigns now belong to history or to tradition, while the art of war itself has been very materially modified. The deeds of brave men belong, however, to all generations and a record of heroism and of patriotism serves to maintain the noblest impulses of human nature.

The narrative in question falls naturally into three divisions: first, an analysis of the causes of the war, second, an account of the conduct of the campaign, and third, the actual consequences of the war.

"The opening scene of the Mexican War aroused the country to a fever heat by reason of the tragic conditions that surrounded it. The first contention was over a narrow strip of comparatively worthless territory, lying between the Nueces River and the Rio Grande. The acquisition of Texas had led to the necessity of occupying the new boundary on the southwest, and General Zachary Taylor with a portion of our small regular army was sent to check any advance of Mexicans into the lately acquired territory.

"He was met at the Nueces River by General Ampudia, in command of the Mexican forces, who forbade him to cross that river, claiming that the other side was undisputably Mexican territory. This demand General Taylor declined to accede to, and, crossing the Nueces, he proceeded at once to the left bank of the Rio Grande, where he threw up a fieldwork, and placing in it a small garrison, he then moved the main body of his troops to the mouth of the river, for the purpose of bringing up supplies and reinforcements. No sooner had he turned his back, than Ampudia with a large force crossed the Rio Grande, besieged the earthwork afterwards known as Fort Brown, and prepared to dispute General Taylor's return.

"This was the situation that aroused the whole Southern Country, especially the people of New Orleans and Mobile, as these were the points of embarkation for the seat of war. It was feared that the fort would be captured and its garrison massacred, and that General Taylor with his very inferior force might be cut to pieces.

"A hundred thousand men would have embarked at once with their own rifles and shotguns if transportation could have been provided for them. All the cities of the South were the scenes of intense excitement, which was only relieved by the glorious news that was soon to come.

"In the meantime, General Taylor, fully aware of what was going on up the river, prepared to return, raise the siege of Fort Brown, and confront the enemy. His little army was composed of superb material. Years of peace had served to recruit a fine class of men at the comfortable and attractive posts on the Northwestern frontier; the troops included school teachers, lawyers,

Introduction

physicians, and merchants, who had found their several vocations overstocked, or who had been obliged to yield the way to men of more push and energy, and had sought a temporary refuge in the army. A more intelligent body of soldiers could not be found in any army in the world. Each man was a host in himself, and each had a personal ambition to gratify. On the other hand, the Mexicans had become inspired with the idea that, compared with themselves, "the barbarians of the North" were an altogether contemptible lot, and so it was with a good deal of confidence that they undertook to interpose themselves between General Taylor and the little garrison of Fort Brown.

"On a beautiful day of May, 1846, on the now historic field of Palo Alto, the Mexican army was drawn up in line of battle, with the artillery in position, supported by a body of infantry, and flanked by squadrons of cavalry. General Taylor, arriving within sight of this impressive array, quickly formed his marching columns into line, and true to his familiar name of 'Rough and Ready,' gave battle at once.

"The field batteries opened their fire with a quickness that astonished the Mexicans, while their rapid discharge mowed down the infantry as with a scythe. For a time the Mexicans, in spite of the terrible fire, bravely held their ground, and many of our gallant officers and soldiers fell before them; but soon their ranks began to waver, and then 'Old Zack' ordered his cavalry to charge, which they did with a terrible effect. It was too much for the enemy, who broke and fled and who could not be rallied. But the American forces, after the fatiguing march in the sun, were in no condition to pursue them, and the army rested on the field it had so bravely won.

"The next morning found the Mexicans recovering somewhat from their surprise, and with renewed courage taking up another position in the rear of the one they had abandoned, known as Resaca de la Palma. It is unnecessary to enter into details. Suffice it to say that the 9th of May by its signal victory added new lustre to the glory of the 8th. The Mexicans were utterly routed, seeking safety in precipitous flight or death by drowning in the river.

"Fort Brown and its heroic garrison, that had so nobly repelled every assault, was relieved, and a new chaplet of fame had been won for our gallant little army. Subsequently the army crossed the Rio Grande into the enemy's country. The capture of Monterey after a hard fought and bloody battle soon followed. And then came the glorious and surprising victory of Buena Vista where the enemy, commanded by Santa Anna in person, outnumbered our brave soldiers more than four to one, but the latter had become veterans of experience.

"The seat of war was now transferred to the Gulf, where the army and navy united in the siege and capture of Vera Cruz and of the strongly fortified Castle of San Juan d'Uloa that defended the harbor. Then began, under General Winfield Scott, who, true to his name, never lost a battle, the long march for the capitol, the halls of the Montezumas.

"Scott was now to achieve, on the lines followed by the great Cortez four centuries before, the second conquest of Mexico. Cerro Gordo, a marvellously strong position, was turned by strategic skill, and city after city threw open its gates until the victorious columns stood on the summit of the mountain range that overlooked the magnificent valley with the splen-

Introduction

did City of Mexico nestled in the centre. Scott had a mere handful of men compared with the legions that the world's great conquerors had led to battle, and if this army failed there was no retreat, and little hope for reinforcement. Down the mountainsides and into the great valley the army hastened, to the accomplishment of the work before it.

"A city on an island, in a lake, with no approach except by narrow causeways bristling with cannon! The army advanced, but not to the place prepared for them, where a victory would have been next to a defeat, but by a flank movement, executed with military genius, it succeeded in turning the elaborate and formidable fortifications at El Piñon.

"Yet there were battles to be fought, and won, before the prize could be grasped. There was Contreras and Cherubusco, Molino del Rey and Chapultepec, and then the Garrittas bristling with cannon was to be captured. These places all fell in turn, some of them with heavy loss. But what deeds of valor, what heroism, what dauntless courage did that little army exhibit! Scant has been the meed of praise those heroes so dearly earned. Few have been the laurel wreaths upon the graves of those who 'poured their life's blood freely out "pro bono publico."'

"There are few deeds in all the history of war to be compared with the contests of that little army that fought its way step by step to the heart of the great republic of the South, and whose campaigns were followed by the acquisition of the vast treasure house of the continent, from which the world has received more gold and silver than in all time it had before possessed.

"To crown it all we restored to Mexico the country that we had so gallantly won, and we gave also sufficient means to enable the race that had so long neglected its opportunities to enter on a career of industry, of usefulness, and of honor. A full measure of prosperity, and a national security never before experienced, have been the result. No one is now more gladly welcomed or more honored in Mexico than an American.

"To us as a nation, the Mexican War was a grand lesson of patriotism and a glorious exhibition of patriotic valor.

"This brief outline of the campaign enables us to understand the part taken in it by Anderson. Nothing could have given him more poignant distress than the decision made by the War Department which designated his company among those that were to garrison the forts on the seaboard.

"Notwithstanding the requirements for troops in Mexico, it was, of course, not practicable to leave the home stations entirely without garrisons. Anderson's company was ordered from Fort Moultrie first to Fort Marion, and then to Fort Brook. This did not meet with the approbation of the young captain of artillery who had left the staff for the line as a shorter road to active service, and he was well pleased when after a second application to the Adjutant-General, orders came for Company 'G' to embark for the seat of war. Palo Alto, Resaca, and Monterey had already crowned the little army with glory, and Genl. Scott was busy with the organization of his army for invasion by way of Vera Cruz."[1]

This résumé of the inception and history of the Mexican War leads us up to the date of the beginning of Captain Anderson's letters to his wife.

These letters are given without comment or notes.

[1] From an unpublished Life of General Anderson by General Viele.

Introduction

All matters of a personal character are eliminated, as this book has been planned to present the events of the Mexican War in which he took part, and not those of his intimate home life.

The letters of the young Captain present a vivid and valuable picture of the campaign. If we compare these pages with other narratives of the campaign, we may be struck with a similarity of wording. Anderson mentions several persons who applied to him for memoranda from his Journal and who afterwards published histories of the Mexican War. He also speaks of Colonel Hitchcock, who on the 3rd October "did me the honor to read to me a proposed Introduction to a number of Letters written in the City on the 20th of August, requesting my suggestion of any alterations that might occur to me." On the 4th October he writes his wife that not until the preceding day did he learn that "Genl. Scott had, about the 19th of last November, made application for me to be appointed Asst. Adjt. Genl. with the rank of Major to enable him to select me as Chief of his Staff."

One reading Anderson's letter giving an account of the Battle of Molino del Rey, would hardly realize that *he* was the hero of the day. I quote from a very long article, entitled "Captain Robert Anderson," which appeared in the *New Orleans Delta*, a few sentences, showing the estimate in which his services on that occasion were held. "The gallant Kentuckian, who from the bombardment of Vera Cruz to the brilliant and perilous assault on El-Molino-del-Rey, has been a distinguished actor. . . . We wish to add some particular details of that heroic exploit, assuredly one of the most brilliant as well as bloody of the war, which have reached us from an authentic source. . . . The capture of this point, against such odds, and Captain Anderson's part in it, were pronounced by a gallant and distinguished officer, who bore an important command on that occasion, as one of the most brilliant achievements of the war. . . . The fighting and excitement being over, Capt. Anderson became faint from loss of blood, and he was compelled to lie down,—to rest literally on the bed of honor."

In closing this introduction I wish to draw the attention of my readers to three salient points in Anderson's character, which shine forth clear as the sunshine in these, his private letters to his wife, and which, with his love of country, distinguished him through life: his deep religious feeling, his self-abnegation, and his modesty. Before the battle of El-Molino-del-Rey, he writes, "Should God spare my life, I will resume this letter the earliest moment after Victory." In one of his early letters, January 28, 1847, he speaks of having a memorial signed by the officers for his "hobby"— the founding of a retreat for old soldiers. From 1837 to 1851, he had worked over this plan. He had five bills introduced into Congress, the first in 1840, and the last on March 3, 1851; this was passed by a large majority. He had wished the place to be called the "Soldiers' Retreat," in memory of the Kentucky home of his father, Colonel Richard Clough Anderson, and of his own birthplace. From the *Louisville Times* I quote the following, which, in view of the fact that his right as the Founder of the Home is now generally ignored, speaks better for his unselfishness and self-abnegation than for the gratitude of republics. "The humane sentiment which impelled Major Anderson to urge the establishment of such an institution, and the unceasing and laborious zeal and perseverance with which he has

Introduction

pursued his conception to its final consummation, confer undying honor on him, and form a beautiful appendix to the glory his sword has so gallantly won in fighting the battles of his country." Anderson's letter of February 24th is very characteristic. Col. Gates had selected him as his associate at Tampico. Col. Bankhead told him, "that next to the officers of his own Regiment, he would rather have me with him than any one else." "General Scott said that he wanted me in the trenches with him." Anderson adds, "There is so much in the preceding which would not be written to any one else but yourself as it looks exceedingly like *egotism*, that I hope you will not read, or let it be read by any one."

My noble father will forgive his daughter for making public at this time confidences which were intended only for his wife. She can but feel, however, that after an interval of 64 years, it is fitting that his countrymen should secure a clearer understanding of his character and of his service. It is indeed proper, if only as a matter of historic justice, that after more than half a century of silence, Anderson's fellow-citizens should realize that his action at Fort Sumter was only a logical consummation of a life spent in devotion to his country. The memoir of General Anderson, as presented in his Journals and Correspondence, is to be published shortly by G. P. Putnam's Sons. The preparation of this memoir has been undertaken by his daughter, not only as a task of filial duty, but also for the service of the community and with the conviction that the world will be richer for the record of the lifework of a high-minded and noble Christian patriot.

EBA ANDERSON LAWTON.

NEW YORK, September, 1911.

ILLUSTRATIONS

	PAGE
GENERAL ROBERT ANDERSON . . *Frontispiece*	
From a miniature.	
MAJOR-GENERAL ROBERT PATTERSON . . .	16
GENERAL WINFIELD SCOTT	46
VIEW OF TAMPICO	60
GENERAL TAYLOR	66
VIEW OF MOUNT ORIZABA FROM VERA CRUZ . .	80
From an old photograph	
THE SIEGE OF VERA CRUZ	92
From an engraving of the painting by Powell	
GENERAL SANTA ANNA	106
From a lithograph	
GENERAL WILLIAM JENKINS WORTH . . .	111
From an engraving by J. Sartain, after a daguerreotype	
ROUGH SKETCH OF THE BATTLE-GROUND OF CERRO GORDO—APRIL 18, 1847	138
PANORAMA OF PUEBLA	170

Illustrations

	PAGE
PUEBLA DE LOS ANGELES	176
MEXICAN WATER CARRIERS	188
From a photograph	
SCENE IN A MEXICAN MARKET	204
VIEW OF MOUNT IZTACCIHUATL FROM THE EAST	242
From an old photograph	
THE PYRAMID OF CHOLULA	252
Redrawn from an old print	
MAKING TORTILLAS	262
A VIEW OF POPOCATEPETL FROM PUEBLA	282
From an old photograph	
SCENE AT THE BATTLE OF MOLINO DEL REY	310
From an engraving of the painting by Chappel	
THE BATTLE OF CHAPULTEPEC	314
From an engraving by J. Duthie after the painting by H. Billings	
MEXICO CITY LOOKING SOUTHWEST FROM THE CATHEDRAL	328

FORT BROOKE, FLA.
Dec. 7, 1846.

GENL. R. JONES, Adjt.-Genl.

General:

I have the honor most respectfully and earnestly to solicit orders for "G" Co., 3rd Arty., to report forthwith for duty in the field. The Company, having been raised to a total of 86 by the arrival of the recruits under Lt. Brown, is now ready and desirous to join the Army in Mexico. From conversations with Lt. Brown, I think I may safely promise, that these recruits will, by the time an answer is received to this application, and before they can sail, be pretty well prepared for taking their places in the ranks of the Company. The place of "G" Co., as part of this command, might, I think, be easily and properly filled by one of the companies of the 1st Arty., now being raised at the North. This arrangement, certainly satisfactory to the officers of the 1st Arty., would enable the War Dept. to send to Genl. Taylor's Army, a company excellently well armed and equipped, which contains a respectable proportion of well educated old soldiers, in place of one of raw recruits.

Hoping that a favorable answer may be soon received to this application,

I have the honor to remain,
ROBERT ANDERSON,
Capt. 3rd Arty.

An Artillery Officer in Mexico

FORT BROOK, FLORIDA,
December 28, 1846.

AFTER gazing from the hill-top, near which we separated, until I could see nothing more of the two rapidly receding conveyances which carried away from me my *all*, I returned with a heavy heart to *our* home. About 9 o'clock the poor Major came in and sat with me for a few minutes. Poor father, his afflictions are very heavy; he read me part of a letter from his son at Pensacola to his mother, urging her to come and live with and comfort his father. The letter was a very affecting one, and had it not been for the insanity of John, would probably have started Mrs. W. for Tampa. Of John, the accounts are somewhat favorable; he is in the Asylum,—but his Uncle thinks that the affliction is rather bodily than mental. God grant that he may be right. The Major has been so kind that I could not help giving the substance of his evening's communication. He spoke of our separation with much feeling.

I am employing myself as busily as possible in getting ready. God grant that I may hear before we start of your getting on well. Some person may come in who met you on the road. Be assured that I shall keep a good lookout that no one may come in without my questioning them about you.

Mr. Capron told me this morning that Mrs. Steiner had, he believed, given up the idea of going across the country. She thinks of spending the winter here, and going to Ohio in the spring. I hope for Mrs. Capron's sake that the original intention may be carried out, as she will be very unpleasantly situated at this out of the way place without a protector. Corporal and Mrs. Hannel come to my room every day to make up my bed, sweep the floor, etc. I have seen the Sutler—he will take all of the eatables, etc., I have on hand. I am to send him the cooking utensils, etc., this afternoon. The carpenters are at work to-day on my camp bedstead, and the tailor is botching my jacket and pants—thus you see that I have not been unmindful of your requests.

The papers which I have examined closely give no certain intelligence about our vessel. A barque cleared from New York on the 11th inst. for Tampico. This *may* be our vessel. It is the *Floyd*. I shall write you by the next mail—that is, you may expect to receive another letter from this post, whether I am here on mail day or not, as, if I leave, I shall write you the day we sail. The men seem anxious to go; everything is now ready for the vessel.

I have not mentioned that I have joined the mess at Mr. Allen's—breakfast 8:30, dinner 1, and tea at retreat. We keep country hours, differing slightly from our household arrangements. Let us see how my calculations of your daily journeys agree with the facts. Last night I supposed you camped near Capt. Bradley's, to-night I shall locate you about ten miles beyond Col. Pearson's. I pray God that no accident may occur on your journey, and that you may soon reach home enjoying excellent health. Our prayers will meet, I hope, nightly in Heaven, as we pray for our own family. This thought will comfort my heart.

Here you have on this part of the paper the information I should have given you before we parted. It may be best to sell the articles through Capt. Hanham, if Col. M. does not want them. Do as you think best. Say to Col. M. that Dr. Curry has just informed me that he will deliver to him at Longwood his two mules for $165. One is a very large one, and works kindly in harness anywhere. Mrs. C., he says, has driven him in a buggy. The smaller one, he says, is also an excellent animal. The large mule cost him $140. Their ages he thinks 6 and 8. If an answer be sent at once the mules may be sent by Dr. Steiner or Mrs. Capron's party. Dr. Curry is to be Capt. Sprague's *medico*. And now I'll wish you good-evening till after tea.

6:30. Just returned from tea. Capt. Sprague thinks that you are to-night about fifteen miles beyond Col. Pearson's, and that to-morrow night you will encamp fifteen miles beyond the Withlacoochee. This is a better allowance for your day's travel than I have given. I do not think that you can reach Col. Madison's earlier than Wednesday eve., he imagines that you may reach there on Tuesday. Oh! that this letter could call to you as you enter the mail boat at Palatka and tell you of its being on board for you. It will be on board the same boat all the way to St. Mary's, and you cannot read it till you reach home, nearly four days after your having been almost within arm's reach of it.

I have not paid a visit since you left. I saw everybody in church on Sunday, but spoke to no one but Mrs. Astell—who kindly approached me and asked when I left you and how I left you. I suppose that I ought to go in to see the Astells—I shall probably go nowhere else. I am sorry for poor Mrs. Capron, and hope something may occur to give her a safe and agreeable escort to her friends.

You must not omit telling your father that Col. Madison left your Uncle John my calf about which I wrote him last summer. She is now about 18 months old, of Mr. Clay's best stock, her mother imported by Col. Morgan of Ky. I left her with Col. Hanson subject to my order—intending to have requested you to send for her in the event of my not returning to St. Augustine—but he neglected her, and Col. Madison very kindly and properly took her away. I wish your father would get her while she is young, as I would like him to have her stock on his plantation, and when I get within striking distance I will either want her again or one of her calves.

You see that I introduce all my business affairs—I do this to keep my mind from my lonesomeness, and also under the fear that after I get away from here my mind may be so much occupied that these trifles may escape me. I had intended writing to one of my brothers by this mail, but I must put it off till the next one. When our boxes are shipped from here I shall request Mr. Clark to inform you of it. And now I must bid you good-night. Let us try to be grateful to Him for the mercies with which He blesses us. I shall expect to find a letter from you in the first arrival from New Orleans after I reach Tampico.

FORT BROOK, FLORIDA,
December 29, 1846.

The expected vessel has arrived—she is a brig belonging to the Government, called *John Potter*, which sailed from New York on the 14th inst. having made therefore a very quick passage. We are to commence *loading* in the morning and will sail as soon as possible. This letter in which I propose writing a little every day will give you the time *when*. Lt. Burke, Adjt. of the 1st Arty., came passenger. He accompanies us to Tampico, as he will remain with Maj. Whiting who will be the commander of the Regt. I have been busy to-day sending down our goods and chattels to the Sutler's.

Dec. 30th. I had written thus far last evening, when the Sergt. came in with some papers for me to examine and sign, and I was engaged until some time after tattoo before I finished my labors. To-day we have been getting some of the Company's property on board—the vessel is so far down (below the island) that we work very slowly. In private business I have done pretty well. Mr. Clark has settled with me as far as he can; he has a Mem. of all the articles left, and has given me a copy. He will take a favorable time for selling everything. I have written to Mr. Adger informing him that one tierce, one trunk, and three boxes would be sent to him. I have requested him to keep them in store until he hears from me or from you. The Capt. of the *Potter* thinks we will run over in eight days. He thinks that we have an abundance of provisions. We shall not touch at the Balize.

Mrs. C. has, I hear to-day, decided to accompany Mrs. S. on the *New Orleans* to Baton Rouge Barracks. If I had Mrs. S.'s money I do not think I would ever think of living at barracks whilst separated from my husband. Poor Mrs. C. would, I suppose, have to go to Kamchatka if Mrs. S. goes there, as she has no one to take charge of her. I thank God that you have not been dependent on any of them for anything.

I hope that we may not get off until after the mail comes in, as I may get a line from my wife. What a relief it would give me to know that you had gone on without accident after I left you. It cannot be possible that I am not to hear from you until I reach Tampico, and probably not until after I have been two or three weeks there! God has been so full of mercies and kindnesses towards me and mine that I cherish the belief and hope that when I do hear, the news will be good.

My camp bedstead and everything is now ready. I have nothing to do but to pack. I have decided not to take sheets. Good-night.

ON BOARD THE "JOHN POTTER,"
FORT BROOK, FLORIDA,
Thursday, December 31, 1846.

This has been a busy day. It being muster day, I have of course had writing to attend to, and we have been engaged sending our stores on board. The distance by the channel to the position of the brig is about nine miles. My private affairs have not been neglected, the cow having been sold at a loss of only one sixth. The carpenters and sail-makers have finished their work for the Company, and all are now ready to start as soon as we can get on board. The chances are now that we cannot leave before Saturday or perhaps Sunday. To-morrow night's mail may bring a letter from you; oh, how sincerely do I hope it may if it be only two lines to say you are well.

Friday Night, January 1, 1847.

The beginning of a New Year. God grant that

it may bring happiness to us—that we may this year so live as to thank our Heavenly Father for the blessings it brought. Not a line to-night from you—this is as I anticipated; my reason told me it would be so; hope whispered that I might hear.

I send a sweet letter to you from Mrs. Clinch. It was written before the receipt of my letter announcing my having received orders. No other letter came but a very affectionate one from William with a short one from his son Tom. I must answer them to-night as it is probable that I shall be on board to-morrow night. Everything or rather nearly everything is now done. It is proposed to get the men on board to-morrow, and early the next day, that we may sail on Sunday. This may therefore be the last night I shall sleep in my old quarters. Although you are gone, yet there is something a little touched with mournfulness in the idea of my going out of the old rooms not to return into them again.

To-day I have packed and had the Company's desk boxed and commenced packing my mess chest. I find that I have plenty of room. I think even of taking the soup digester with me. Good soup would not be amiss even at Tampico. Some of the ladies expected, I am told, New Year's calls. I have been so much engaged that had I been ever so much inclined, I could not have gone round. Without anything to do, my inclination would have kept me at home. As my red ink is boxed up, I must attempt crossing with this. To-morrow you will perhaps leave Longwood.

Saturday Night, January 2, 1847.

Here I am on board our good brig; nearly all the men are down; to-morrow morning we shall sail as soon as the remainder (about twenty) are on board with the Major and other officers. I preferred coming down to-day with the Command, so as to give Lt. Capron as much time with his poor wife as possible. I called to say good-bye to her, and she was very much affected. I called at Mr. Astell's but they were at tea. I did not have time to call at the Doctor's, every moment of my time being taken up. Capt. Sprague received a long letter from Mr. Judd. He writes from Tampico, and says that he has very pleasant quarters there. Col. Gates and Lt. Col. Belton are there. We expect to find Genl. Scott there with a large force, as the papers are filled with accounts of the movements of Volunteers towards that place. There was a rumor to-day of Col. Andrews being on his way—if so, you must have met him. I hope if he comes in to-night that he will come down to-morrow.

I am exceedingly anxious to hear from you, or to see some person who has met you. I fear, however, that I shall have to sail without this last satisfaction. You are, I suppose, on the road from Col. M.'s to Palatka. God grant that you may reach home in good health, and that you, finding how much joy you impart to others, may soon begin to look upon the bright side of things. I shall write you by every opportunity, but you must not worry if you do not receive a letter every mail, as opportunities *may* not occur so often even as that. As the Postmaster is to be on board to-morrow, I shall not close this letter to-night.

On Board the "John Potter,"
Sunday Morning, January 3, 1847.

The last boat load of the Command is now coming, and the Capt. of the brig has gone in his boat to bring the rest of the officers. This looks like moving. I had thought until last night that I was about taking my departure from the United States, but the Capt. says that he took papers from New York exactly as if he were going from one port to another in the United States. Indeed the march of Democracy is progressive.

How different to-day from the Sundays when we were together—then all quiet, now all bustle and confusion. The officers do very well on board, but the accommodations are not sufficient for the number of men. We have a very comfortable, airy, and commodious cabin on deck, they have lines of berths extending the length of the hold, badly lighted and scarcely ventilated at all. Fortunate will it be for the men if our trip is short. The nights are so pleasant that many of them will sleep on deck.

Major Whiting received a letter from his wife by yesterday's mail. She had heard of his orders and writes to him cheerfully: tells him that the Power who has thus far preserved them will continue his protection; that he must not be worried about her; that she and the children will get on very well. But the best of her news is about their son, whose condition is favorably mentioned. Do not forget to mention to your father that the *Intelligencer* and *Courier* are still probably sent to Charleston; they had better be discontinued; it is useless to send them to me as I shall never get them.

We take as passengers out with us from Tampa Bay —the Clerk of the Court, Mr. Wan, and the brother of the Postmaster. They go to Mexico to seek their fortunes—anything for a change. The United States will be depopulated by their conquests. Each State, as it is conquered, will be considered the most desirable part of the world. Florida is no longer the land of promise. I have directed Mr. Clark to forward the proceeds of the sale of the articles left with him direct to you. I gave our poultry and some few things away. It was useless to take many things with me, and hardly worth while to send others to sell. Having now nearly reached the bottom of the page, and finished rewriting the whole, I must now bid you adieu.

BRIG "JOHN POTTER,"
January 25, 1847.

Here we are at anchor off the bar at Tampico, and the steamboat is now approaching to tow us to town. Hoping that an opportunity may present itself for sending this letter, I have determined to attempt writing, though I fear from the rocking of the boat, and the confusion of all on board, that my scrawl will be illegible. We have had two or three pretty severe storms, but preserved by the Father of all mercies, we are now at our destined port. To-morrow week we were where we *now* are, and were blown off by a Norther. We are reduced to a short allowance of provisions and water, so that it is well for us that we are to get in to-day.

You do not know how full my heart has been constantly of you. You will be, I know, wretched at not hearing from me,—will think that we are lost. Place your confidence, I beseech you, in God who has showered so many blessings on us since our destinies have been united. He has protected both of us in many dangers, and will not forsake us unless we forget Him.

We have a Mexican subject on board, but as he does not speak a word of English, and we have no one on board who speaks Spanish, we can get *very* little in-

In Mexico

formation from him. We do not know whether Genl. Scott is at Tampico or not. As the steamer is now alongside, I will stop writing a few moments, and finish as we go up the river.

We are now safely over the bar, and a small boat is on the point of leaving us for the *Ellen and Clara* which is to sail to New Orleans in the morning. I shall send this scrawl as I may not have an opportunity of writing again. A steamer is now coming down from Tampico to tow us up—we having sent the one that brought us over the bar to tow a bark, which is said to have troops on board. As I shall not have an opportunity of sending this off I will take it up to Tampico with me.

Off Tampico. Finding that the letter I have written since we anchored is but little better written than this, I think I shall send this. The next time I write, I hope that my hand and head will both have recovered from the effects of sea-sickness. I am truly rejoiced that you had no sea voyage to take to reach home. All on board, except Major Whiting, suffered very much; the Major has improved very much. He looks much better than he did at Tampa Bay.

I hope to find a letter from you in the first mail from New Orleans. Were it not that I am exceedingly desirous you should hear from me by the earliest opportunity, I would not send you this letter as really I am ashamed of my writing. But as I am writing, or rather attempting to write, on a ship's table, and at this time with a very bad light, and as it is probable that I should not write any better to-morrow, I *will* and *must* send this. You can make out what I mean. Finding that I will have a little time for writing a few lines in the morning, I will now bid you good-night.

TAMPICO, January 26th, 9 P.M.

Finding that the mail would not leave until six o'clock to-morrow, I have kept this letter open that I might give you the last news. I have attended to-day to landing the Company, etc., and to getting them made comfortable in the quarters. To-morrow I shall move them into other quarters where I am to remain till we leave here. We shall be very comfortable. I am now writing at Lt. Austine's table. Col. Gates has just left the room to allow my finishing my letter. He has been talking a great deal about his wife and child. From his own account it seems to me that the Col. depended too much on himself in attending to his child. He says that Mrs. Gates became strongly attached to the little boy.

To-day I have been looking around the town—it is not a Mexican or Spanish town in its construction. Most of the good houses being constructed by English or German residents, the walls are very thick and surrounding courtyards. Until the Volunteers came, the citizens appeared inclined to be sociable. But now many have left, and gone into the interior. Genl. Whitman's Brigade arrived within ten miles of camp, and is there encamped. I have seen many of my old army friends here to-day. Capt. Myers will sleep in the same room with me to-night. I have not seen him yet. Mr. Brown, whom I saw this morning, expresses himself anxious to join me. He will, I expect, be assigned to-morrow. Lt. Andrews has been assigned to the Company temporarily to-day. Mr. Judd, tell Mary, looks exceedingly fierce with his moustachios. He does not shave at all—I wonder that he is not alarmed at his own likeness in the glass. I must now bid you farewell for the present, as I know Col. Gates keeps early hours for retiring, and I fear that I am keeping him up. No news from Genl. Scott—he is daily expected. Maj. McCall inquired very kindly after Genl. Clinch to-day.

BRIG "JOHN POTTER," TAMPICO,
January 25, 1847.

We are here at last, and fearing that you may have heard through the newspapers of our reported distress for want of provisions, etc., which we find prevailing here, I hasten to write the first moment after our anchoring. We have had two severe storms, one very severe, but Almighty God, who has ever watchfully preserved me, has brought us into safety, and we are now so grateful that we think lightly of the dangers we have passed. I can never forget it, as I was aware at the time of the danger we were in, and placed my reliance on the only Power which could save us.

The first person who came on board to see me was Adjt. Austine; he gave me all the news. Lts. Steptoe and Judd have returned to this place from an expedition about fifty miles to the north a few days since. There are now three companies of the 3rd Arty. here quartered in the city—the Company I bring makes the third. You see that I am fortunate again, as the barracks are excellent. Poor Maj. Whiting is to go into camp—joining Lt. Capron's Company to three others already here. Genl. Patterson arrived yesterday with his Division. Our two companies raise the force now here to a fraction over 7000 men—a very respectable force. Genl. Worth is reported to be on his way with all the regulars from the Monterey Army; Genl. Twiggs came with Genl. Patterson; Genl.

Shields was here, but left yesterday for old Tampico —a few miles hence.

Genl. Taylor had advanced as far as Victoria, and was ordered back to Saltillo or Monterey. Genl. Scott is expected in about a week. What we are then to do, no one knows. Rumor says that the City of Vera Cruz is to be taken—that Genl. Taylor is to advance towards San Luis de Potosi, to keep Santa Anna in check, whilst Genl. Scott takes Vera Cruz—the *invincible* Castle of San Juan d'Ulua will not be attacked. When the city is taken, it must fall, as our Navy will cut off their supplies by sea, and the Army in possession of Vera Cruz will prevent succor by land. An English gentleman who arrived from Vera Cruz yesterday reports that there are not more than 4000 troops in Vera Cruz, and that if the city is approached by an army of 5000 or 6000 American troops, it will surrender without a struggle.

Of Mexican news the reports are contradictory; one is that the Congress consents to renewing diplomatic relations with our Govt. by a vote of 300 to 250; another report, that they decide *against* renewing these relations, by that vote. It is stated, however, that the Mexican Congress have enacted a law requiring the priesthood to assist the Govt. with money—and this law will produce a revolution which may lead to peace. After I get on shore I will write you a more connected letter than this—I merely give you the floating rumors in this.

Our cousin Saml. Anderson came to see me soon after we anchored. He looks very well and says that all are delighted with their position here; the market is very good—an abundant supply of everything, and at very reasonable rates. What think you of teal ducks fifty cents per dozen!—common ducks twelve and one-half cents a pair. These were the prices asked when the troops first came here—now they are a little higher. The town, in which I have not yet been, looks very well from our boat. The streets are well paved, and the houses well built—the large have courtyards enclosed by them. A splendid house is being fitted up for Genl. Scott.

Capt. P. is here; he is Sutler and Postmaster; if he keeps steady, he will soon make a fortune. His nephew, David Wells, arrived yesterday. Col. Gates is, I am told, looking very well. Drs. Hawkins and McLean are both here. Lt. H. Brown is also here. Brig. Genl. Shields has attached him to his Staff. Adjt. Austine told me that Col. Gates would at once apply for Mr. Brown to be assigned to my Company. I would be very happy to have Lt. B. again. We are fortunate in getting all the men here in pretty good health. Corp. Hannel has a slight touch of the jaundice.

One German sang every mild night of our passage over. I find the band of the 3rd Arty. here, also the bands of three other Regts. They alternate in playing on the Plaza every night. Your first letter will, I hope, give me full news. What would I not give to be one half hour with you! I will, however, apply myself closely to my duties, and do all that in me lies to bring this war to a close.

Do always write me fully; your letters may be sent to me, Tampico, Mexico, via New Orleans. As this is now a United States city, it will not be necessary to pay the postage on your letters. My heart leaped with pride when I saw the United States flag flying over the City of Tampico, but that pride was soon checked when I thought of the power of the United States, and the weakness of Mexico. God grant that peace may soon be effected. This letter is so badly written that I will not attempt to cross it. I pray you to burn it as soon as you have read it.

No. 1. TAMPICO, MEXICO,
January 27, 1847.

I moved to-day, Wednesday, 27th of Jany., into very good quarters near the principal Plaza of the City. I hope that the Company will soon get on their land legs, and become again decent to be looked upon. I paid my respects to-day to Brig. Genl. Patterson—found him very affable and gentlemanly. He thinks that we have a sufficient force now assembled in and near the City to take Vera Cruz, and is very anxiously expecting Genl. Scott daily. Genl. Worth is, he says, on his way to this place.

We have already more rank than I ever saw together— Major Genl. Patterson, Brig. Generals Twiggs, Pillow, Quitman, and Shields, Genl. Patterson being the Genl. of this Division of the Army. Volunteers raised for the war are hourly expected. Those who are now here are, at this time, indulging somewhat freely in frolicking, as a reward, I suppose, for the abstemiousness necessarily practised during their long marches. Your old friend, Yawn, joins Genl. Patterson's Military family to-morrow as clerk. He conducts himself so well that it gives me pleasure to advance his interests. I spoke to Genl. Patterson to-day about him, mentioned under what circumstances he enlisted, the estimation in which he was held by the business men of Charleston, etc.

Breakfasted with Capt. Myers, and a friend or two at a café—fried fish, venison steak, eggs, buckwheat cakes, fried bananas, and coffee, all neatly served and well cooked. Dined at the same house with a mess—

MAJOR-GENERAL ROBERT PATTERSON

In Mexico

Drs. Harney, Satterlee, and Cuyler—soup, baked fish, broiled and roasted duck (excellent) with lettuce salad, Irish and sweet potatoes. From these bills of fare (omitting, as I do, an excellent bottle of champagne at dinner) you will find that there is no danger of my starving. Were you here, I could live as happily and comfortably as at any other place.

Miss Chase, the lady (Irish) who distinguished herself by raising the American flag as our Navy was coming up to town (three miles) from the bar, has invited Mrs. Col. Gates to come and take a room at her house. The Col. has sent the invitation but does not know whether she will come or not. I would not experience the anxiety I should entertain at the idea of your being on your way to this place for anything in this world. The Col. writes her that he will probably leave this place before she can get here.

Intending to write you daily, I will now close this day's letter by wishing you good-night.

Thursday, January 28, 1847.

To-day I dined with Maj. Morris, *Chef de police de* Tampico. He deserves very great credit for his untiring zeal and attention to his duties. His authority is necessarily very extensive, all being subject to his supervision. Yesterday he sent a Capt. and Lt. of Volunteers to the guard-house. He orders any house where there is rioting or unnecessary noise to be instantly closed, and his authority is undisputed. To-day I am Officer of the Day, and have the right of exercising nearly all the above mentioned authority, but as my plan and desire is, to prevent rather than to suppress, I have already stopped by timely advice one or two incipient cases of riotous conduct.

10:30. Just returned from the American Theatre, which I had to visit as Officer of the Day—heard "O'er the Mountain Brow" melodiously sung by the favorite of the night. There were plenty of good subjects for a row, but the fear of the bayonets of the Guard who were present kept them moderately quiet. On my return, I passed round and found the town unusually still. Another *Norther*—as the storms from that direction are called—is now *screaming* its approach. The term screaming is strictly applicable to the storm as it exerted its fury on our vessel whilst under its influence at sea. No news from Genl. Scott or from the northern portion of the Army. Saw Genl. Persifer Smith to-day —he is looking very well.

I THINK OF CIRCULATING A PETITION TO CONGRESS RELATIVE TO ARMY ASYLUM, as we have now a very large portion of the Regular Officers within a few miles of this City, and I find I have active friends in each Camp who would take pleasure in aiding me. I have been looking round for something for you, but have seen nothing very rare or nice.

Friday, January 29, 1847.

To-day I marched fifty of the 3rd to the Camp of the 2nd Arty. when under the command of Capt. McKenzie, we *rehearsed* the ceremony of receiving Genl. Scott hourly expected from Brazos. I play the second fiddle—the escort of honor is composed of 200 men. Genl. Pillow's Brigade has moved its camp nearer town—sorry for it, as we shall have an additional number of the *boys* to keep in order.

I have just returned from dining with our friend, H. Brown. We had an agreeable party and a very

In Mexico

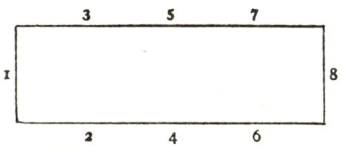

good dinner. Guests: Genl.⁵ Shields, Adjt. Austine,⁷ Dr. Hawkins,³ Lt. Lovell,⁶ and Capt. Anderson.² Hosts (or Mess): Col. Kinney¹ (Texan Danl. Boone), Lt. Brown⁸ and Lt. Collins.⁴ I will not describe the dinner, as it was an American, not a Mexican dinner. Col. Kinney is an extraordinary man, and probably knows more of the Mexican character than any one with the Army. I was rejoiced to find no animosity in his conversation towards the Mexican common people, which I expected from him as the Texan Ranger; on the contrary he concurs with me in sympathizing with them. Genl. Shields is the "Commissioner of the Land Office," and a devoted friend of the President. I THINK THAT I HAVE IN HIM A GOOD FRIEND OF THE ARMY ASYLUM. A few such men will carry the measure through Congress. I am to give him a copy of the Bill. No. 3 looks as though he was not quite so sedate as when Nancy was with him. No. 4 is A. D. C. to No. 5. No. 6 is the son of the late Surgeon-Genl., and the young gentleman you saw at Old Point. No. 8 received me very warmly.

I learned from conversation at the table that some of the principal men of this part of the Country are now considering whether they shall not at once raise a Mexican force, attach themselves to our Army, and declare at once against the Govt., either holding out the flag of annexation, or of a separate Govt. under the protection of ours. Thus far it seems that our course here has conciliated the inhabitants, and it may lead to important results. All think that if the troops were withdrawn in a short time even, that their presence and the attending introduction of our goods at a rate so much cheaper than the poor Mexicans have ever before purchased them, with the swarm of enterprising Yankees introduced into the Country, will eventually produce, inevitably, the downfall of the Spanish influence. A Mexican is said to have arrived this day with important news from the interior. I have not heard whether the rumor be true or false.

As a mail is to go to New Orleans to-morrow morning, I shall close this letter to-night. One month and three days (five weeks) have gone since I saw you—and I have not one word from you. 'T is not your fault as I know that you write constantly—too frequently for your health I fear. You must, I entreat you, be careful of *yourself*. Could I only be assured by one word that you were well, how warmly I would thank our Heavenly Father—as it is, I must rely upon His protecting mercies for what He has done, with an earnest hope that He has, and does, still guard and provide for my darling wife.

How you would enjoy what I scarcely now hear, though playing near my Quarters, the bands of the 1st, 2nd, and 3rd Regts. Arty.—the band of the 4th has not yet arrived. One band is now playing—they alternate in playing every other night.

A mail arrived this evening from New Orleans *via* Brazos—it brought nothing for me but a Volume of Tactics from Washington. I cannot learn that any news of Genl. Scott's movements was received. All are in the dark here—eagerly, anxiously looking for his arrival. No one knows who his Staff Officers are to be. It seems to be expected that Congress will give him another Asst. Adjt. Genl., and that he will not deprive either of the Genls. now in the field of theirs. I see no good reason for this suggestion as he can call very properly for either of them, and let these Genls. select Lts. to perform the duties of A. A. Genl. in their Military Families. I find that I have been unintentionally led into a Military discussion. A truce with all such stuff.

You have a right to expect from me some remarks upon the Mexicans, but as yet I have seen nothing of them except of the lower class, who differ very little in social position from our slaves. They work for us, unload our vessels, assist in throwing up embankments to the fortifications around Tampico, etc.; in fact, they seem to evince no dissatisfaction at our presence.

You must know that our troops have been busily engaged ever since their arrival in fortifying the town, as in the event of the movement of the Army from this place a garrison sufficiently large to defend the City will be left here. Each Regt. hopes that it will not have to remain. Col. Bankhead is on his way out —he cannot be fit to go into the field, and would make a very respectable Governor. Major Whitney cannot go into the field. I am rejoiced to hear that he has been assigned to quarters in the City.

Our flagstaff is planted in the centre of the platform on which it was intended to erect a monument to Santa Anna. To what strange uses are the vain purposes of man sometimes applied! I will here narrate an anecdote connected with the raising of our flag here, which was told at dinner to-day. An old Mexican about ninety, when it was raised, observed to a man standing near him: "Well, I am not sorry to see that flag going up. That flag has been my ruin. I came from Spain, and I was then young, and was sent into Louisiana; that flag came and I then went into Florida; in a few years the same flag came, and I then came to this place expecting never to be disturbed by it again. But there it is—the same flag, the same people." This was substantially the comment of the old Spaniard, and evidences in a few words the astonishing increase and growing power of our Country. God grant that it may be all for the best.

As I intend writing you a letter every day so as to give you a bulletin by each of your weekly mails, I shall now close this letter that it may leave in the mail of to-morrow, as I do not know when I shall have another opportunity. Do write me how you are. I will not close without saying that I have entirely recovered from my sea-sickness, and that I can now relish very well a good dinner.

No. 2. TAMPICO, MEXICO,
January 29 and 30, 1847.

I have this moment (9 P.M.), returned from a dinner given by the officers of the 2nd Infy. to those of the 2nd Arty. Though feeling very little like dining out to-day, I thought I could not refuse the invitation, as it would enable me to become acquainted with many young officers of those Regts. whom I did not know. The dinner was abundant and pretty well cooked, but it was not served in the *home style* always indicating the supervisory care of woman. Genl. Patterson was the principal guest and gave us speeches enough to last for half a dozen dinners. What he said was very well, but too much of it for a festive board. Compliments were bandied from the Regts.—the hosts and the guests, and many witty, and some very smart

In Mexico

speeches were made. When Genl. Taylor and some others of the Mexican conquerors were toasted, the utmost enthusiasm prevailed. Good old Genl. Brady was warmly toasted. No toast was given to Worth—and none, except one not understood by one half at the table, was given to Genl. Scott, until towards the close of the dinner, and that one was very coldly received. Genl. S. is not known and is therefore unappreciated by these gentlemen. I venture, however, to predict that at the close of the first campaign under him, these same gentlemen will warm at the mention of his name. I rejoice at his approach.

Genl. Taylor feels hurt, I fear, at Genl. Scott's having stripped him of most of the Regulars with whom he has won so much glory; he should, however, reflect that Genl. Scott's success is a national, not a personal one. We learn this evening that Genl. Worth has arrived at the Brazos with his Brigade. It is probable that we shall not see him here, as we presume that his command will concentrate with the Volunteers under orders for the seat of war at the Lobos Islands—about forty or fifty miles to the south of this place—where it is said that the vessels will have safe anchorage. Good-night, etc.

Sunday, 31st.

It is so late, that I can write you only a few lines before retiring. The Sloop of War, *Albany*, arrived this morning from Vera Cruz with Lt. Rains (Old Point acquaintance) on board with dispatches from Commodore Conner for Genl. Scott. Lt. Rains was, I understand, in the City of Vera Cruz—there are about 1500 men in the City and 800 in the Castle. Troops may be safely landed under the protection of the guns of our Fleet, about three miles from Vera Cruz, when the City may be taken without exposure to the fire of the Castle d'Ulua. The City is not defended, or defended badly, from a land attack, and must readily fall. The Castle would of course follow.

From all that I can learn, it seems that Santa Anna can not succeed in exciting the common Mexicans against us—the kind treatment received from us contrasts so forcibly with the harsh conduct of the Mexican officers and officials as to operate very much in our favor. Many contend that we ought to live on the country to make them feel the horrors of war, and that then they will sue for peace. Perhaps not. It may be that a change of policy on our part would excite the common people so much, as to make resistance to the death a cardinal principle with them; hence would result an enthusiasm which would render the country unconquerable. Every City and Town might then fall before the force of our Arms, and still we would meet with enemies in every mountain recess, and behind every burn. Good-night. God bless you.

Monday, February 1st.

Tampico is a very pretty town—but its people do not look like any you ever saw. Everything here would look strange to you. The men wear large palmetto hats, or broad brimmed and high black polished hats with brass knobs on them, which they think make them look pretty. They wear blankets thrown over their shoulders—some of these blankets are of very rich colors and cost as much as $60 for one. The people here would make you feel sorry for them, if you could see what heavy loads they carry on their backs. They have a strap, passing over the top of

In Mexico

the forehead, which is fastened at each end to a thick soft pad which rests on the shoulders—this pad keeps the heavy things from hurting their shoulders. I saw a small Mexican carrying, the other day, a barrel full of loaf sugar. Four men will, with these pads, carry very large boxes, as big as your largest box—the two men at the corners behind bend their heads down so low that the box rests on the pads. Some of the men wear very curious-looking pants—they have a white pair made with very large legs; over this comes another pair open on the outer seam almost all the way up to the top.

You must not think that I do not get enough to eat —oysters and fish are nearly as good as those at Tampa. A fish called "barilla" is perhaps better than those we had at Tampa. Oranges four for a sixpence, wild geese twenty-five cents, ducks four cents apiece, and very good they are—in the market I find more kinds of peppers then I ever saw anywhere; one of the large peppers is called *dulce*, and the skin has a sweet taste. I am getting seeds of the different kinds of peppers and beans I see. Every day lettuce, sweet potatoes, Irish potatoes (brought here), tomatoes cultivated and wild, egg plants, and several kinds of vegetables which do not grow in the places where you have lived, are found in the Market. The Mexicans sit down on the pavement in a large square, and have their market goods near them. You might buy a cup of chocolate in the Market and some nice fresh rolls or cake, as they are always there for sale.

I can buy a nice little pony here, but it could not be sent safely by water. The sea is so rough when it blows strong from the north that the horses on board ship are almost always badly hurt.

Tuesday, Feb. 2nd.

The newspapers give you so regularly and constantly the last news from the Army, that it is hardly worth while for me to chronicle events as they transpire, or to detail rumors as they fly. Of rumors I am too old a campaigner to repeat one twentieth of what I hear. I shall generally give you only what I know, or believe to be true, or think very probable.

This day has been peculiarly prolific in items of news—the most important is the fact of the stranding of a ship from New Orleans with Col. De Russy and four Compys. of the Louisiana Vols. on board. The ship is on shore thirty miles south of us. They saved most of their guns, their tents, provisions, etc. and all the men—one only was lost. Pack mules under an escort of Cavalry will be sent down for them to-morrow.

Last evening some of the officers of the N. Y. Vols. came up to town—they left N. Y. Jany. 4th, and came here *via* Brazos, where they left Genl. Scott about five days since. Their orders are to go as far south as the Isles de Lobos, and anchoring, to remain till further orders.

The anxiety increases daily in relation to Genl. Scott. All want to see him—because all think that Vera Cruz can be easily taken with the troops now here. Genl. Scott will not move till his plans are well matured, and will not strike a blow until he knows it will tell well. Great anxiety is entertained here by Genl. Scott's friends relative to a bill before Congress to make a Lt. Genl., as we know it is aimed at Genl. S. and designed to place some politician above him. If Genl. S. can take the field with a strong force, carry Vera Cruz, and compel its boasted Castle to surrender, and then establish himself safely in the interior across the mountains, before the arrival of the Lt. Genl., his being superseded will make him President, in spite of the manœuvres of politicians.

I rode this evening to the camp of Genl. Twiggs's Brigade, about two and one half miles from town. Their Camp is prettily situated on rolling ground, with a very pretty water prospect. The Officers say they cannot step into the woods outside without being covered with ticks. Say to the Genl. that his old friend Col. Riley desires to be particularly remembered to him. Maj. McKee, a relation of Mrs. Clinch's, also requested to be presented most warmly to the family. As I feel a little fatigued after my ride, I shall now bid you good-night.

Wednesday, Feb. 3rd.

Postmaster Perkins informs me that he expects to send a mail to the United States to-morrow. I shall then, instead of keeping this letter for another mail, close and send it by that mail. I am more anxious that you should hear from me by every opportunity now, as I fear that when we leave this place, it will be impossible for me to write as regularly as I now do, and that the chances of communication with New Orleans will be very much decreased.

Not a line yet from my wife—as there has been no mail direct from New Orleans since my arrival, none could have arrived. And yet it is hard that just at this time when I am so anxious to get a letter, the mail should be so much behind. To-morrow will, I hope, bring us a vessel from New Orleans with the mail. Dr. Cuyler says that he hears from his wife more regularly than any one else here, because he has his letters sent under cover to Col. T. F. Hunt, Deputy

Q. M. Genl., New Orleans. Mrs. C. pays the postage to New Orleans and Col. H. forwards them. Do try this plan; it may, and I hope will succeed with us. With a good Postmaster in New Orleans, there would be no use for any other than the ordinary direction on the letter, but he, it is said, has some inattentive persons in the office.

We heard from the interior to-day, that about six hundred Mexicans were defeated near the Paso del Norte by four hundred of Genl. Kearney's troops. This you probably heard a week ago, as it is said to have taken place more than a month ago. We hear not a word about the doings of the Mexican Congress—their not acting precipitately augurs that they consider the question of peace or war one on which they will reflect—that they have not met with the determination to prosecute it at all hazards. Nothing from Genl. Scott. An escort was sent down this morning with pack mules to Col. De Russy's command—they will join us in about four days.

The band of the 4th Arty. is now playing your old favorite "Love not"—some musicians with the very instruments to which we have listened together. What emotions throng to my heart—God grant that we may again enjoy—and now they are playing "Oft in the Stilly Night"—I can write no more till they have finished. I think I can safely promise that this war being over, nothing save the most imperious necessity will ever separate me from my family except for short periods.

Before closing, I may as well give you a little insight into my household arrangements. Behold me then seated before the old Company desk in my parlor of 24 by 16 feet—the walls about 30 ft. high and 2 ft. thick, the piazza in front paved with marble.

Having described my parlor, I will enter no further into details about my drawing-room and bedroom, than to say that exactly the same description *verbatim et literatim* will answer for them. I am still messing with Doctors Harney and Cuyler one square from my Quarters. In a day or two we intend changing to a Frenchman who is said to keep a better table. I have not yet found a servant, though Dr. C. told me to-day of one who would go with me. Derr is attending to my few wants now—we get on very well.

I must invite some friends to assist in eating the fine jar of oysters you made me bring. I opened my Mess chest to-day and found them in excellent order. I omitted mentioning in my last letters that the married men are well—indeed there are none but slight cases of indisposition in the Compy. The houses here have no fireplaces—the Mexicans you find sleeping under the piazzas, or in the open square every night, having merely wrapped themselves up in their blankets which they always wear, using their hats as pillows and at the same time covers to their heads.

I omitted stating the other day that I had seen Maj. Buchanan; he commands the Baltimore Vols., who, they do say here, behaved most cowardly at Monterey; their Commander, Col. Watson—a brave man—was sixty yards ahead of his men when he fell. As I must put this letter in the mail to-night, I must now close. Give my love to all the family.

No. 3. TAMPICO, Feb. 4th.

Is it not too tantalizing, that a vessel has just arrived from New Orleans in seven days without having brought the mail. Not even a newspaper did the stupid dolt bring. He deserves not to hear from his family for a year. And to think that he *might* have brought me news from you as late as the 15th of last month! That is indeed a long time back, but still how delighted I should be to hear from you as late as that. I really am so much out of patience that I cannot write. But as I cannot omit writing a single evening whilst I can do so, you must make all excuses for me this evening.

This day has been nearly barren of rumors and reports—the newsmongers seem to have exhausted all their powers of invention during the last two days. To-day I have been in company with some of the distinguished of the battle of Monterey, and am sorry to say that their want of modesty detracted very much from my estimation of their deeds. No one admires courage more than I do, but I always regret to hear the hero trumpeting his own fame—however weak the blast may be, it had better been left for other lungs to swell the strain.

All agree, however, in representing Genl. Taylor as perfectly cool and collected during the fight—they say that he exposed himself unnecessarily—that he was frequently in the advance when he might have left the duty of reconnoitring to others. The Genl. preferred perhaps to look with his own eyes. AMPUDIA is represented as both drunkard and coward.

The band, it must be the 3rd, is now playing that medley you remember—"Some Love to Roam," "Love not," etc. They play better than I ever heard them. I can scarcely think it is our band, and yet in some parts the instruments sound very much like those of the 3rd did in olden times at Fort Moultrie. Now they play the old *American Museum* tune. How well do I remember the many evenings you have heard those notes when we were so happy together. Memory is to me a very great blessing—with some sad thoughts, she presents me many bright and happy ones. These continue through life to present to me occasionally the panorama of life's acts, and of my mind's thoughts and hopes. Good-night. I can write no more to-night.

Feb. 5th. A mail from New Orleans, but bringing no letter from you—to-morrow it is said that we are to have a large mail left behind somewhere with later dates than those brought to-day. Then *assuredly* I shall hear from you—I shall indulge at all events in that sweet hope till the mail comes. I hear that Genl. Scott is to be here next week. On reflecting upon what may be the state of affairs at Vera Cruz I do not see why it may not be better to remain where we are until we can get a battery of heavy battering guns, a siege train —as it may be that we shall have good uses for it.

The newspapers, months ago, stated that our friend Capt. Huger was to sail about the 1st of Jany. with one hundred men well instructed in the management of mortars and heavy howitzers, which he was to bring with him. He may perhaps be now to the south of us. No one can tell who is to remain as Governor of Tampico. As Col. Gates had the honor of landing the first detachments of troops here, it may be his ill fortune, but we hope that the 3rd will not be kept with him. As yesterday was pay day for the Compy. I have been pretty busy to-day settling accounts, sending off checks, etc. By the bye, I think it will probably be advisable for me to send some of my surplus funds to you. The amount will not be so large as to endanger your safety in keeping it—nor have I any very great fears of your becoming *purse proud* in consequence of its possession.

Entre nous, I saw a letter of Genl. Worth's to-day, dated Nov. 23rd extolling Genl. Taylor in the highest manner. I have no doubt of Genl. T's richly deserving the encomium and hope Genl. W. may not, from a fit of passion, alter his opinions. That Genl. Scott will place Worth in every position where distinction can be won, I am sure, and I fear that this partiality may not be acceptable to others in the Army who will wish to share honors with the gallant—I presume we may now say—Major General. I find that I am encroaching on to-morrow's sheet. God bless you and keep you in happiness and in health.

Feb. 6th. Another night and day have passed since we have talked together, and no mail has come with a letter from home—where you two are, is my heart's home. Dr. Cuyler and myself have talked so much to-day of our family feelings, as to make me, I fear, a very poor correspondent for my to-night's letter.

Monday, Feb. 8th, 9:30 A.M.

Rumors have been received from several sources during yesterday and the day before, that the Mexicans were surrounding the Command of Col. De Russy, which I mentioned in my last letter as having been wrecked about thirty-five miles to the southward yesterday morning. Lt. Magruder was sent down to see what the Command was doing. After his departure reports were received to the effect that Col. De Russy was attacked by Genl. Coss and 980 men, and that Capt. Brooks, sent to him with supplies, was also engaged—that the attack commenced on the 4th and that so great was the disparity of the force (Col. De Russy having very few muskets, and no flints) that there was every probability that they had been captured or cut off by the Mexicans.

Genl. Patterson about sunset last evening ordered two

In Mexico

Companies to embark. Col. Gates placed me in command of the Companies selected and directed me to report to Genl. Patterson for orders. I called on him and received orders to proceed in an armed schooner down the coast to reconnoitre the position occupied by Col. De Russy, to afford him and the troops sent to his relief every assistance if they can be found—assuming, when I join them, the command of the Arty. Compys. (4). If I find no persons where the vessel was wrecked, I am to examine the ground to see if an engagement has taken place—then to proceed south to a small town, Tamagua, near the Islands, where our forces are to concentrate.

We met on the bar this morning the steamboat which took Lt. Magruder down, and attempted to communicate with it, but failing to do so, and knowing how important it was that we should not go off on a wild goose chase, I determined to recross the bar, and dispatch an officer to Genl. Patterson, to mention the state of facts, and to ask his instructions. We are in fact better inside the bar than being at sea, as the wind is dead ahead and we should be drifted by the strong current to the north here. I expect the officer back in an hour—when I think it probable we shall be ordered to return to Tampico.

My Compy. was not selected because of its containing so large a number of recruits. Poor fellows, many of them appeared very anxious to go. I will here stop until the return of Lt. Beckwith—the officer sent. Our cousin Lt. Anderson commands one of the Compys., and Lt. Wyse the other one on board this vessel—which is the schooner *Ella* now under the charge of Midshipman Smith. Midshipman Maury is with him. The two companies muster about 140 men—enough to whip 500 Mexicans in fair fight.

MY OWN QUARTERS IN TAMPICO, 8:30 P.M.

As I expected, Genl. Patterson sent orders for me to return with my Command; on arriving I immediately reported to him at his Quarters, and gave him my reasons; he approved of my course and directed me to order the companies to their quarters.

The Genl.'s statement of the events reported to him by the officer who came up from Col. De Russy's troops is this. On Thursday Genl. Coss summoned Col. De R. to surrender—to the second note the Col. replied that he wanted till 9 o'clock the next morning to consider the demand. Night soon came on and early in the night the Col. took up the line of march leaving his tents standing, with candles burning in them. By daylight the next morning he had marched about twenty miles. He then met Lt. Miller with his party, and a few miles farther he received the Compys. under Lt. Magruder which were landed from the steamboat we met this morning on the Bar. He then felt himself so secure that he determined to report his position to Genl. Patterson who he thought might send him reinforcements sufficient to authorize his attacking Genl. Coss. This Genl. Patterson declines doing, as from the nature of the country the chances are that Genl. Coss would escape without the possibility of being caught by our troops. Col. De Russy has been ordered to join our forces. This ends this expedition.

We expect soon to sail for Vera Cruz as we hear this evening that transports are arriving at Brazos from New Orleans. Those ordered to this place may be soon expected. An officer of the Navy arrived this evening four days from Vera Cruz—he reports that there are only 4000 troops in the City. You will see, I fear, before this reaches you, an account of my having been sent out on what will be called undoubtedly a *perilous expedition*. You have all the facts above and will learn how to appreciate such reports. Editors must of course manufacture interesting paragraphs for their papers.

Tuesday night, Feb. 9th.

Col. De Russy and his Command arrived this afternoon. Nothing was seen of Genl. Coss after Col. De R.'s leaving his camp. No mail yet from New Orleans—it does seem that we are never to get a mail. Whilst I was absent the other day I looked forward to my return to Tampico with the greatest pleasure, because I hoped, till I was almost certain, that there would be a mail—that I should find a letter from you. You will nearly have received my first letters from this place and I have not received one of the many letters which I know you have written. It is too bad.

We hear a rumor to-day that Genl. Santa Anna is marching all his forces to crush Genl. Taylor. It may be true but I do not credit the report. If he makes the attempt, although Genl. Taylor has not many Regulars with him, he will prove a very ugly customer, and again if he moves with all his forces to Monterey, he leaves the road to San Luis and the City of Mexico open to one part of the Army, and even success against Genl. Taylor—hardly a supposable thing—will not atone for the injury we shall inflict on him by cutting him off from the Capital, and our obtaining and securing possession of the tablelands, the garden of Mexico, where alone an Army can be subsisted in the Republic.

Genl. Scott, who is still at the Brazos, will soon be informed of this movement of Santa Anna if it be made, and will at once give Genl. Taylor such additional reinforcements as to secure him in his possession. We must not suffer any reverses in this war. Not a man must be surrendered to the Mexicans. Fortunate was it for us that an ex-Army officer was in command of the wrecked Louisianians, as a raw volunteer would have been very likely to have surrendered under similar circumstances—at least he would not have thought of escaping by a ruse. How foolish Genl. Coss must have felt on approaching the empty tents!

I was introduced this afternoon to Col. Jackson of the Georgia troops. He is said to be one of the best of the Volunteer Officers in the Army. Col. Baker, member of Congress from Illinois, was pointed out last night to me—I saw him seated in a crowd—he looked like a regular electioneering hero. I did not think so highly of his speech in Congress, just before his leaving Washington, as many of his Volunteer friends do. Regular vote-asking—praising the Volunteers to the skies. Nearly all the Volunteers are encamped on a very extensive plain just below the City where they have room enough to drill. It is a level piece of land, overflowed in the Spring, extending about two miles along the river bank, and from a quarter to a mile broad. Having obtained some few articles of clothing for the "G's," I am just beginning to take them out of the yard. To-day I marched them down to the plain, where I gave them a good drill.

Extremely desirous of not missing the mail, I will now close begging to be remembered most affectionately to Genl. C. and all at home. That our Heavenly Father will secure your present and eternal happiness and soon restore me to you is my constant prayer.

No. 4. TAMPICO, Feb. 10, 1847.
No boat can come, nor can any boat go, during the

In Mexico

time when the "Northers" are blowing here, and vessels that are at anchor outside the bar, at the mouth of the river, have frequently to get under sail in so great a hurry that they have not time to raise their anchors. These high winds do not generally continue, the residents say, longer than the middle of this month.

No news has been received to-day from any quarter. I saw Col. De Russy to-day, but had no time for conversation with him; he looks very well. The Mississippi troops, reported to be suffering very severely from a malignant dysentery, who were off the bar yesterday, must have been blown to sea by the storm.

I shall send you by mail a No. of the Tampico *Sentinel.* It is conducted by one of the Editors Lumsden, of the New Orleans *Picayune.* You will find mention made of some movements alluded to in my letters, and full accounts of some particulars to which I have not alluded. In fact the Editor has to make the most of the few incidents which happen in our midst, where nothing is done but "drill" and look out for the mail.

To-day I have been engaged as President of a Court trying some soldiers. The big Sergeant, as you used to call him, was before us. He could not resist temptation and took one more than the authorized frolic. I overlooked the first frolic all, or nearly all, had on landing. I find my military frock so warm that I am getting another *drap-d'-été* one made. A franco-espagnol mulatto promises to make me one that will fit me well.

My old friend Dr. Harney was quite unwell last night; he feels better to-day, but I fear he may have a very bad time—a severe fit of sickness. The Dr. has reached that period of life when the constitution has frequently a severe struggle with the arch enemy. Dr.

Wright says that if the Dr. survives this attack the chances are that he will be in feeble health for about a year, and that then he will enjoy a green old age. The Drs. are making arrangements to establish a Mess, and Dr. Harney insists upon my living with them as a guest. I told him that he must let me pay my portion of the Mess bill, and that I would join them with pleasure.

Genl. Scott will not, I presume, allow us to mess here much longer. What would I not give to know that at this moment you were well. With how much more alacrity and zeal could I attend to my duties, had I but that knowledge daily! My men, even, must find me much changed, and I expect wish you were here as I am much more rigid with them than I was at Tampa. God grant that this ill-fated war may soon be closed and that I may again see my wife. Goodnight.

Feb. 11th.

The wind has abated, but the waves are so high that boats can neither come in nor go out. I fear that there will be no possible chance of a mail's coming in before Sunday. If one comes I must certainly hear from you. Major Whiting found a letter here from Mrs. W.—she writes, he tells me, in fine spirits. The Major will soon break down—his Command are in tents—he is quartered in town.

I went to the Court House for the first time this morning to hear Col. Baker of Illinois, M. C., and Col. Jackson of Savannah. Col. B. is acting as Prosecuting Attorney, and Col. J. appears for the prisoner—an American arraigned for the murder of another American. The Georgia gentleman is not sufficiently cool

In Mexico

for his antagonist, who is very calm, and a much abler man in debate. The Court is composed of three American citizens, and has been organized by the order of Genl. Shields whilst in command here for the trial of all civil and criminal offences. I am not sufficiently conversant with the "custom of war in like cases," consequently am not quite certain if the Comdg. Genl. is vested properly with any authority to constitute Courts, appoint judges, etc. The question may be brought before Congress. I do not think, if they find the man *guilty*, they can venture to hang him. The Court must feel morally certain that they are legally authorized to act, or in case of the reverse, they would be guilty of murder were they to have the man hung.

It is now cold enough for a fire—if it continues as cold to-morrow, I must purchase an earthen pot, and have a charcoal fire in my quarters. We have a report to-day that Santa Anna has been declared Dictator. This can hardly be true as the people are already disaffected, it is said, towards him and he is too shrewd to risk popularity of so high-handed a measure. Having encroached on my to-morrow's page, I will now bid you good-night.

Friday night, 12th.

To-day the weather has been uncomfortably cold—sufficiently so to make sitting by a fire very comfortable. I have spent the greater part of the afternoon with my friends the Doctors, where there is the only fireplace I have seen in Tampico. This cold weather reconciles me to my position in the City. I have, ever since my arrival, been urging the Adjt. to induce Genl. Shields to send me into one of the camps. Last night and to-day I feel exceedingly grateful for the privilege of being in comfortable quarters, and subscribe that *what is*, is for the best, is very good doctrine.

We hear to-day of the capture of Capt. Cassius M. Clay and his Company of Cavalry by the Mexicans. Capt. Clay had seventy, the Mexicans were said to have been 1500 strong. The newspapers will doubtless give you more particulars than we have now, as it reaches us through the Mexican papers. Per contra, our troops to-day have captured 500 head of cattle. They are still greatly in our debt, and we will soon, we hope, balance the account.

The august Court of Tampico, Chief Justice Capers, ex-Sutler 8th Infy., and Associate Justice Lumsden of the *Picayune* are engaged in trying a Mexican for the murder of the American mentioned in my yesterday's letter. The American first arraigned for the murder is to be tried as an accessory to the murder if the Mexican is convicted, as it is said that he got the Mexican to kill him. Col. Baker appeared as prosecutor in the case of the Mexican, and the jury (probably the first one impanelled in Mexico) will, I think, find the man guilty. The jury is composed of American citizens. I am sorry they did not give him a jury consisting in part of his own countrymen. It would have a better appearance. It would have been well to have associated one of the Alcaldes with our Judges. The Mexicans were watching the trial with great interest.

To-morrow we are to commence Messing. Dr. Harney and I are to look in at the market occasionally to see that the servants do not cheat us too much in the prices. The Dr. is much better, but says that he will take another dose of calomel to-night.

My letter No. 3, was, I am told, sent on board a vessel which went down to the mouth of the river this morning. I fear, however, that the bar has been too rough for any vessel to go out, and that it will be delayed one day longer in reaching you. I think I shall venture some more Treasury Notes in this letter. I may be robbed some day or night when I am out of my Quarters, and the chances of their being lost in being sent by letter are so few that I think it best to send them. Others I find are doing the same thing. Were I certain that Col. Andrews or any other Paymaster is to remain at Charleston, I would send on my pay accounts, as the safest way of sending funds; but Col. Andrews may by this time be under orders for the Army.
Good-night.

Saturday, 13th.

Another long, long day and no mail. A vessel came in from Baltimore, but brings us nothing later than papers to the 19th Jany. We are indeed out of the U. S. Tampa Bay we used to consider far enough out of the U. S.—so far *out* that the mail was exceedingly irregular, but this is rather worse. To be sure I was not quite so deeply interested in the arrivals of the mail there as I am here.

To-night there is every appearance of a Norther; should it come on to-morrow, we may not have a mail for three days. I *will* however indulge in the hope that we shall be made happy on to-morrow by hearing good news from our families. How truly will it be a day of rejoicing to me if I receive one of your letters telling me of your safe arrival at the Refuge[1] and saying that

---

[1] Genl. Clinch's plantation. General Clinch's wife's father, John Houstoun Mackintosh, owned Ft. George Island, near the mouth of

you were well and in good spirits about me. I shall do admirably well if I can only hear from you now and then and know that you are well.

Sunday night.

Thank God the mail brought me to-day a letter from you. It was your letter from the Withlacoochee bearing the Tampa Bay postmark of Jany. 19th. I had hoped to receive a letter from you after your arrival at the Refuge. But I am thankful, very thankful, for this one. The few words you wrote about yourself present in the strongest light what I knew would be your sufferings. I pray Heaven that you may have been saved from sickness and great suffering—which your grief and exhaustion were so well calculated to produce.

Dr. Cuyler received by this mail letters from his wife, dated 31st Jany. Assuredly I must receive two letters from you by the next mail. I received by a gentleman from Brazos a letter from Genl. Scott, which I intended enclosing to Father, but as I may have good use for it here, it will be better for me to send an epitome of its contents, which will show how wisely Genl. Scott had made his arrangements, with how great forethought he acted, and how cruelly his plans have been thwarted by delays.

The Secretary of War on Genl. Scott's requisition ordered in Dec. ten large transports to be sent in ballast; nothing has been heard of them. Genl. Jesup went on the 3rd Jany. to New Orleans to take up ships, etc. On the 22nd he had chartered almost enough for

---

the St. John's River, Florida. During the Spanish troubles Mr. Mackintosh removed his family and slaves to a tract of land on the St. Mary's River, Georgia, and called the new home the "Refuge." This tract was a grant from the Crown to his mother's father, Sir Patrick Houstoun, President of His Majesty's Council of Georgia.

8000 men and 1200 Arty. and Cavalry horses. They were to have left New Orleans on the 24th; but the time necessary to make extra water casks, the sailors striving for higher wages, and finally a fog which lasted for one week have so delayed them that only one had reached the Brazos on the 11th inst. Of the heavy supplies of Ord. and Ordnance Stores ordered, only a small part has been heard of. Was ever such ill fortune!

The Genl. will leave Brazos as soon as the transports or most of them come up. He will stop here only a day or two and will hasten to Lobos, etc. We must make an attack on Vera Cruz in a few weeks, or abandon it until Oct. or Nov. Healthy portions may be found in the interior, sufficiently near to haul our supplies from this place. Col. Bankhead arrived to-day—he looks very well—we, or at least many, think that he will be the Milty. Governor of this place instead of Col. Gates. I think this will be entirely as Col. Bankhead wishes—he is an old friend and favorite of Genl. Scott's. Gates is neither the one nor the other. As I must reserve some space for another day's memoranda I will now close.

Monday night, 15th.

I have just been informed that a mail will be closed early to-night to go in the morning. As it is uncertain when another one will be sent, and as I am determined that you shall have a chance of hearing from me by every mail, I have determined though there be no stirring incidents to season my epistle, to close and send this letter.

This day has given us no news. Col. Bankhead assumed command of the Regt. to-day without taking command of the City. This looks a little like a disinclination on his part to interfere with Col. Gates in his Gubernatorial capacity. Genl. Scott will probably leave the selection of the Officer to be left in command here to Genl. Patterson. I hope that Genl. Scott will take all the Regulars with him leaving some 1500 Volunteers here.

A ship is reported off the Bar this evening; whether it be one of the delayed transports or one of the ships containing the Mississippi or the New York Volunteers, we know not. I did not mention among the other items of Genl. Scott's bad luck, the fact that the Mississippi Volunteers, which were ordered to the Brazos for Genl. Taylor's Division of the Army, have come down here! Genl. S. is now doubtless expecting them at the Brazos.

Major Kirby is to join Genl. Scott as he passes this place. Whether he will be with him merely as the Senior Paymaster-General or that he is to serve in some other capacity on the Staff, I know not. Kirby, if he be sincerely attached (which I hope is the case) to Genl. Scott, will be a very good adviser. He is a prudent man, and prudence is always a virtue in the Staff of a man like Genl. Scott, whose indignation, though justly excited, may sometimes lead him to express himself too harshly. Maj. Van Buren is with the Genl. I don't think much of him as an adviser. You know the Major however as well as I do; a very amiable gentleman. I hope that Capt. De Hart may be in the General's Staff. He has a very rough and unpleasantly independent way of speaking sometimes to the Genl., and this frequently vexes him: but his business habits, his acquaintance with details, and his attachment to the Genl. render him a very valuable man to him. Genl. Scott should now have men around him who will at the risk of incurring for a time his displeasure, speak the truth fully and freely to him. His magnanimity will always cause him to make promptly the *Amende honorable* when he has been vexed by a person's not agreeing with him, and he will esteem them all the more for it. Of one thing I am certain, as I said in a former letter—one Campaign with this Army will give Genl. Scott a popularity which he has not at present. The Army has been lying idle here so long, that the croakers are busily at work; a little active service will send this gentry into their dens again.

No. 5. TAMPICO,
Tuesday, 16th.

I mailed a letter to you in a very great hurry, and hear this evening that the mail was not sent, and what is more vexatious that none will be sent to-morrow. I shall however commence and continue this, as though the other were off, and may probably send both under one envelope should no mail leave before I finish this.

Col. Bankhead assumed command to-day, and the first act of his administration was to order his predecessor into Camp with our two companies; so that this is probably the last letter I shall write you from quarters in Tampico. I do not know the position of the site selected for our Camp, but hear that it is a pleasant and healthy one. We shall be about three quarters of a mile from where I am now quartered. The Camp will be composed of the three Companies of the 3rd Arty. now here, viz.—"G" Co. and the Companies commanded by Lieutenants Steptoe and Wyse.

The probabilities are in favor of our being moved again in a few days, as we learn that the transports are rendezvousing rapidly at the Lobos Islands, a vessel which arrived this afternoon reports fifteen large ships at anchor there, and that she met four others on her way up. The inference is then certainly fair, that those ordered to this place may very soon arrive.

The important point now discussed is what troops are to remain. The general impression seems to be that Col. Gates is to be left. *Nous verrons.*

Among the rumors of the day, credited by some knowing ones, is an old one revived; that the commandant at Vera Cruz has received instructions from Santa Anna to evacuate the place, on the arrival before it of our Army, as was done here. This comes from a Mexican lady of this place. I would not be astonished if it was done, if we go there with a heavy battery (without which we ought not to approach the place) and a well organized force.

Genl. Scott, I am confident, feels the full importance of entire success, and will not run the risk of a failure. His enemies are on the watch; his friends are keenly and sensitively alive and will leave nothing unattempted in their power to ensure success.

Tattoo call has just beat; and it is time for me to visit the Theatre. I have, I believe, omitted telling you that among the duties of the Officer of the Day, are those of going to the Theatre, the Fandangoes, and all places of amusement. Such a collection as I saw at the only Fandango I have attended you can not conceive of— from the Vol. Colonel to the drunken private soldier and the black Mexicanesses—I soon became disgusted, but had to remain for fear of a row, to close it. The Theatre is filled with noisy Volunteers some of whom are taken away from their frolics there every night and given a place on the floor of our filthy guardhouse. At all places of amusement are found sentinels with

GENERAL WINFIELD SCOTT

In Mexico

their fixed bayonets; they are even on the ballroom floor. And this is necessary to keep our free and independent citizens in order! Good-night, it will be so late when I return, that I can write no more to-night.

Wednesday night, 17th.

I am now writing from camp, having vacated my quarters in town at 4.30 this evening. Mr. Wyse came in when I had finished the last sentence to talk about the chance of our remaining here. It seems that the question has been discussed to-day, and he says that Col. Gates and our two companies will form a portion of the garrison. Genl. Scott may change the arrangements entered into by the gentlemen here. I shall therefore give myself very little trouble about the affair.

I saw to-day Genl. Twiggs's Brigade drilling on the plain near our camp. I never saw so many Regulars together: there were about 1400 men; of the Rifles, 1st, 2nd, 3rd, and 7th Infantry. They made a very respectable display; the day was intensely warm and two or three of the men fainted in the ranks.

Of rumors we have a full budget—one, that Genl. Taylor has had a fight with and whipped Genl. Santa Anna; a second report says that Santa Anna can not raise money to organize an Army, and that Vera Cruz will certainly be abandoned on our approach. *Nous verrons.* As I am not yet well arranged for writing, I will here finish—wishing you good-night; the discordance of two camps beating tattoo at the same time makes not a very pleasant music.

Thursday, Feb. 18th.

We are now comfortably fixed in our Camp which

has been well and thoroughly policed. I find that I am too far from my own Mess in town to continue a member of it; I shall therefore organize a Mess tomorrow in camp. I brought, you know, all the furniture, etc., necessary for this purpose. Finding, however, that my pewter is not quite genteel enough for a Tampico Mess, where we *greatly profess gentility*, I went to the heavy expense of 75 cts. for a china bowl and plate. The pattern is a very pretty one, as you may see some day from the fragments. I have not succeeded in finding any curiosities or rarities which I thought worth procuring and keeping for you.

When in town this morning, I called to see Maj. McCall, Genl. Patterson's Adjt. Genl., in consequence of Mr. Wyse's conversation with me last night, and asked him whether the designation of the companies to remain here was made by him or by Genl. Scott's Adjt. Genl. He said that Genl. Scott would designate the garrison. Thus falls to the ground the castles which our knowing ones have been building for their friends during the last few days.

We had a report this morning that Capt. Huger was off the bar to-day. I could not trace the report to a reliable source, though I thought it might well be so. He must have been under orders in Dec. or Jany.; and should have arrived before this time. Genl. Scott will be here at 7.30 to-morrow.

Why does not Congress act on the Army Bills; the President's earnest recommendations have not been acquiesced in. It is highly important that Genl. Scott should have the ten Regiments of Regulars so strongly recommended by the Secretary of War, at the earliest moment, and yet, at our latest advices from Washington, they were gravely discussing the question of giving Volunteers in place of Regulars. Had Congress been serious in desiring to prosecute the War vigorously, they would have passed the Bill proposed, or some other for increasing the Army, in the first two weeks of its Session, and some of the Regts. might have been now in the field. Now the passage of any Bill augmenting the Army can do no good until next winter. Our armies are not sufficiently strong for invasion; we may occupy the seaport towns and healthy positions near them, but can not throw our forces far into the interior.

I learn to-day from a very reliable source that there is much bitter feeling between the Volunteer Generals. I fear that this feeling may be extended by them towards Genl. Scott, who comes to an army, I am sorry to say it, strongly prejudiced against him. Bragg in the Arty. and Lt. Don Carlos Buell in the Infy., or, at least, Genl. Scott's action in their cases, have had much weight in producing this feeling. You can readily conceive the anxiety I feel on this account. I am apprehensive that the prejudice is so strong as to mislead many honorable men, who can not give his acts a fair trial. Once in a campaign and in a glorious action, and all must be, will be, right—envy and malice will [*not*] then be so powerful to injure as now, and the very men who now dare to speak slightingly, and disrespectfully of him, will be loudest and most fulsome in his adulation.

I hear to-night that a mail from New Orleans will leave early in the morning, and as I am not now so near the Post Office as when in town, I will not be able to spoil this letter by cross writing. Mr. Wyse promised to call for my letter after tattoo, and as the call has beat, I must now close.

No. 6. In Camp, Tampico
Sat., Feb. 20th.

Thank God I have at last received letters from you. Yours of the 7th, 14th, 21st, and 29th, Jany. were received yesterday morning. With what gratitude do I thank our Heavenly Father for having restored you to health. And you have suffered so severely, my poor wife. What wou d have become of you had you been among strangers, worn out by worrying about me? Now I feel that you are surrounded by those whose love and affection will anticipate all your wishes, whose devotion encircles you with care and attentions which strangers would never think of, and which in the sick room are so much needed, so highly appreciated. Is it not true that in this case all was ordered for the best? I will not ask you to thank all the family, the attentions of each of whom have been so warmly dwelt upon in your letters—this would be too cold and formal. But I do thank God for having given us relations with hearts so warm and so true.

I will not attempt to state the feelings which pervaded my heart when I read your most, most welcome letters. How often did I have to stop reading—some sentiment of yours brought you before me so plainly, and yet so far are we separated, and so much uncertainty is there about the time of our meeting again. God will, I know, continue to protect and bless you.

As my scribble on the side of No. 5 indicated, Genl. Scott was that night off the bar, and arrived yesterday morning. He was received and escorted to his quarters by four companies of Arty.; Capt. Wm. McKenzie, Commander, Capt. A. Compy., the right Compy. The Genl. looked, on arriving, somewhat worried;

In Mexico 51

he went off this afternoon, I think, in better spirits. He issued yesterday his Orders naming his Staff Officers, and declaring Martial Law to prevail wherever any part of the Army might be. I send a copy of the newspaper containing them.

I met many of my old friends—Major Smith, Engineers Col. Totten, Capt. C. F. Smith, Capt. Joe Johnson, Lt. Scott, A. D. C., Capt. Swartwout, A.D.C. Williams, etc., etc., etc. All are in fine spirits. I have not mentioned my old friend Capt. Huger, who dined with me to-day on "Armadillo" and other nice dishes. He has brought out the heavy Ordnance, the arrival of which has been so anxiously hoped for. Col. Gates will remain here with one compy. of Arty. and 1200 Volunteers. Col. De Russy has been ordered to remain with the Louisiana Volunteers; this is a bitter pill for them to swallow. I saw very little of Genl. Scott; knowing how busy he would be, I purposely avoided going near him. He enquired most affectionately about Father and the family; says that the Genl. owes him two letters. I wish you would ask Father to write to him, directing to the care of Col. Hunt, who will forward it. Having largely trespassed on my to-morrow's pages, I will now bid you good-night. God bless you.

Sunday, 21st.

The Norther which raged last night with considerable force, must have carried Genl. Scott down to Lobos early to-day; he is, I suppose, safely anchored there to-night. Last night reminded me of some of the stormy nights we had at Tampa Bay. Luckily the Sentinels of our Camp are not far from each other, and it did not take me long to visit them. I took advantage of a lull, and paid my visit rapidly between two showers. To-night the wind is pretty high, but there is no rain.

I have this evening distressed Lt. Judd by telling him that I intended applying for him to join my Compy. He has just succeeded in having Lt. Steptoe's Compy. organized as a Compy. of Foot Artillery, and it will go hard with him to have to leave it, but I must now have all the officers who properly belong to it, if I can get them. Col. Gates said this evening that he would order him to the Compy., but he may change his mind to-morrow.

An English gentleman of high character informed us last night that he had received advices from Mexico to the 13th inst. stating that a bearer of dispatches had been sent by our Govt. to the Mexican; the nature of the communication was not known. It is said that the bearer of the dispatches is a Mexican, who has been during the last year in some official correspondence with our Secy. of State, and who has constantly taken the ground that a peace might be honorably adjusted by the two Govts. News from San Luis Potosi to the 7th was also received by Mr. Whitehead, which represents that Santa Anna has advanced 50 leagues towards Genl. Taylor and that he had then halted, having learned that the Genl. was stronger than he believed him to be. Information also states that the Mexican Congress has informed Santa Anna that no money can be raised for him, that he must subsist his army as best he can. Before this reaches you, you will have heard whether these rumors are confirmed.

Genl. Twiggs's Brigade will commence embarking as soon as the bar becomes quiet enough for them to cross. It will be succeeded by the other troops as rapidly as they can be got off. A large steamboat was reported off the bar this afternoon; it is supposed to be the *Alabama* from New Orleans. She has probably run out to sea again; and will, I hope, return to-morrow, and give us a mail with later news from my wife. I must leave a little space for to-morrow on this side. That our Heavenly Father may protect and guard you, and soon restore me to you is my earnest, my constant prayer. Good-night. The Taps have just been given.

Monday, 22nd.

Washington's Birthday. I am, with my company, in the City to-day guarding the City. Col. Bankhead showed me the order of Genl. Patterson directing the Arty. companies to be embarked next after Genl. Twiggs's Brigade, which will, I suppose, commence its removal to-morrow. The steamer reported off the bar yesterday has not yet come in. She is thought to be the *Alabama.*

Of news we have nothing to-day. I am seated in Dr. Harney's parlor, with the Dr. in front of me on the sofa. Lt. Beckwith, 3rd. Arty., is on my left, and Lt. Van Vliet is walking across the room;—as they are talking I find that I shall have to defer my writing till I can steal a more favorable moment, when I shall resume and finish to-night, and mail will go to-morrow.

9.30 P.M., Monday.

I had intended writing you a good long letter, but as Officer of the Day, I shall have so much to do that I shall have to content myself with this letter with a slight addition to it. It will be useless for me to keep it out of the Post Office to-night for the chance of the mail's not going off until the afternoon of to-morrow, as I learn that I am named as Judge Advocate and Recorder to a Military Commission to try a Mexican Spy to-morrow.

This is the first Board organized under Genl. Scott's order declaring Martial Law. The Commission is composed of Col. Bankhead, Col. Gates, Col. Campbell, Tenn. Vols., Lt. Col. Belton, and another Vol. Officer. I regret exceedingly being placed on the Commission, as it is a question which will attract much attention, and should be managed by an officer of much more experience and talents than myself. Capt. De Hart should have been sent here to act on the Court.

I do not think that the Prosecuting Officer will be able to sustain the charge, as I can not conceive the necessity for the Mexican General having sent a spy to this city, whose inhabitants are in daily communication with their friends in the Army and elsewhere. Again it may be apprehended that if he be found guilty and executed under our sentence, the Mexicans may cause Lt. Rodgers of the Navy, a prisoner in Vera Cruz, to share the same fate. Joaquim Nogales, our prisoner, is said to be a Sergeant in Genl. Urea's part of the Army, and was apprehended by Major Morris, who prefers the Charges.

I shall not be able to send you by this mail the copy of Genl. Scott's order which I intended sending. You will find a copy in the next newspaper which I send. Maj. McCall has just sent me word that he wants to see me, and I must go over.—I have just returned; he gave me the order detailing the Military Commission and the charges against Nogales. They are hardly strong enough to convict him of being a spy. I must study the case. Good-night, may our Heavenly Father bless you.

No. 7. TAMPICO.
Wednesday, Feb. 24.

As I was engaged yesterday on the first "Military Commission," I did not feel like writing at night, and retired at early candle light. This morning I received orders to prepare my Compy. for embarkation, and as I have much to think of and to arrange to-night, as we embark early to-morrow, I fear that my last letter from Tampico must necessarily be a short one.

Before commencing my daily narrative of events, rumors, etc., since the close of my last, I may as well tell how near I was being kept here by Col. Gates. My last mentioned that the Col. was to remain here with one Compy. of his Regt. This decision was made the day Genl. Scott left. That morning, Adjt. Austine informed me that Col. G. had selected me. I immediately went to his Quarters and asked him if that was so. He answered me in the affirmative, said that he had been treated with great discourtesy in being separated from his Regt., and that, saying divers complimentary things, he had selected me to remain with him. I stated that, from the relations which had always existed between us, I knew that he would not misunderstand me, when I informed him that I would appeal from his decision; that as the ranking officer of those in command of Companies of the 3rd Regt. here, I claimed that I was entitled to be first sent on armed service. He said that there would be no misunderstanding between us.

I left him, and had barely seated myself to write my appeal, when Col. Bankhead's orderly came in and said that Col. B. wished to see me, at his Quarters. I went, when he informed me that it was strange that Col. Gates had misunderstood him; that he had informed him as plainly as he could speak the English language that he, Col. B. would, to prevent any heart-burnings between him and his officers, make the selection. He then said, that next to the officers of his own Regt., he would rather have me with him than any one else. And wound up by stating that he would not make the selection till Genl. Scott left.

Immediately on Genl. Scott's leaving, he informed Mr. Wyse that his Compy. would remain. Col. Bankhead told Col. Gates subsequently, that Genl. Scott had said that he wanted me in the trenches with him.

So much for being too *popular*. I have made a very narrow escape. There is so much in the preceding which would not be written to any one else but yourself, as it looks exceedingly like *egotism*, that I hope you will not read or let it be read by any one.

The Company is to embark in a very fine sailer with accommodations for about thirty men more than the company musters. I have to leave "Ruh" in the Hospital here. He was shot accidentally in the calf of his leg, by a revolver in the hands of one of Mr. Wyse's Compy. and will not be able to go with us. I must have him sent on to join me as soon as he gets sufficiently well. Mr. Judd has managed to keep from joining the Compy., as he prefers remaining with Mr. Steptoe whose Compy. he managed to have converted into a battery of Foot Artillery. But I think, as he has not been transferred from the Compy. I will get him back as soon as I get to Genl. Scott's Headquarters.

And now about the grand "Military Commission" which met yesterday to try the spy. On the assembling of the Court, after a few remarks, the names of the members were called, when, before the prisoner was brought in, I presented the question as to our competency to try a *spy*, and stated that we were debarred from doing so by Genl. Scott's order, and by the Rules and Articles of War, which declare that spies shall be tried by Genl. Courts-Martial. The question was put —the objection sustained—when I wrote a letter communicating the fact to Genl. Patterson; the moment I explained the grounds of our decision, he stated that we were right, and informed me that he would have an order issued dissolving the Commission. Thus was I relieved from a most unwelcome and troublesome task. The fates are decidedly in my favor—I ask pardon, I am no fatalist, even in jest, and firmly believe that the Great God orders all events. He speaks to us whether in the gentle zephyr or in the raging storm.

Adjutant Austine goes with us. Col. Gates was quite angry when Mr. A. told him he must go; but afterwards consented. The Col. keeps the band; we take the Colors, and the Adjt., Col. Childs, and Capt. Vinton will be with us.

We have rumors again that a messenger has been sent to the Mexican Govt. with an offer to take north of a line running through Matamoros, to embrace a part of California, Santa Fé, etc.; and that we will give her twenty millions from which the claims of our citizens on her Govt. are to be discounted. These terms do not appear to me very liberal. Whether the Mexicans will accept, no one knows. I believe that the Govt. at Washington would do any honorable thing—may be that word is too short—to prevent Genl. Scott from conquering a peace. We will see.

Friend Derr and I get on very well together. He goes on guard with me when I am Officer of the Day, and does not therefore miss any of his duties. I will reserve a little space for to-morrow morning, when, if possible, I will add a few words more. Good-night, my wife. Good-night.

February 25th.

My Compy. is now on board, and I am waiting for the return of the lighter to go on board. Col. Belton and Lt. Andrews are the only officers who go in the same vessel. The wind is now ahead, and it seems doubtful whether we shall leave to-night or not; it is now 2.30 o'clock. Genl. Patterson will, it is said, leave the day after to-morrow in the steamboat *Alabama*. For safety and the chance of making snug harbors I prefer our little schooner, the *Regina Hill*. I intended sending another trio of drafts, but as I am separated from my baggage, I cannot.

No. 8. TAMPICO,
February 27th, Saturday.

It appears now, my wife, that my last, very hurried letter might have been finished at my leisure. A Norther was brewing as we went on board, and yesterday morning the breakers were so high on the bar that no vessels went out. The wind is now lulling and it is probable that the gallant little barque will sail tomorrow. I very innocently came up to see my friends the Doctors on Thursday night, as I thought a night on shore would be better for me than one on board, but they refused to let me return, and here I am separated from the Company by a cold. They have given me no medicine but one dose of magnesia; but say that I shall not expose myself by unnecessarily accompanying the command in a small vessel without medical attendance, when they can take me with them in the steamer *Alabama*, which, leaving to-morrow, or the next day, will reach Lobos before the *Regina Hill*.

My cough is less violent than when I left the vessel. You know that generally I am very little affected by colds, recovering frequently from those that are very severe in one night. I have no pains or aches, simply a cough, and hope that with a change of weather I shall be again well enough to rejoin and go down with the Compy. I have a piece of news for you.

Did I not mention in one of my first letters that Mrs. Gates had been invited by Mrs. Chase (the lady who first raised our flag) to come on? She is now here. I have not seen her, but intend, if to-morrow is a mild day, to call on her. Her arrival will, I hope, make our Col. better satisfied with his position here. She had, I hear, some difficulties to contend with, in getting here. The Col. will, I suppose, tell the whole story when I see him.

Mr. Wyse called to see me this afternoon; he seems very well contented, and talks about his Company's being mounted. It is very well that all men are not constituted alike. I feel very certain that with all my attachment to my profession, I would have resigned and gone to Vera Cruz as a Volunteer, rather than to have remained here. I am glad, however, that I was not put to the trial.

8 P.M. Mr. Judd has just left, having called to see me. He expects to start to-morrow or the next day.

Before I stop I will take you a walk through the market. In the first place you see the "Flag of our Country"; it is placed on a platform intended to receive a statue of Genl. Santa Anna. The house is the guardhouse; the square is paved with stones. Let us commence with the people farthest from the river. I have marked the line 1.[1] Here you see tables and people—soldiers and others—drinking coffee and chocolate with cakes and bread. The coffee is kept hot in large tin urns with charcoal burning under them. You ask me what that Mexican woman is doing there, turning a stick between the palms of her hands as she stoops over that earthen pot on the fire. She is making a cup of chocolate for some one. She will pour some out, then put it on the fire and turn her stick in it again, and then pour more out; now she puts a piece of sponge cake into the saucer, and hands it to that man; he pays her sixpence for it, and she smiles as pleasantly as if he had made her a present.

A little farther on you see a pile of curious-shaped earthen pots; they are used for cooking, some are for meats and vegetables, others for chocolate, and others are water jars. Next you see several straw hats; they are worn by the people of the country; the prices are from 25 cts. apiece to $1.50. That man is selling coarse Mexican blankets and some common cotton goods.

Now we will commence with the next line; here you see no tables, the articles are either in open boxes slightly raised on one side, on coarse matting, or upon the pavement. The first box contains a large dried black pepper; this is the sweet pepper; next are green peppers, bird's-eye peppers, the true cayenne, and another kind somewhat larger. There are black beans, the favorite bean, about the size of our garden pea; next the large kidney, then the common pea; then a small flat bean much used with rice, a box of which comes next; take care that you don't tread upon that fine large lettuce or upon those egg-plants.

[1] A diagram was enclosed in letter.

VIEW OF TAMPICO

In Mexico

But what is that man doing? See, he has a kind of bag, which seems filled with moss, and he is taking something out of it and opening the moss which is made into a kind of ball; they are eggs which he has brought to market on the back of a donkey. Each ball holds an egg carefully wrapped. See, there is another man who is opening corn shucks in which he has fastened his eggs.

Most of them in this and the next line have nearly the same things; here is a vegetable something like the egg-plant in its form, but that it is flattened; it has a deep crease at one end, and a piece projecting out like a tongue; the plant has small points on it which do not stick you; this plant is cooked like the egg-plant, but I think it is much better. I have tried to get the seed, but was told that the fruit itself was planted, and that the part looking like a tongue will grow into a vine on which some fifty or sixty of these will grow. I will try to take one to Father. That pretty red bird you see there is the pink curlew; its feathers are beautiful; you must have some to make a fan; he asks 12½ cts. for it and says it is good to eat. It is not very good. That basket-looking coop made of corn-stalks holds chickens. Ducks and turkeys you see here. That man has sugar cane and plantains for sale; the next one bananas, $1.00 for a bunch of green ones; we won't give it—we may find some ripe ones farther on.

But come, we must make haste, and return home; we have not the time to see all the things this morning and will glance along as we run through these lanes of market people near the river. In the boats are very fine fish; look at those turtles with supple twigs tied around their bodies between their shells and their legs, so that they can't move their legs; there is corn, rice, dried corn, coarse salt, Mexican soap, raisins, onions, garlic, cabbage, mint, *parsley* in small bundles, *cigaritos* (small paper cigars smoked by *ladies!* as well as gentlemen); the most beautiful white lard you ever saw; sweet potatoes, Irish potatoes; tomatoes, some very small—the wild tomatoes—others red like our common ones, and some of a very rich yellow; radishes, green peas—see those long strips piled up on those cow hides—that is jerked beef.

Look at that donkey, see his tail trimmed. He has naturally, the poor creature, very little hair on it. On his back you see four layers or steps of bottles. That is a common drink of the country made of cane juice. There goes another donkey carrying water; he has four kegs; when the man stops to sell his load, he places a wide leather strap over the eyes of his donkey; this keeps the animal quiet and still—a pair of *leather spectacles*. But here we are at home. We may take another walk through the market in Vera Cruz.

1.30, Sunday morning, Feb. 28th.

I have heard that Genl. Worth is off the mouth of the River, and that a mail has been received at the office. I will run down to see if I cannot get a letter from you.—3.15. Thank God the mail did bring me two letters from my wife.

My letters, which you will have received long ere this, will have removed all cause of uneasiness about the uncertainty of my arrival here, and subsequent letters will have informed you how well I have been taken care of since my arrival. Place your confidence, and place it freely and fully, in Almighty God who has always been more careful of me than I have deserved, and you will then feel that all will go right. Repine not that He has separated us for a while; He knows what is best; we can not look wisely ahead for a single hour. The end will convince us of His foresight, our shortsightedness; His wisdom, our folly.

You express apprehensions about your letters, that I may never receive them. I think I have them all: Jany. 7, 14, 21, 29; Feby. 4 and 12. In your letter of the 4th of Feby. you say that it is your *fifth;* such you see my table of letters received makes it. You ask whether it is worth while for you to send the *Intelligencer;* scarcely, because I see from the loose manner in which business is transacted here in the Post Office, that any person can go in and help himself to any papers he chooses. I hear from my friends who read papers, all the news. I do not feel much like reading.

I have just heard that Genl. Patterson has notified the gentlemen who are to accompany him that the *Alabama* will leave at 9 o'clock in the morning. The *Regina* is still at the mouth of the River, and I think it probable that I may leave the *Alabama* and get on board with the rest of the "G's."

Dr. Cuyler received a letter from Mrs. Cuyler as late as the 13th. She writes that she had heard from Miss Johanna Wade that the Major had been ordered to Tampico. Col. Gates will, I presume, detain the Major with his Compy. at this place—he will meet his brother-in-law, Major Buchanan, here in command of the Baltimore troops.

The Army Bill I see has passed; it may help me a little. I am very much pleased with the synopsis you give of your newspaper readings. I learn from it many things which I had not before heard.

You must not write me such long letters—one page telling me that all are well and that you are walking about and getting strong again, would give all the pleasure I can receive from any letters, and particularly when I know that the effort necessary to write those long letters tires you. Let me urge you by all the love you bear me, and I know its weight and its worth, to take care of yourself. Look at events which have passed. Do you not see how groundless were a thousand fears which have harassed and worried your life out? The uncertainty of the departure of our mails, though I have put you on your guard against it, has caused you, I know, many bitter hours of anxiety and uneasiness. This letter I leave under a promise from the Postmaster that it will go the day after tomorrow. It may, however, remain here a week. When I shall have another opportunity of sending a letter off, no one can tell. That Genl. Scott will have his letters as frequently as practicable, I know, but he may not care about reporting until he has executed something to make a report about. I shall reserve my vacant space for a talk with you to-night and to-morrow morning.

7.30. Major Capers came in soon after I had finished the above; he is as big, consequential and important as man can well be; he said that he had been down to see Genl. Worth who had sent for him. The Genl. was on the Steamer *Edith* at the mouth of the River. I was sorry to hear that the Genl. looks badly; he is said to be in fine spirits, says that of course we shall whip the Mexicans at Vera Cruz, does n't believe any of the rumors we hear about Genl. Taylor's likelihood of being defeated by Santa Anna.

Dr. Wright received a letter to-day from an officer serving under Genl. Taylor, who writes that Genl. T. had advanced ten leagues from Saltillo on the road

In Mexico

towards San Luis, and that the report there was that Santa Anna had withdrawn his forces from San Luis and intended opposing the landing of our Army at Vera Cruz. The next thing we shall probably hear of Santa Anna, will be an attack made on some place he may hope to surprise.

You must not allow yourself to be worried by the thousand reports with which the papers will now be filled. Every paper must have some items of interest to publish about the Army at Vera Cruz. Show anything you may see to your Father, and he will tell you how much credit may be attached to it.

We shall not be able to disembark the Army much earlier than the 15th of March, so that you can not hear any thing certain from its operations sooner than about the last of March or 1st of April. I must save the other side for to-morrow. Good-night.

Monday morning, Feb. 29th, 9 A.M.

The wagon has just come for our baggage, and I must bid you farewell. Rumor reports that an attack was recently made by 2000 Cavalry on one of Genl. Taylor's posts, and that the Mexicans lost four hundred men; the attack was said to have been made at night.

No. 1. STEAMSHIP "ALABAMA,"
OFF ANTON LIZARDS.
March 5, 1847.

Anchored at last, I resume my correspondence. The date of my last letter I do not remember. The little vessel with my Compy. crossed the bar at Tampico, Sunday, 28th ult. As the Doctors, in consequence of my having a cold, refused to let me go on board with the Compy. I was perforce compelled to come on board this ship. Genl. Patterson with his Staff were fellow-passengers. One Regt. of Tenn. Foot, and Capt. Walker's Compy. 6th U. S. Infy. are also on board.

We got on board Monday the 1st inst., crossed the bar the next morning, and getting under weigh about midnight, reached the Lobos Islands early the next day, where orders were received to proceed South. Genl. Scott had already left Lobos. Yesterday we lay to for about eight hours in a Norther and arrived at our anchorage here about 10 o'clock this morning. Genl. Scott came in about two hours afterwards, and at the suggestion of Col. Campbell commanding the Tenn. Regt. he was greeted with three hearty cheers as he passed us.

We are about thirteen or eighteen miles south of Vera Cruz. There are at this time, 5.30 P.M., sixty-four ships, etc., at anchor in sight; the vessel with "G" Co. has not yet arrived, but as the wind is fair, I presume she and nearly all the others that are due will be in to-morrow. Genl. Worth has just entered our stateroom; I must stop to shake hands with him. Genl. W. looks badly; his old wound has given him a good deal of pain within the last month.

I heard yesterday that the Genl. thinks that he will be killed in this attack. I cannot think that a man who has so bravely passed through so many dangers as Genl. W. would give expression to such feelings, even if he entertained them.

Glorious news has just been received from Genl. Taylor's Army. The news comes pretty direct. A British Man-of-War which communicated this morning with Vera Cruz, on coming out gave the last Mexican papers to some of our Naval Officers—in one of

GENERAL TAYLOR

In Mexico

these papers was Genl. Santa Anna's report to his Govt. He states that he fought Genl. Taylor on the 22nd of Feby. at Aguanueva, not far from Saltillo, and again the fight was resumed on the 23rd. That he, Genl. Santa Anna, having lost in killed and wounded 1000 men, found it necessary to fall back to "Incarnation," whence, after having taken care of his sick and procured provisions, he would again advance to attack Genl. Taylor whose loss he estimates as 2000.

This paper also mentions that there had been fighting for three days in the City of Mexico in consequence of the attempt to raise money by forced loans from the Clergy. This is certainly most glorious news, and coming as it does from the Mexicans, we may fairly infer that it has not been colored too strongly in our favor. Genl. Taylor has then whipped their great man! This news will have a fine effect on our troops; all are even more anxious than ever to be led to the attack.

The news from Vera Cruz is that there are about 3000 Regulars, and a little over 2000 *ir*regulars. Our troops will be, including 200 marines, about 13,000. The result no one can doubt. Genl. Scott will not make his attack in such a manner as unnecessarily to sacrifice life. If possible, he will take the place without the loss of a man.

I have a Volunteer captain who wishes to accompany me. He is a gentleman who raised a fine company in Uniontown, Pa. which the Secy. of War could not receive, as the Regt. from Pa. had been filled up before the Capt. went to Washington. Determined to be in the fight himself, as soon as he found that his Compy. was refused, he started for the Seat of War, and is now here. I shall go with him to Genl. Scott to-morrow and request that his wishes may be complied with.

Capt. Austine has declined an offer he received to-day of the position of Lt. Col. or Major, in the 1st Regt. Pa. troops, both these positions being vacated by the sickness of those officers. He says that he prefers being with me to going into the field with that Regt. He is full of zeal and will be of assistance in inspiring my Germans with a determination to go ahead.

Our anchorage is, I hear this evening, eighteen miles by land from Vera Cruz, and fifteen miles by water. If we land here, we shall have to cross a small river about two hundred yards wide; on the way up, there is a mill where the stream can easily be waded which will make our march somewhat longer. The Naval Officers say that no opposition will be made to our landing. As I wish to reserve some space for to-morrow after my interview with Genl. Scott, I will now close by wishing you good-night. That God our Heavenly Father may guard and protect you is my earnest prayer. Good-night.

Saturday, March 6th.

The *Regina Hill* bearing Col. Belton and "G" Co. has not yet arrived. I do hope they will arrive to-day, as a rumor says that we are to land to-morrow, and it would be hard, after all my endeavors to get this Compy. into active service, if they should now miss this opportunity for distinction! Genl. Patterson told me last night that if the Compy. did not arrive, he would be very happy to have me with him. This would not suit me.

I called this morning at Genl. Hd. Qrs., but Genl. Scott had gone off on a reconnoitring party. All his

Milty. family went with him. I saw my old friends Capt. C. F. Smith and Capt. Vinton. I heard a bad translation of Genl. Santa Anna's report. He states Genl. Taylor's force at between eight and nine thousand men. He has nearly doubled the General's force, which could not have exceeded six thousand. The action took place at Buena Vista, a strong position about six miles from Saltillo. He says that he thinks of falling back the following morning (24th) as he has not a piece of bread or a pound of rice for his sick.

We have received no mail since we came down. We hope that we may have one to-day as the last Norther ought to have brought us down on its swift wings, vessels from New Orleans. The next mail ought to bring me letters from you as late as the 10th Feby. I am very anxious to hear that you are well enough to be walking about, and that you have made some arrangement which will remedy some of the many inconveniences which Elizabeth's leaving you has given. I must now stop writing, as I see that Col. Ward Burnett, New York Regt., has entered the cabin. I shall take up my pen again as soon as the reconnoitring party returns, as I can then state with some certainty when the landing is to take place.

Monday, 8th.

The reconnoitring party went so close to the Castle on the 6th as to draw a fire from the Mexican battery; no harm was done. Yesterday Col. Belton arrived with "G" Co., and I was so much occupied that I could not write. We are now momentarily expecting a steamer to take us to Sacrificios where the landing of the troops is to take place.

The 3rd Arty. with a company of Sappers and Miners

constitute the Reserve of Genl. Worth's Brigade, which leads. It is not anticipated that any resistance will be made to our landing. I have confidence in the protection of our Heavenly Father who has thus far protected me with the most fatherly care. This letter may not be sent until after the engagement, in which case I hope to accompany it with another.

Monday night.

As no movement was made to-day, in consequence partly of an expectation that a "Norther" would interfere with it, I have the pleasure of continuing my nightly conversation with you. Genl. Worth's Brigade has been increased to-day by the addition of about one hundred and eighty Marines, who under Capt. Edson form part of the Brigade Reserve under Lt. Col. Belton, which as ordered will consist of three Compys. 3rd Arty., Capt. Vinton's, Capt. Anderson's; Lt. Col. Childs under command of Capt. Taylor, Sappers and Miners, Capt. Swift, and the Marines, amounting in all to about four hundred and twenty men. As the barometers indicate the approach of a "Norther," it is probable that no move will be made to-morrow.

Lt. Judd has arrived with a part of Lt. Steptoe's battery. He reports the arrival of Genl. Jesup at Tampico in the Steamer *New Orleans*. We are daily, indeed hourly, expecting her arrival here with a mail. Capt. F. Taylor is here with a battery of the 1st Arty. Lt. Col. Duncan is to arrive. The expected Norther will bring, we hope, all the absent vessels.

All who are here are impatient to make the attack, as many dread being detained here during the next month, when they apprehend greater danger from the yellow fever than from the balls of the Mexicans.

The yellow fever commences in Vera Cruz about the 15th of April, so we have five weeks for operations before a necessity will exist for our moving into the interior.

The mountains are occasionally plainly visible from our present anchorage. The peak of Orizaba towers proudly 17,500 and some odd feet above us. We can move to delightful and healthy positions among the mountains. Such will undoubtedly be our destination as soon as we take Vera Cruz. I am anxious to get through this affair as I know that you will imagine thousands of dangers which never existed, and nothing but the certainty that the City is ours will relieve your anxiety.

This will, I hope, be the last war I shall take an active part in. I think after the declaration of peace, I may safely promise that I will go "a-soldiering" no more. I think that no more absurd scheme could be invented for settling national difficulties than the one we are now engaged in—killing each other to find out who is in the right!

I enjoyed this evening the singing of our Germans; they sang several of the songs we used to listen to at Tampa Bay. God grant that not many months may elapse before we shall enjoy *together* our pleasures again.

I have not received a line from either of my own family. Indeed, I have not written to any one but my dear Mother. I have devoted every spare hour of my evenings to writing to you and have indeed felt very little like writing to any one else. I feel that you are entitled to all the time I can take from my duties, and indeed I do not feel that I ought to retire to my bed without having first held my converse with you.

As I shall want to add something more to-morrow, I shall bid you good-night.

Tuesday, 9th, sunrise. The signals for sailing are up. We shall commence transferring our men to the transport which is to convey us up immediately. Good-bye. May God Almighty bless and preserve you.

No. 1. Camp near Vera Cruz.
March 12, 1847.

I have this moment (sunrise) arrived in Camp, and hear that a mail is to leave this morning. I fear that I am too late for it, but shall scribble a few lines in the hope that my good luck may not fail me in getting my letter off. My last letter informed you that we were on the eve of landing.

The landing was effected without any attempt to prevent or molest us. That night a little skirmishing occurred, by which the Mexicans had, a French Naval Officer reports, twenty men wounded,—one or two of our men are said to have been hit by spent balls. The result of the next day's skirmishing resulted in killing six Mexicans.

Yesterday, Lt. Col. Dickison of the S. C. Vol. was wounded in the breast, Capt. Alburtis, 2nd Infy., killed, and a private of the Rifles killed, a Lt. of the Rifles and seven privates are said to have been killed —per contra seventeen Mexicans were killed. The City is now completely invested (surrounded by our troops) and I presume that some of our mortars will be in position to-morrow, when they will begin to feel the horrors of a siege.

Why the Mexicans did not meet us on the beach

In Mexico 73

when they might have annoyed and cut us up most unmercifully, is most unaccountable. They act very foolishly, throwing shot and shells at small bodies of men at distances so great as to make the chances of their hitting us almost nothing.

I am in excellent health, and in good spirits, as Genl. Scott has an army of about 14,000 who are in good tone for serving. All are zealous and anxious to close the siege. 'T is true that all our heavy Ordnance has not yet arrived, but still we have enough to bring them to terms before the sickly season commences.

No. 2. March 13th, 1847.

The scrawl sent, or rather written on the 11th, will I presume be received by the mail which takes this. My note book presents nothing worthy of being recorded; I shall therefore have very little to say of Army matters. Our tents and boxes are landing to-day, so that we shall soon be able to make ourselves as comfortable as the circumstances of a siege will permit of our being. Night before last I was, as I think my last note mentioned, on duty with about one hundred and forty men to assist Capt. Vinton in the event of his being attacked. I passed, of course, a sleepless night, but was afforded no opportunity of distinguishing myself.

To show how inaccurate Camp reports are, I will here correct one which I propagated in my last letter, and which had come direct from two of Genl. Worth's staff. 'T is not true that a Lieut. of Rifles and seven privates were killed, nor is it true that seventeen Mexicans were killed.

To-day we hear that the large thirteen-inch mortar, with the firing of which they have been amusing themselves, has burst, and we also hear that eight hundred men passed through our lines last night and entered the City; these men were from Jalapa. I give but little credit to both of these rumors.

I will, to ease your mind in relation to the Military prowess and skill of these people, say more of our operations than I had intended. Had they planted a battery on the beach where they must have thought we intended landing, they might, with the unimportant loss of their cannon, have killed and drowned a thousand of our men.

As it was, the landing was a most thrilling and exciting affair; it was effected in about seventy large surf boats containing from fifty to eighty men. The ships and steamers which brought us up from Anton Lizards, with the vessels of war, American, English, French, and Spanish, formed a fine background to the picture; the surf boats were drawn up in line, the first attached to the Steamer *Princeton*, the others successively to each other; the commands were given to wheel to the right and advance.

I suppose that every man on board these boats expected to be fired upon as we approached the shore; the first boat landed, and such a shout was raised throughout the whole line as never was heard before on these shores. Why they made no attempt to oppose our landing, no one can tell. And since we have landed they have kept up a pretty constant round of firing; scarcely a quarter of an hour passes without our hearing the noise of the firing and flight of a harmless shot or shell, nearly all of them falling far short of our lines. At night, too, we frequently hear their *escopettes* or large guns, injuring us in no other way than by rousing us from our slumbers or by causing us to get up and stand by our Arms for a quarter of an hour or so. Thus have they, in not attacking us when we landed (a work necessarily always accomplished with great confusion) and in the useless daily waste of powder, shewn a great absence of Military skill.

To-day an attempt will be made to land our heavy Ordnance. One battery will probably be sent to Capt. Vinton whose position is about three quarters of a mile from the town. Yesterday the aqueduct which supplies the City with water was tapped by the Compy. of Sappers and Miners; this may distress them very much. We do not know, however, what resources they may have or what supply they may have in their cisterns.

Capt. Vinton being on detached service, places me in the position of Acting Major of this battalion as I find, on comparing my date with that of his appointment, that I rank him. This may separate me from my Compy., but as the battalion is small it is hardly worth while to place me on duty as field officer.

Our sutlers have not yet arrived, so that we are now living on the commissary stores, or have to pay the prices asked by the sharpers who follow us. This morning I priced a few *luxuries* as follows: Irish potatoes $6.00 a barrel, sheep $5.00 apiece, and pigs $2.50. You may readily suppose that we cannot indulge frequently in such expensive luxuries. I find everybody here, many of my old friends whom I have not seen for very many years.

I saw Genl. Scott a few moments since; he gave me a very hearty shake of the hand, but as it is mail day, I did not stop to see him. As you always feel an interest in the "G's" I am glad that I can give a favorable report of them. Our old friend Derr takes most fatherly and affectionate care of me. He frequently comes to me with a nice piece of pork or bacon which he has put aside for me, and every morning and evening brings me a cup of coffee or tea. The married men are all well—indeed there is only one man in the Compy. who is on the sick report.

The Steamer *McKimm* arrived yesterday without a mail. This is really too trying. 'T is not often we have opportunities of hearing, but that the vessels which arrive do not bring in letters is too bad. I must soon receive your letters. I know that several are on the way for me. I hear our men criticising our Navy, as they say that a ship has just entered the harbor of Vera Cruz having evaded the blocking squadron.

The weather to-day is very pleasant, and from the appearance of the skies, I think we may hope for a continuance of it. As soon as I get my tent, which will be to-day I think, I shall resume, as far as my camp duties will permit, my daily talks with you. That mode of writing is much the most satisfactory one to me, as when I lie down at night I feel much better satisfied with myself than when I have not written.

Tell Father that the sight of our Army on the beach, the morning after we landed, before we had dispersed to take our positions around the City, was a glorious one—about ten thousand men under arms, and most of them in motion. We have now about fourteen thousand men, as our numbers have been daily increased. Some of our troops are not up yet.

Saturday, March 13th.

I feel at home, almost, with my pen in hand, seated

In Mexico

in my tent commencing one of my regular talks with you. My company baggage was received this evening, and I am seated for the first time in my own tent.

Captain Austen of the Pa. Volunteers who, I mentioned, wanted to serve with me, returned to camp to-day. He accompanied us, the day after we landed, to our position immediately in front of our present encampment, and was so unwell as to be compelled to return to the steamer. I learn from him that he is a regular correspondent of the New Orleans *Delta*, and of the Baltimore *Sun*. He tells me that in his last letter to the *Delta*, he mentioned that I was well. This information was most kindly meant for you, but he did not know where you were, or he would have had a copy sent to you. I am sorry that he mentioned my name at all as the custom of recording everybody's deeds has become so common, that it is almost more creditable *not* to be among the distinguished.

Col. Totten has been reconnoitring to-day, and has decided, I presume, to place several mortars at Captain Vinton's position on the sea beach. I would attempt a sketch of our encampment, but for two reasons; firstly, that I am pretty certain the newspapers will present you with an authentic map of the encampment of the besieging army of Vera Cruz, and secondly, that my talent in that line is so well known to you, that I am convinced you will readily excuse me for not making the attempt.

I have just returned from Tattoo; we are very military here: all the officers attend roll-calls, and as I expect the enemy will be alarmed again to-night, and commence firing, which will call us up, I shall very soon retire. Unless I can get a good night's rest, I shall be worth very little, and we have advanced so far, that we may be called to our work at any time. Derr has just brought me a cup of coffee: the kind creature knew that I had had none for supper. Good-night, good-night.

Sunday night, March 14th.

The investment of the City being complete, an advance was ordered this morning, from each brigade. The companies were ordered to drive the Mexicans and their pickets into the City. The advanced detachments are this evening within about seven hundred yards of the City.

Genl. Scott sent an answer this morning to the French and Spanish Consuls who made some application to him, probably in relation to protection. The Genl.'s answer is said to have been equivalent to this: "As far as posssible you shall be protected, but when the batteries open on the town, I can give you no assurance that you or your property may not be injured; you had better leave the City; I will give you a safe guard to enable you to do so." There has been but little activity in the firing to-day.

A Norther has been raging all day, and a detachment of two thousand two hundred men has been sent towards Anton Lizards to look after a ship, reported to be ashore, with Lt. Col. Duncan's battery on board. It is now so late, my tent having been full, till after Tattoo, of Naval officers kept on shore by this storm, that I will bid you good-night. To-morrow night, I hope that I shall be master of my own time. Good-night.

Monday, 15th.

As it is blowing very violently to-night, I hope that

In Mexico

no one will interrupt me. Yesterday, we had a very respectable blow, which lulled after midnight, and this morning, though there was a cloudy horizon, I enjoyed a most magnificent view of the peak of Orizaba. I will not attempt a description of its glorious beauty; towering among the clouds with its rosy peak reflecting the rays of the sun—which was invisible to us—rising as it did, behind dense clouds, with its sides concealed from view by broken masses of clouds resting on them, it formed a glorious and majestic object. Would that we could have enjoyed the sight of it together, but I do not want you to come here to partake of this enjoyment. We will be well contented to participate the delight of seeing more unpretending scenery in our own dear land. I hope that among the thousands congregated here, there may be some with a sufficiency of our friend Weir's talent to paint the landscape presented to our view this morning. We are now witnesses to the truth of the saying, that when the Orizaba is plainly seen, you may be sure that the Norther is close at hand. The wind commenced freshening about nine this morning, and soon became a gale which is now sweeping the sand so rapidly through our Camp as to make it very difficult to find our way from one tent to another. Our only chance of comparative comfort is either to remain *at home* with closed tent, or to move with handkerchiefs closely drawn over the head.

A vessel got on the breakers in attempting to run into our anchorage at Lizards; she will, I fear, if this Norther does not soon abate, be a total wreck. Col. Harney is said to be on board with some three or four companies of the 2nd Dragoons. Our friends in Vera Cruz have been throwing a few shells at us to-day, some coming, accidentally, rather nearer than was comfortable.

Last night, a mail was intercepted; the letters say that there is a scanty supply of provisions which will last but a short time. Addresses in bad English were also taken at the same time, calling on the Volunteers to desert, promising them rich lands, in healthy regions, where the best tropical fruits grow, etc. This morning a courier was taken who was the bearer of a despatch from the City Authorities to the Governor of this state, complaining that no aid had been furnished, stating their condition, the scarcity of provisions, etc. They are, in fact, so completely surrounded by our troops, that it must be a dangerous thing for even individuals to enter or leave the City.

Genl. Scott has decided, I suspect, not to commence firing upon the City, but to open his batteries on the Castle. He does this, knowing that if the Castle be brought to terms, the City falls as a matter of course, and that we will then be masters of the City, without the dreadful effusion of the blood of women and children, which must ensue from a bombardment of the City. This is just like him, ever instigated by the most humane and generous feelings. I have been interrupted, and must now bid you good-night. God preserve you.

Tuesday, 16th.

The day has passed, without the occurrence, as far as I have heard, of any things of note. A few Volunteers, who strayed some miles out of our lines report that they were fired on by some hundred Infy. and about two hundred Cavalry. They are supposed to be troops from Alvarado who desire to enter the City. Whether they

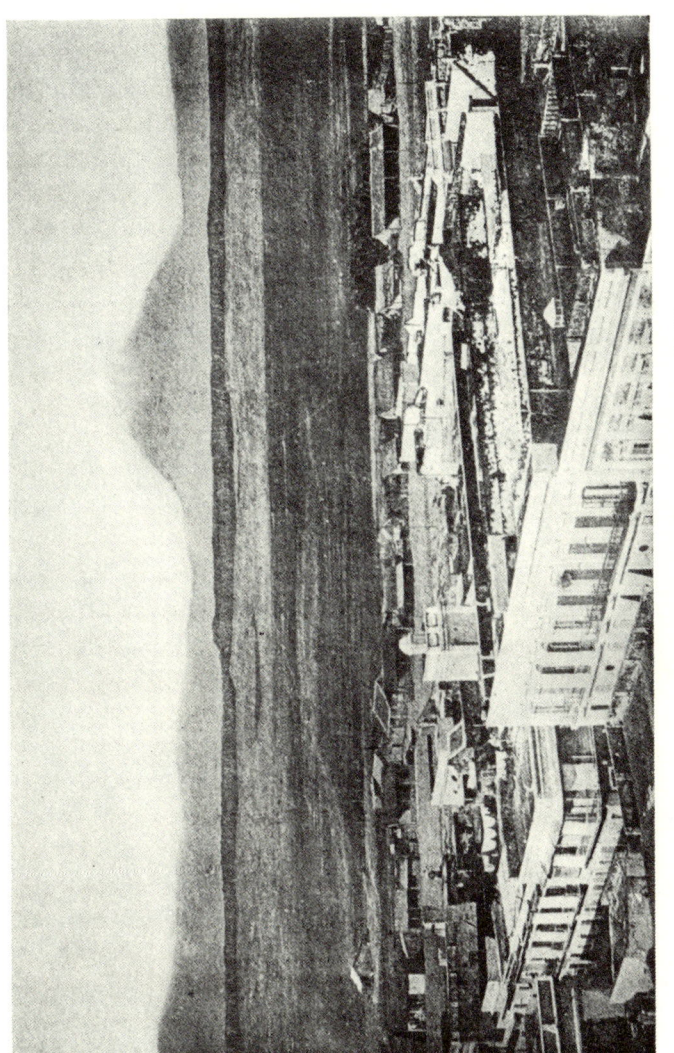

VIEW OF MOUNT ORIZABA FROM VERA CRUZ
From an old photograph

will attempt to force an entrance, and on finding how closely the City is invested, will abandon the attempt, the occurrences of the night will prove.

This morning among some prisoners taken, one dropped a club near one of our guard fires, which on examination was found to contain a letter from a man in Vera Cruz, to a brother in Puebla, underrating our numbers, and stating that if any assistance was to be given, it should be done at once, as the supply of provisions was small. This club was very cunningly devised, for a *mail club*. A hole had been bored in the centre, the letter introduced, a plug of the same wood driven in, and then the stick sawed off through the plug. The fact is, I presume, that the poor families are already feeling the horrors of a siege, and are eagerly looking around for succor. Would that the siege was over!

I fear that all Genl. Scott's foresight will not be able to guard against, and prevent the perpetration of most shocking acts of brutality in the taking of the City. I shall exert my powers to the utmost to aid him in stopping such unchristian and brutal acts.

Major G. just stopped at my tent and asked to whom I was writing, and said he would return as he wanted to send a message to Genl. Clinch, whom, he says, "You know I adore very much." He has now gone to his tent, to see whether his command is under arms to go out to-night or not. Capt. Vinton designs attempting to take a Cavalry Vidette which has been for some nights in his neighborhood, and three companies have been ordered out to assist. This is the duty Maj. G. thinks he may have to be occupied in to-night. The Maj. has not, I am sorry to say, become a *teetotaler*. He has been drinking very deeply before coming down. I shall try and keep him from throwing himself away, as he is too gallant and noble-minded to be permitted to destroy himself.

Fearing that we may be kept awake by alarms through the night, I will now retire, praying that God may give you that peace of mind and happiness enjoyed by good Christians. Good-night.

Wednesday, 17th.

The mail, thank God, brought this evening your letter of the eighteenth Feb. The mail preceding your letter had brought you news from Tampico up to the day we arrived there. Your next mail must have given you at least two letters from me. I know now how miserable you must have been made by each arrival of a mail bringing nothing from me. You have, however, since that time, unless the Post Office has played you false, received some letters. Every succeeding mail must have given you one and generally two letters. You must not, my wife, be uneasy if you do not receive letters by every mail. For although I shall write by every opportunity, still you must recollect that the vessels carrying them may be several days on the passage. We were, be it remembered (I am sure *you* always will), twenty-two days from Tampa to Tampico. Again, letters may remain some time in New Orleans, and a mail may well be missed at Savannah. All of these might keep you from receiving my letters for two or three mails. This will try you severely, my wife, but it is best to look at the worst shade of the picture.

I think that I shall close this letter to-night, for the chance of a vessel's going to-morrow, as I know that until you hear of Vera Cruz being taken, you will not have one moment's peace. But, with such an Army as we have and against such an enemy, the chances are that after one hour's firing of our Mortars, the City will raise the white flag. This leads, of course, at once, to a capitulation. Genl. Scott will be as liberal towards the Vera Cruzians as his duty to his own Govt. will permit.

You write that the ten Regt. Bill has passed, and ask if I am not going to be promoted. My wife, you have forgotten the provision of the bill requiring the President to make the selections of Cols., Lt. Cols., and Majors during the session of Congress. Those of us who are here could not possibly through our own agency have exerted the least influence in procuring advancement, as all the appointments must have been made before our letters could have reached Washington, and perhaps before they might have reached New Orleans.

No minor appointment would I, of course, agree to take. I would not give up my Captaincy in my Regt. for anything below a Lt. Colonelcy or a Majority in one of the new Regts. From the decided hostility evinced by President Polk to the Army, and his eager desire to secure political influence in his appointments, I have no doubt that all the exertions which might have been made by my friends would have been disregarded. The President in his appointments for the Rifle Regt. when gratitude towards gallant men, who by their valor had saved his administration, demanded some recognition, spoke as plainly to the Army as actions could speak, stating that we need expect nothing from him. For myself, I am becoming pretty thoroughly disgusted with the way in which the Army is treated, and care very little about remaining in it after the close of this war. This disgust is felt by very many, some of whom will undoubtedly resign as soon as peace is declared. God grant that the happy tidings may soon be heard in our land.

Everything has been pretty quiet about the lines to-day. A few shells and shots have been thrown, but no one has, I think, been injured. The storm so far abated to-day as to permit us to resume the landing of our Mortars and guns; ten of the former are now on the beach. To-morrow, I hope, will place us in possession of fifteen or twenty more—and then a few days only will be required to place them in position. That want of food would soon compel the [City and Castle to surrender (?)] is a very general camp impression; but on this point, as well as on all others relating to the siege, Genl. Scott's information is much more accurate than ours. I have just heard that another mail is here. I will reserve the rest of this space for to-morrow, as I may hear from you again.

Tuesday, 18th.

I have just received orders to go out with our Battalion to establish a Mortar Battery and will not be able to write any more to-night.

March 19th.

We were out engaged in making a battery for Mortars all night, returning into Camp at half-past four o'clock. We worked without being discovered. *I threw the first shovelful of earth in breaking ground for the attack on Vera Cruz!* I think, from their firing to-day, that they have discovered our work, as they have fired over a hundred shot and shell since ten o'clock.

Lieut. Hill has just informed me that the *Massa-*

chusetts will go to New Orleans to-morrow. I must, as he is waiting to take charge of this letter for me, now close. May God Almighty protect and guard my wife. Be of good cheer, I shall continue, as punctually as practicable, my daily letters, and hope to give you good news. Love to Father and the family.

No. 3. March 19th.

Having deposited No. 2 in the Post Office this afternoon I now commence our evening's chat, with No. 3, though to say the truth I feel so stupid that I shall prove very sorry company. As it will be impolite for me either to go to sleep, or to evince great stupidity, it will be well for me at once to excuse myself by stating why I cannot act *better*.

Last afternoon, at the request of Genl. Worth, I accompanied a party of officers on a visit to the outposts, the Genl. stating that our command was destined for the advance pickets to-morrow night. On my return, I flattered myself with the hope of having a comfortable sleep, as the enemy had been very quiet through the day, having thrown very few shot or shell.

Our Camp (3rd Arty.), I may as well here state, is south of Vera Cruz, say two and a half miles off, and having a high sand hill sixty or eighty feet high between us and the City, forming an excellent protection. We are just at its base, in a little triangle having smaller sand hills on the two other sides. My hopes of having a quiet night were, however, doomed to be sadly wrecked.

We had just finished our frugal evening meal when we heard the well known clatter of the sword of the Staff Officer, who usually brings orders to the Camp.

Col. Belton's call for Mr. Austine soon followed, and we were informed that two hundred men were required from our Camp, to report immediately to Col. Totten on the beach, the men to have their arms slung, with one half dozen cartridges in their pockets. "G" Co. was soon ready.

We marched to the Engineer depot where the men were furnished with picks, spades, and axes, each man having two of *different kinds* of these articles. A young Engineer was our pilot and we silently took up our line of march in single file.

The night was very favorable for our obtaining our position unperceived, the night being dark, with a mist amounting almost to a gentle drizzling rain. We lost our way and approached to within five or six hundred yards from the City, where we could hear the voices of the sentinels and men in the town very distinctly. Our young Engineer took some two or three men and searched for the position we were to occupy; after an hour's absence he returned and led us on. We found Capt. Lee and Lt. Smith expecting us. The men were at once ordered into the area enclosed by the cords marking the outlines of the battery and set to work cutting away the brush or digging and throwing the earth into an embankment designed as a protection against the balls of the Castle and town for those who will man the battery to be placed there. *I, of course, threw out the first spadeful.*

With occasional relieves from some forty Marines, the men of "G" Co. worked till about half-past three, when the relieving Engineers came. Our men then placed their working tools in order on the ground, and resuming their Arms we quietly retraced our way to Camp, where we arrived a little before five, not having been honored with a shot or shell from Castle, City, or even from a stray *ranchéro*.

We met the men who were to relieve us, on our way down. They must have reached their work about the time we reached Camp. We left the work in such a state as to protect them pretty effectually from the shot of the enemy. They have not, however, succeeded in accomplishing their tour of duty (twelve hours) unperceived and unsaluted, as the enemy have been firing at their embankment ever since about eleven this morning when they were probably first noticed.

Our party commenced two works about one hundred yards apart and three quarters of a mile from the town. Capt. Edson was at the other work. To-night I presume the relieving party will take up timber to make a platform for the mortar beds to rest upon, and to-morrow night I suppose the mortars with the shells will be put in place.

We hear this evening that another ship has arrived with Ordnance; I hope that she brings about twenty mortars, as we can use that number to great advantage. We hear also from a captured Mexican that there has been a *pronunciamiento* in Mexico (the City) declaring that those who made the war might fight it. Doubtful.

Now as you know that I am no *sleeper* in the day, am I not excusable for being stupid? Tattoo is now beating and I must attend. I attend with my officers all roll-calls now, as we are in the presence of the enemy. Just returned; as the town is quiet, I *hope* they will let me have a quiet night, though they may attempt annoying our working parties; if so it will annoy me more than I wish.

March 20th.

How vain are our hopes, some of them. Instead

of being permitted to pass my night quietly in my tent as I hoped, I was on picket all night with the Compy. I had just composed myself for sleep when I heard a few musketry shot from some of the outer pickets; this was soon followed by the *generale* when I was quickly at the head of the Compy. After the expiration of some fifteen minutes a staff officer galloped up to where Col. Belton was standing and directed him by order of Genl. Worth to detach a Compy. of his command for outlying picket service. It being my turn for service I was soon en route and took post for the night. Not an enemy, or anything a sane man could have taken to be one, was seen. During the night there was some firing by the camp pickets, but the cowardly fears of the sentinels caused them.

To-night our battalion goes out as the advance pickets, but, as the Navy is going to amuse the town during the night by throwing shot and shells, I presume that we shall have very little to excite us. The object of the Navy's firing to-night is to withdraw the attention of the Military in the City from our batteries, which it is intended to arm during the night.

Ten more mortars have arrived so that we shall now have an armament which will authorize us to open our batteries with every prospect of success upon the town. Yesterday they threw, as counted by one of the officers, one hundred and seventy-four shot and shells, and not a single man was hurt. One man, as he was stooping at his work, lost from a shot his suspenders, which were in a kind of knot at his back. Two Mexicans were killed by the pickets of the 2nd Brigade, in an attempt to pass through our lines from town.

In Mexico

Our Army in the line of investment, extends about seven miles. You may imagine how difficult it is for any person to state the daily events which take place in the Army. The health of the Compy. with very few and trifling exceptions, is good. All the married men are well, except Corp. Devit who has had a slight touch of ague; he is, however, nearly fit for duty.

My health, with the exception of the cold which separated me from the Compy. at Tampico, has been better than it was when I was at Tampa Bay. In my tent I have more comforts than almost any one I have seen in camp. And I have india-rubber cloth and my old cloak which protect me from the dews of night, and keep me warm enough when I am on detailed service from our Camp.

When we go out on duty, we leave a few men to guard the Camp, and leave everything standing. Each officer and man takes with him in his haversack provisions to last him his time of service. Old Derr I sometimes take, but not always, as he is frequently more serviceable in taking care of my things than in accompanying us. As yet we have only been enjoying the comforts of the soldiers' rations, but as the Sutlers are now arriving, we shall soon be supplied with anything we want.

As I spoiled the last letter by crossing, I think I shall not cross this one, but continue it by taking another sheet. This method presents, too, this advantage, that as soon as I hear that a vessel is about to sail, I can at once despatch the sheet or sheets which I have finished. Every few days I thus have a letter on hand for the mail. I shall now make some preparation for going out to-night. Good-bye, etc., etc.

Sunday, 21st.

Tattoo. You see by my closing lines that I did not intend crossing this letter, but as I hear that the *Princeton* leaves the Squadron to-morrow for the United States, I must, at the risk of giving you a little guessing, add a few lines. We have just returned from our tour of advanced picket duty. We had a quiet night as the enemy made no attempt to harass us. The platforms for the Mortar batteries were laid for six mortars to-day. The mortars will be taken to their positions to-night, and probably to-morrow we may commence firing. I do not think the City can stand many days' firing, and would not be surprised were my next letter addressed to you from the City of Vera Cruz. Good-night. May God guard and protect you.

Tuesday morning, 23rd.

The Engineer has just told me that six mortars were placed in position last night.

No. 1. BESIEGING CAMP, VERA CRUZ, MEX.

March 23rd.

Again has my plan of writing a little to you each day been interfered with. Yesterday morning I went into the trenches and took charge of one of the Mortar batteries. We remained on duty twenty-four hours, and as we were engaged every minute of that time either in firing, or in something connected with that duty, I had neither opportunity nor time for writing. The operations are now rapidly advancing; a new battery of heavy guns under Naval Officers was opened this morning.

[1] This letter "No. 1" of March 23d appears to be No. 4 of the series written from the Camp near Vera Cruz.

In Mexico

To-morrow morning a heavy battery of twenty-four pounders and of eight-inch howitzers (six pieces in all) will be opened. In addition to what we are using, eighteen Mortars arrived yesterday. These, when in position, will give us twenty-eight Mortars which, with the batteries of heavy guns above alluded to, must soon compel the City to surrender.

In my last letter I think that I mentioned that Genl. Scott had summoned the City to surrender, and that a civil negative was returned. Our Mortars commenced firing the moment that answer was received, and have continued the fire night and day. We have no means of ascertaining the amount of injury inflicted on the City, but I fear that the destruction of life must be very great.

It really goes to my heart to be compelled to do my duty when I know that every shot either injures or seriously distresses the poor inoffensive women and children, who have neither part nor lot in the War. On our side the loss in numbers is trifling.

I regret that I have to announce the death of an Officer of the 3rd whom you saw at Charleston. Capt. Vinton was killed by an eight-inch howitzer, which appeared to have struck him on the side of his head, and to have rolled along down his face and breast. So near was the force of the shell spent, that the skin on his side face was not broken.

I make my men protect themselves carefully in the battery and have had not an injury of any seriousness among them. Sergt. Foster will be excused from duty for a few days in consequence of a slight cut made by the fragments of a shell. In my own case, I look with confidence to the protecting care of our Heavenly Father who has shielded us both in many dangers.

I hope that my next letter will inform you that Vera Cruz with its celebrated Castle is in our possession. The moment we are Masters here, I presume that we shall be marched into the interior to some healthy position. Genl. Scott suggested that, the day of the summons. I was dining with him on that day; the summons was sent by Capt. Johnston, Topographical Engineers.

Great enthusiasm prevails throughout the Army, and all cheerfully perform the duties required of them. The Companies are sometimes on duty three days in succession, as was the case with "G" Co. last week, but there was no grumbling. And, although they were on duty all day yesterday and last night, there was no exhibition of dissatisfaction when I mentioned that they would be on the same duty to-morrow. An Army with such feelings will never flinch from the performance of any duty.

I shall leave the remainder of this sheet for this evening's news, as I hope to have a half hour to myself, in which I shall resume, for this evening at least, my delightful night's chat with you.

Evening.

Nothing of interest to communicate to-night. I have just returned from a visit to Col. Totten, the Chief Engineer, to see his map of the City. Lt. Scammon has kindly furnished me with a copy indicating the points of most interest to us in our operations. I sincerely hope that a few days firing will show them the inutility of longer delaying the surrender, and that the taking of this, connected with Genl. Taylor's glorious whipping of Santa Anna, will have a favorable effect in tending to an early termination of this un-

THE SIEGE OF VERA CRUZ
From an engraving of the painting by Powell

fortunate War. I think that killing people is a very poor way of settling National grievances.

I hope that we shall stay long enough in Vera Cruz for me to procure you a few articles of Spanish brass, etc., which I will send by some vessel returning to the United States. Genl. Scott told me to-day that this letter must be sent to his quarters early to-morrow; I will therefore not run the risk of keeping it open till the morning, as I might not have time to close and direct it, before leaving camp. I shall therefore be compelled to make a short letter of it, and give it to Yawn to-night; he will be left in camp to-morrow, with instructions for him to take it to Genl. Scott's Hd. Qrs. soon after breakfast.

You must not worry yourself by the idea that this constant work is wearing me down; my health is excellent; the only thing I have to complain of is that having lost the plug from one of my teeth it annoys me by feeling sore. Thus you see that I have a personal interest in inducing the Vera Cruzians to let us enter their inhospitable gates. I shall expect to be blessed with a series of letters from you on returning from this tour of duty. Give my best love to Father and all the family.

No. 5. BESIEGING CAMP NEAR VERA CRUZ.

March 27, 1847.

"Te Deum Laudamus." Commissioners were asked for by the Mexicans yesterday, and from the suspension of the firing this morning, the inference may fairly be drawn that terms are now being discussed for the surrender of Vera Cruz. But as this is a most important event in our Army affairs, and as yesterday was an important and interesting date in *our own*, it may be best for me to give as distinctly as I can trace them, the incidents connected with my last day's tour of duty in the batteries.

The morning of the 25th, leaving camp at four A.M., we reached the batteries in about a quarter of an hour; in a few moments we opened our fires on the devoted City. My position was in Battery No. 1 where I had been on the 23rd. Finding that there was a pretty good supply of ammunition, I soon accelerated the rapidity of my fires, till we threw a shell from the battery every minute, giving them twenty shells an hour from each of my three pieces. The Mexican batteries for a short time paid particular attention to us, but finding that they were also under a heavy fire from the other batteries of our line, they were compelled to make a more equitable distribution of their favors and we were soon left to the enjoyment of *only* our share of their shells.

Sometime in the afternoon, perhaps between four and five, I observed a white flag approaching the Mexican battery nearest to our lines. I instantly suspended the fire of my battery, and sent word to the commanders of the other batteries to do the same. The flag approached, a shot was fired over the heads of the party bearing it (an officer, interpreter, and sergeant) and a white flag rapidly run up and down at the battery; the flag again approached, another shot was thrown over the party, which halted for a minute or two, and again approached; another shot brought the party to a full halt, when in a few minutes a party of three Mexicans was seen approaching our flag. A polite salutation informed us that the conference had commenced. It lasted but for a few moments, when the parties separated and returned.

In Mexico

Our flag, it appears, was an answer from Genl. Scott to an application received the day before from the Consuls requesting that they might be permitted with their families to leave the City, and that this permission might be extended to the women and children. Genl. Scott's answer is said to have been a *negative*.

The excitement at the battery when the Mexicans fired the second and third shot over our flag was intense. They were anxious for me to open my fires upon that battery, but knowing that the language of the shot was simply, "Don't advance," I declined doing so. Col. Belton came up a short time afterwards, when I reported to him my reasons for discontinuing the fire; this was approved by him, and also by Col. Bankhead our "Chief of Artillery."

About nightfall I was ordered not to fire until the Mexican batteries opened their fires, and then to return it vigorously. This order was, however, limited to the time of the completion of some work on which the Engineers were employed. Finding at twenty minutes past two on the morning of the 26th that everything was ready, I gave the signal by firing one of the mortars at the Castle of San Juan d'Ulua. The thundering boom of this piece was soon answered by our whole line; in about twenty minutes I heard the notes of a bugle in the City; it discontinued and was again repeated. I told Col. Belton that it was a signal I was not familiar with, and that I supposed it might be a "parley." On hearing the same notes a third time I was authorized to cease firing. This was done in the expectation of the flag of truce being sent to one of our batteries. A picket was advanced to receive him, but as no one approached, after a silence of about half an hour, we resumed and continued our firing till we were relieved at five o'clock yesterday morning.

On our way home we were overtaken by the severest Norther I have experienced; on coming into camp, blinded with dust, we found many of the tents down. Mine still stands, a wreck, the fly torn to pieces and the tent torn nearly through along the ridge pole.

Yesterday morning very early, a Mexican came to Genl. Scott's tent with a note from the officer second in command (stating that Genl. Morales was sick) asking the appointment of Commissioners to make arrangements for the surrender of the City. Genl. Scott replied that he had already named Commissioners (Genl. Worth, Genl. Pillow, and Col. Totten). To this Genl. Morales replied by stating that he had appointed Commissioners to meet ours to enter into arrangements for the surrender of the City and Fort.

The Commissioners met and disagreed; it is said that the instructions given to the Mexican Commissioners authorized them to assent to the surrender, the troops to march out with colors flying, taking their Arms, etc. This was of course, declined by ours, and they separated with the understanding that if the white flag was not raised at six o'clock this morning, our firing would be resumed.

No firing has yet taken place, the Commissioners are now in the City, and the white flag is occasionally passing and repassing, coming, I presume, to Genl. Scott for specific instructions on the points raised during the discussion of the terms.

I omitted mentioning in the proper place that the Mexican batteries did return our fires yesterday morning; thus has the 3rd the honor of being on duty when the parley was sounded, and (if this discussion leads to a surrender) when the last gun was fired from their batteries.

I commenced this letter, intending to send it by the *Princeton*, but as I learn that a mail is being made up for a ship to New Orleans, and as the *Princeton* may delay till the termination of the discussion which may be spun out for a day or two, I think I shall send it to New Orleans.

Genl. Scott deserves, and I hope will receive, all credit with his countrymen for the almost bloodless triumph he will attain by the surrender. God grant that this may lead to an arrangement by which this unfortunate war will be closed. The Navy have suffered very severely at their battery; during their first day's fire, they lost four sailors, and on the second day, Midshipman Shubrick and one sailor were killed and two were wounded.

In a skirmish on the 25th we lost a few men—the numbers I do not know. But all our loss is very little compared with those of the other battles which have taken place during the war, much less than any one could reasonably have expected. The Mexicans have fired with great accuracy, but our men have been well protected, *firstly*, by the position of our camp, and secondly, by the parapets, etc., formed for the protection of our batteries.

We have peculiar reasons for remembering the 26th; let us then unite with all our hearts in thanks to our Heavenly Father for so glorious an addition to our reasons for thankful rejoicings at the return of that day. I have been thus far shielded from danger by His hand, and pray that He may soon return me to my darling family, to leave them no more.

A quarter past one P.M. The Commissioners have

not yet returned, and as I am fearful that I may miss the mail, I think that I had better close my letter and mail it at once. A mail may go without my being informed of it. The rumor now is that Genl. Scott has, in consideration of the value of the acquisition of the Castle San Juan, etc., consented to permit the soldiers to go into the interior as prisoners of War.

No. 6. CAMP WASHINGTON, NEAR VERA CRUZ, MEX.
March 27th.

No. 5 has been sent to the Post Office to take its chance for a mail to New Orleans; this will, I think, go by the *Princeton* which will bear Genl. Scott's despatches.

I have this moment returned from Genl. Scott's Hd. Qrs. where I learned that the position of the negotiation is this. The Mexican proposition was that the Officers and men were to march out with arms and equipments, with colors flying, to go into the interior to some designated point, the citizen soldiery not to be molested for the part they had taken in the War, the citizens to be protected in their personal property, their religion not to be interfered with, that in the event of hostilities being resumed, the women and children to be permitted to leave the City, etc.

Genl. Scott declined their first proposition and demands that the officers and men should be surrendered as prisoners of War, the officers to be paroled, and finally consented, that the men instead of being sent to the United States, might be sent into the interior, on a pledge from their officers that they should not serve during the War; of course he assented to the request about private property and not interfering with the religion of the people; to the request about the women and children leaving the City, if hostilities were resumed, he gave a prompt denial.

The details of the affair will be drawn up by the Commissioners under the instructions of the Genl., which are very particular, and you will soon see them in all the papers, as the Editors of the *Picayune* are here collecting everything that takes place.

As I mentioned in my letter No. 5, General Morales resigned, turning over the command to Genl. José Juan de Landero. Genl. Landero now states that Genl. Morales did not place him in command of the Castle of "Ulua" and that its commander is not responsible to him. The Commissioners express an apprehension that the Castle may not consent to the terms agreed upon, and one of them had, at the last advices, gone to the Castle to ascertain whether he could not bring the garrison to consent to the terms proposed.

The difficulty appears to be this, that, though we have inflicted most serious destruction on the City, the soldiery has, as yet, suffered very little, and they fear that it may be thought that they ought to have suffered more before surrendering. We are now well prepared for commencing operations against the Castle, as, the City being ours, we can turn all of our guns against it. One of Col. Bomford's Columbiads has been received, and it will be found a very formidable addition to our Armament.

I think that I am not too sanguine when I assert it as my opinion that this celebrated Castle will fall in about one week's firing. Genl. Scott will probably keep the soldiers here until our forces make one or two marches into the interior. But I will make no further speculations as I may to-morrow be able to give you an epitome of the treaty.

Luckily I have not been sent to the batteries to-day and am not under orders for to-morrow, so that I shall get a good night's rest, make up for the loss of sleep this siege has caused me. Good-night, may our Heavenly Father watch over and protect you.

Sunday morning, 28th.

I learn this morning that the Articles of Capitulation have been signed and approved, and that the *Princeton* will leave early this morning with Genl. Scott's despatches. This event is a glorious one for our arms, and has been effected principally by Arty.; indeed not a musket has been fired against the City; some skirmishes have taken place with a few lancers and other troops hanging around the outskirts of our Camp. I shall now take my letter to Genl. Scott's Camp where I may learn some facts which may be of interest.

Genl. Scott is so much engaged that I have not approached him. The Articles have been signed, the troops are to evacuate the City and Castle to-morrow morning at ten o'clock, to lay down their arms, the Officers retaining their side arms, to be paroled, pledging themselves that neither they nor their men shall serve again during the War, unless exchanged, the Officers to retain their private baggage, the Castle, Town, and Forts surrendered with all their armament and public stores, the private property of the citizens to be respected, etc.

We are this morning very much disgusted with Commodore Perry, who, after the terms of the Capitulation had been agreed upon and signed, wrote a presumptuous note to Genl. Scott, demanding the right to affix his name to that paper. Genl. Scott has deemed proper to admit him to sign it as a matter of courtesy. The fact

In Mexico

of his signature being affixed will be taken as proof positive that he was of material assistance in reducing the City, when the fact is, that since he came, but little has been done. The Naval battery was established by the orders of Commodore Conner, and Commodore Perry's first official communication to Genl. Scott declared that he could not supply their batteries with powder.

Commodore Conner and all under him exerted themselves to the uttermost to assist, but they could, from the circumstances of the case, etc., do but little more than give us the all-important aid of their sailors. For all this, Genl. Scott will in his Order give them full credit. I would have a greater right to demand my name to be affixed because I commanded a battery during the siege, than Commodore Perry for what he has done since his arrival!

No. 1. JUAN D'ULUA, MEX.

Tuesday, March 30, 1847.

My cousin, Lt. Anderson brought me this morning your letters of the 26th Feby. and 5th of March. Thanks be to God for his care and protection of my treasure. This information that you were well, gave me much greater true pleasure than any I have experienced for a long time. I find that I must again give you a hurried letter, as I learn that a vessel is to sail to-morrow morning for the United States. I shall therefore give you a few of the details of the closing events of the last two days; which will explain why I have changed the No. and heading of my letter, or, why I am here.

The 28th inst. we received orders directing Genl. Worth, with his Brigade, to receive the arms of the

Mexicans at ten A.M. That night, for the last time, I hope, in this war, I was at one of the batteries. The next morning about sunrise, Lt. Austine came to my command, and directed me to return to Camp, as my Compy. was one of those designated to garrison the Castle of San Juan d'Ulua. I immediately repaired to Camp, and at half-past eight marched with the rest of the Brigade to a large plain, taking our position, the right of our line about one half a mile from the main gates of the City, near the road to the City of Mexico.

The Brigade of Genl. Patterson's Division was facing us and say a quarter of a mile. We had been on the plain but a short time when we heard the Mexican bugle, and soon afterwards a salute to their flag, which was lowered at Castle and Forts. Next was heard the music of approaching bands, and was seen the head of their columns.

The interesting period was now near when I was to see a large Army lay down its arms at the feet of its conquerors. After much passing on the part of our gallant Genl. and his Aids, and infinite confusion on the part of our Col., we were put in march, with several other companies (destined to garrison the surrendered Castle and Forts) towards the City gate—meeting and passing close by the advancing prisoners of war.

I will not attempt to describe their troops; they wore dresses of various colors, blue, red, and white predominating; none of the companies looked to me like well drilled troops; they were, however, a conquered army, and, of course, could not have felt or exhibited much of the haughty pride of the soldier. Again I may as well confess that I did not look at them critically or closely, as I was afraid they might detect something of *triumph* in my countenance, when I thought them so humiliated by their surrender that none should have been exhibited, though we could not help feeling it.

But upon entering the City, having passed about five thousand of the Mexican Army before we reacheb the walls, all feelings of pride were gone when I witnessed the awful evidences of the deadly work of our destructive shells; not a step was taken that we did not see or stumble over the ruins we had made; in many of the houses shells had fallen, and burst, blowing everything within them to ruins. The police had been entirely neglected, and the smell of the filth was very offensive.

Occasionally we saw men, women, and children standing in the doorways or looking from the windows upon our rapidly advancing troops; there was no scowl or frown, but on the contrary no smiles welcomed us; the countenance bore more of sadness and sorrow than of anger. I saw but little of the City; my eye rested only on the ruins, and it was with feelings of relief I reached the end of the City, where we found boats ready to convey our command to this place. A few minutes landed us on this formidable work.

A Salute was fired, and the Stars and Stripes raised. I then felt that we were in an American Castle. Soon afterwards *I fired a second Salute to the "Princeton,"* as she passed us on her way home; this salute was joyfully given, as she bears two or three letters to my wife informing her of the capture of City and Castle, and of God's having preserved my life through the dangers of the siege.

To-day we have receive orders that for the present

the three companies of the 3rd Arty. under Col. Belton, are to compose the garrison of this place. I shall therefore have ample leisure to study this work. We find the quarters excessively filthy; they will not answer for our men; we shall have to construct temporary quarters on top of the present quarters which are not sufficiently ventilated.

The troops in the Castle are said to have lost but one man who was killed by the bursting of a shell thrown from one of the mortars of the battery. I commanded the last day of our firing. We were dealing destruction so heavily on the town that I thought I would see if I could wake the Castle, hence the unauthorized shell which killed this poor man.

Of the casualties in the City, I am afraid to enquire; most heart-rending scenes undoubtedly occurred. The British Consul lost a daughter about fifteen years old, killed by the bursting of a shell. The Consul does not blame any one but himself as he says he should have left the City when Genl. Scott gave them passports to do so.

To-morrow, or as soon as transportation can be procured, Genl. Twiggs will advance to the National Bridge, thirty miles distant on the road to Mexico. Jalapa is, I presume, to be the place where the Army will take summer quarters. It is represented as enjoying a delightful climate, perfectly healthy, and sixty or seventy-five miles from this place. I hope that as my good luck has, with the blessing of God, thus far prevailed, I may not now have a change and be settled down here during the summer months. I have no great dread of the yellow fever, but do not wish to be separated from the Army when *something* may be done. The 3rd has had the good fortune to have been at the batteries more than half the time the firing lasted.

I had the honor of firing with "G" Co. and a compy. of the 2nd Arty. the first two Salutes ever given by the U. S. troops in this justly celebrated work. The United States in getting possession of this work, gets many very valuable guns, and a large quantity of Ord. Stores. Many of the large guns are old Spanish pieces of the 17th Century filled with curious devices and inscriptions. The brass contained in the bronze of which they are made, is of itself valuable. Here are also fine English, French, and American pieces, some bearing the well-known stamp W. P. F., West Point Foundry.

As Col. Belton is to take this letter to town, and as the boat has just been reported ready, I must close. Give my love to Father, Mother, and the girls.

Before I close, let me beg you not to defer writing till the last day. 'T is the worry of writing so long a letter that gives you pains in your back. Do not make writing so much a matter of business; write not more than one page at a time and close it on mail day. Try this and resolve not to break your rule of one page a day, and all will be well.

No. 2. Ulua, Vera Cruz, Mexico.

Thursday, April 1st.

Presuming that I may consider myself as *at home* for a few days at least in this "Fortaleza," I commence my daily chat with you on my largest paper. The other day I wrote so hurriedly, that I merely thanked you for your letters, but my answer like most purporting to be such, did not give a reply to a single one of your queries. Some of them are very hard to answer, but still I will give the best I can. Before commencing, let me say that I found a sweet little violet in the letter, which I have placed among my treasures.

I have said nothing about your joining me, because everything has been and still continues uncertain. I could not write for you to come on, even if ordered to remain at a given place, because the very next day might order me to a remote part of the Country. What effect the glorious taking of Vera Cruz and of this place will have on the question of peace or war, we cannot tell.

Some of the Mexican officers who were received as prisoners of war on the 24th inst. said that it would protract the war. They probably spoke from the effect of deeply mortified feelings. Could Genl. Scott *now* be enabled to enter into correspondence with the Govt. I would hope for the best results; a few months might then restore me to your side. Let us hope for the best.

Mexico is, however, exceedingly crippled; her great General, he who was to rouse the slumbering energies of the Nation, the Army's Hero, Santa Anna, has been beaten by Genl. Taylor, and here we are in peaceable possession of her strongest tower of defence.

The value of the armament of this Fortress, and of the defences of the City is enormous. One hundred and forty good guns are in this place, many of them fine iron guns cast at the West Point Foundry, most of them good bronze Spanish and French pieces, which are very valuable. We find but a scanty supply of provisions, but powder, ball, shells and guns, howitzers or Columbiads, and mortars in the greatest abundance.

We learn from citizens of Vera Cruz that they had

GENERAL SANTA ANNA
From a lithograph

no idea that we were engaged in erecting our batteries till a short time before we opened our fires. The expectation was that we would take the place by a storming party; everything was well prepared for this, every street had its barricades, and most of the houses had sandbags at the doors and windows, and on the roofs. We should have met with very heavy losses had we not approached the town as we did. This fortress was also prepared for an assault, as the direct passage along every part of the work is cut up by piles of sandbags forming what we call "traverses."

My promise to get you to me or for me to take myself to you, will, you may be assured, be performed as soon as either can with propriety be done.

Your suspicions about Corp. Hannel's jaundice being yellow fever, were fortunately groundless, as a day or two after reaching Tampico he was quite restored. To your appeal for me to urge matters with my friends to gain me promotion, my last letter from camp, and since then the indecent conduct of Mr. Polk has given a full answer. The President or his advisers resorted to a practical lie to reward some of their pets. The law of Congress declares that the President is authorized to appoint an additional Major to each Regt., "who shall be taken from the Captains of the Army," and what does he do but send to the Senate a man's name for a Captaincy in the Army, and probably the very next meeting of the Senate, nominates this individual as Major. Such conduct is, I think, disgraceful.

Major Geo. Talcott received in the same envelope his commissions as Capt. and Major. Could I do so with honor, I would resign to-morrow rather than hold a commission under an administration which has, from the first day of its existence, shewn that it used all means to destroy the pride and trample on the rights of the Army particularly when that army has by its gallant deeds plucked its drowning honors from the deep. I cannot think with patience of the gross acts of injustice practised towards some gallant men in the Army.

Look at the case of my friend, Charles F. Smith. He has been foremost in every battle in which he has been engaged, and he has been in all save Genl. Taylor's last, and he has not even received the notice of an empty brevet. A man known and admired by all the Army for his well-tried courage, his cool self-possession in danger, and his high military attainments, and over this man's head are placed a score of men whose sole recommendation is that they or their friends have proved faithful in their worship of the President's party. Enough, enough.

It appears from letters received in camp from Maj. Bliss and some others in Genl. Taylor's army that the Illinois and Arkansas Volunteers ran like sheep from Genl. T.'s battle-field. Poor Lincoln received his death wound in trying to rally one of the Regts. Lt. Col. H. Clay, it is said, was deserted after he had been wounded, and was lanced by the Mexicans. And still Genl. Taylor does not in his despatches consign the cowards to merited infamy. This looks very much like a squint at the Presidency.

A quarter past eight P.M. Col. Belton, Adjt. Austine, and some others of our officers have returned from town; they have sought to ascertain whether we are to remain here, or to accompany the Army into the interior. Their impression is that not more than one Compy. will be left, that this Fortaleza and the armed works in the City will be dismantled and the guarding of this place be left mostly to the Navy. Should this be true, I have a chance of spending the summer at Jalapa, celebrated for its healthfulness, etc.

Capt. Wade has been kept by Col. Gates, at Tampico. Capt. Wayne is here, as small as ever. The illustrious patron keeps away from my company. The promotion of Bvt. Capt. Taylor and Lt. Steptoe to fill the vacancies of Bvt. Col. Childs, made Additional Major, 1st Arty., and Capt. Vinton, killed at his battery, will give the patron command of the Compy. he is now serving with, which is the Compy. about whose fate your letter expresses solicitude.

Derr is still my right-hand man, and as kindly attentive as he can be. I approve your suggestion about Lassie and will thank you to ask Father to dispose of her; he may make his own bargain. Her pedigree which is before me, written by the Editor of the *Spirit of the Times*, is, Lassie by Gohanna out of Isabella by Sir Charles, her dam by American Eagle, g.g. dam by Independence, g.g.g. dam by Jim Crack, g.g.g.g. dam by Impd. Sharke out of a thoroughbred mare. American Eagle by Impd. Spread Eagle, dam by Im. Sharke, g. dam Atalanta by Lyndsay's Arabian, g.g. dam Impd. Kitty Fisher. (See *Turf Register*, vol. 2, page 622.) For Independence (grandson of Mary Randolph and Annetta) see *Turf Register*, ditto for Jim Crack's pedigree in full. This is horse learning enough for you. I send her pedigree in full, because any one who wants blood will find that of Lassie as pure and good as any stock in the Country. I shall dislike parting from her, but I know it is best.

Maj. Whiting, I hear, leaves Mexico for the United States; he is not able to stand a summer's campaign here. You know, though, how weakly he is. I have not heard of Mrs. Hawkins, but she would *perhaps* do a good wife's part by joining her husband

April 2nd.

Having written at such length yesterday, I shall write only a few lines to you to-night. News from the City of Mexico informs us that they are there engaged in a struggle, of the Peace party under Herrera and the Priesthood with Santa Anna, and Gomez Farias heading the War party. It is said that the parties have been fighting for three or four days in the streets.

The Army which surrendered to us on the 29th have in the progress into the interior committed all kinds of disgraceful excesses laying the country waste by pillage and fire as they passed in.

The expedition to Alvarado under Genl. Quitman met with no resistance; indeed I learn this evening that a deputation was received by Genl. Scott from the authorities there, a short time after the departure of the expedition, offering to surrender to the Army and Genl. Scott. An expedition of about one thousand men left this morning for some little place, Antigua, some fourteen miles hence, where there are said to be seven hundred Mexican soldiers. Could we *now* advance, the chances are that we might march direct upon Mexico without having to fire a gun before reaching that place. Rumor says that Genl. Taylor is advancing to San Luis; doubtful. Col. Riley, another visitor to Ulua, sends message to his dear friend the General [Clinch]. Time for retiring, will bid you good-night.

April 3rd.

I commenced crossing No. 2 but recollecting that

GENERAL WILLIAM JENKINS WORTH
From an engraving by J. Sartain, after a daguerreotype

In Mexico

you had but one mail a week, and that a series of letters had been sent but a few days since, I thought it would be better to give you a letter which could be read, without that difficulty always existing with badly written and crossed letters.

As our Fortaleza is separated from Hd. Qrs. by one half mile of water, I can only give you the rumors which *float* to us from the City; many of them are, subsequently to our first hearing them, found to be incorrect; such as are important I will always try and give you the last and true version of, but the minor ones are not worth re-mentioning.

I find by orders received yesterday, that we (the 3rd Arty.) are brigaded with the 2nd Arty. and 4th Infy., the brigade commanded by Col. Bankhead. This promises that we may accompany the Army into the Country, as it makes it Col. B.'s interest to keep us with him, and he has much influence at Hd. Qrs. Major Genl. W. G. Worth has issued his order dividing his old Brigade into two Brigades, he commanding them as a Division so that we belong now to the 1st Brigade, 1st Division.

I shall, if I can obtain a copy, send by this mail the first number of the *American Eagle* published at Vera Cruz. It gives a different version to the news from the City of Mexico from that written yesterday by me; this may be correction No. 1 of the Camp rumors. Genl. Santa Anna is there stated to have joined the Priests' party, and opposed Gomez Farias. This gives us a President *versus* his Vice-president.

Sunday morning, April 4th.

I was prevented by a succession of visitors from writing more than the above note yesterday and must write as rapidly as I can till breakfast, as the steamer *Edith* leaves this morning, I hear, for the United States and I *must* have my letter mailed in time.

The news from Mexico is reported to be, that Santa Anna has placed himself in the governmental seat, but that both parties are for prosecuting the war (correction No. 2).

Genl. Scott thinks, I was told yesterday, that the difficulties between the two Governments will be arranged in a few months. Genl. Worth, as you will see by this paper, sent by this mail, is Governor of Vera Cruz and this place. He is exerting himself to clean the city, having pressed into the police service some two hundred Mexican laborers. He feeds them well, and they, I fancy, do not overwork themselves. Confidence seems gradually gaining ground, shops which were closed for the first three or four days are now opened.

If the Vols. were at home we could so govern our soldiers as to check outrages now hourly committed. Capt. Marshall states that as he was walking in the streets night before last, he saw just ahead of him a man with a musket and before he reached him, the scamp struck a Mexican with the butt of his musket and knocked him down. This is a slight enormity compared with some that have been committed. A Milty. Commission has been instituted by Genl. Scott to try all cases which can not legally be brought before Courts-Martial, and I hope that Genl. S. will have every convicted culprit punished as fully as the court and law direct.

Major Wade's Compy. has been ordered from Tampico to join the Regt. here. Unless Col. Gates can offer very weighty arguments against its being withdrawn from that place, I presume that we shall enjoy the pleasure of seeing the Major here. Col. Gates seems very anxious to increase his *regulars*, as he has detained two compys. of Infy. who accidently touched at Tampico on their way here.

I have omitted mentioning that this grand army is honored by the presence of a lady, and who do you suppose her to be—no less a personage than Mrs. ————. She visited our Fortaleza the day we took possession, but I did not beg an introduction. She remained on board ship during the siege; where she is now, I do not know. I presume that she intends accompanying us to Mexico. Could she hear the remarks made about the indecency and indelicacy of her husband's having allowed her to come, I am sure that her ears would burn.

I am sorry that Duncan has set his heart upon entering the service at this time. Those of us now *in*, are thinking seriously of getting *out*, so that the new *ins* stand a *chance* of good promotion. The recent promotions will place me the third captain in the Regt. Capts. Burke and Wade are the two above me.

As we are soon to go into Summer quarters, I must put you on your guard about listening to or rather believing the ten thousand reports you will hear and see about the health of our troops. I find that letter writers who are with us write lies, either through ignorance, inattention, or design. I will inform you if there be any unusual degree of sickness in our Army. Should I be taken sick, you may be pretty well assured of my being sent out of the country, as no *useless* mouths are wanted with an army which will have to draw its supplies as far into the interior as we are going.

You enquire about our friend Major Whitney; he has gone home; he stayed through the siege, and was sent off the day before yesterday. It is well that he should return; he was present at the *siege and capture of Vera Cruz*, and as this will be regarded as the great feat of our war, he returns now satisfied and will find in the incidents of the siege anecdotes enough for repetition for the last days of his life, rapidly, I fear, drawing to a close.

Our friend Austine has been for some time anxious to give up his Adjutancy, if he could get anything better. He applied on receiving the recent law giving a Rgtl. Q. M. to each Regt., for that appointment to our Regt. but Lt. Col. Belton, who assumes that he has authority to appoint, gave the appointment to Lt. Van Vliet (gone to New Orleans sick) on the ground assumed by the President towards the Army, in not giving appointments in new Regts. to officers of the Army, "that Lt. Austine was already well provided for."

Capt. Taylor, who desires to be remembered, has just informed me that the letters are to be sent to the *Edith*, and that the boat is to go very soon. I must therefore close. That God may bless and guard you is my earnest prayer.

When shall we spend our sweet Sundays together? How different this day from what it was when we were together.

No. 1. Camp Surrender, Vera Cruz, Mexico.
April 5th.

Again in Camp, and very much I assure you, to my own gratification. I had been a little apprehensive that it might be my fate to be among

In Mexico

those to be left behind, and was delighted to receive orders to leave the pleasant quarters of the Fortaleza de Ulua, where, though we revelled *not* in the Halls of the Montezumas, we had the honor of being bitten by day and night by fleas which might have legitimately descended from the Conquerors of this Country. Defend me from a summer residence in the justly celebrated Ulua! I would, I am certain, be very unwilling to rank among its conquerors again, were a residence there a necessary consequence. I am sure that I would gladly vote for its re-delivery, in preference to remaining there, I mean. Tell Father, no disparagement to Florida when I say that Ulua can beat her and give her odds, in producing fleas and mosquitoes. I must send a phial of them to the National Museum at Washington to be placed among our trophies. Stay, I need not do it, the flag and articles to be forwarded will carry the breed.

I have just returned from reporting my arrival in Camp to Col. Bankhead, our new Brigade (2nd Arty., 3rd Arty., and 4th Infy.) Commander, and am sorry to find that in consequence of his not getting on well with our *new* Division Commander, Major Genl. Worth, he is soon to leave for the United States. The order states that in consequence of his health and distinguished services in the trenches he has been selected to convey to the President the Flags, etc., captured in the City and Castle. Col. B. is a selfish man, but is always a gentleman; I am sorry to lose him, though I know that he is too infirm to accompany us into the interior.

I also learn that the *Edith* for which I wrote so hurriedly, day before yesterday, has not yet gone, and that she *will* leave to-morrow, hence this *hurried* scrawl in place of one of my old-fashioned family talks. Having reached Camp about twelve, I dined with Cousin Sam, and enjoyed the best dinner I have had since I landed—bean soup, rice, tomatoes, sweet potatoes, green peppers as a salad with the tomatoes.

At the Castle we have had fresh beef twice, but really, the taste was such that I was not certain it might not have been a spare cut from the rump of some poor donkey killed by one of our shells during the siege. Last night, hunger and the novelty of seeing *fresh* meat made me relish a piece, but this morning, I could not *go it*, like a second bad egg; I left the enjoyment to those who liked it. I am told that by sending to market early, we can purchase vegetables, etc. I think that one of our men must wake to-morrow *bien matinée!*

I met Dr. Cuyler in the City as I passed through it, and was told that he was to do duty with the 3rd. Dr. Potter is now our Surgeon; he is, I find, a great favorite with some of the 2nd, with whom he has been serving; they are both, I believe, good surgeons, and we shall be lucky in having either. By the bye, I met young Dr. Steiner in the City; he had an army cap and informed me that he was on duty with the 4th Arty.

I find that much has been done to cleanse the City since I first passed through it. The sandbags have been taken down, and some of the filth removed, but much yet remains undone; you see many piles of rubbish, with here and there fragments of the murderous shells. Doubtful of the proper name of this Camp, I have given it a name, descriptive of its locality, as it embraces the ground occupied by our troops on the 29th, when the enemy laid down their arms.

No one pretends to guess the day of our departure; the fact is that our knowing ones have been so completely found amiss in their speculations that they cease to be regarded as prophets.

I this moment hear a mocking-bird warbling his sweet notes; the Band of the 2nd is practising, and this sweet bird seems answering to some notes he loves. How many, many miles do those notes bear my thoughts, my wishes, from this dull camp. How delightful and still how tinged with sadness those thoughts! They tell of home, of a beloved wife, but yet of a home that I do not enjoy with her. Sing on, sweet bird, there is joy mingled with the sadness of your song. I may soon be as free as you are and return on wings of love to my own mate. Why not? The storm is now over and we may expect a calm. Gentle Peace will soon, I hope, spread her healing wings over this distracted country, and will send us *hopping* glad to our homes again.

Having reduced my baggage to nearly the campaign allowance, you must expect nothing but scrawls from me henceforth. My Compy. desk has been deposited with some other, etc., in the Castle. I now write on the top of my little hand trunk placed on the old camp bedstead. My seat is the campstool which was broken in our march to Tampa Bay. These three articles with my dressing-gown and large pillow have been great comforts I assure you. I shall be sorry when I have to leave any of them behind. 'T is said that we are to have very limited means of transportation when we leave for Jalapa. I must manage to have my favorites taken by my friends, *los medicos*, whose means of transportation are very liberal in all well-appointed armies.

Heigho, an order has just been handed me stating that in consequence of the limited means of transportation all Compy. and Regt. Books must be left. I fear that some of my good friends will have to stay behind. *N'importe*, they were in the Siege; they have had glory enough to make all stay-at-home, small trunks, bedsteads, and chairs blush for their lack of spirit in not having gone into the field at their Country's call! Who can conceive what thrilling stories these said articles of furniture may attempt telling you some of these days when they are in the mood?

I must stop cross writing here or you will make nothing of the whole letter. As Col. B. proposes leaving in a few days, he will probably be the bearer of my next despatches?

No. 2. Camp near Vera Cruz, Mexico.
April 5th.

Though a letter was written and sent to be mailed since my arrival in camp to-day, I must have my evening's chat with you before I retire. My conscience has reproached me, too, with my ingratitude in having omitted in my list of comforts, my mosquito bar (the daily admiration of Derr), my coarse towels, and dressing-gown. Two luxuries I shall have to part with, my white wash basin and pitcher; these I can replace, however, at Jalapa. The others are home tokens containing either your work or executed under your directions. An order requiring my separation from them would be met with a very ill grace.

April 6th.

I had written the first four lines last night, when Capt. Taylor and Lt. Thomas came to my tent, and talked nonsense till my candle was burnt into the socket; having, unfortunately, no other, I could not write a

In Mexico

word more and was compelled to go to bed. The only piece of information communicated was, that we were authorized to send and receive letters free of postage. This is not much of a boon to me, as the postage on my letters is always most freely given.

This morning I, being for the first time where I could indulge that extravagance, tried a little marketing; here are some of the items: sweet potatoes, about the medium size, $6\frac{1}{4}$ cents apiece, turnips as large as two fists $12\frac{1}{2}$ cents, tomatoes 2 cents apiece, something between a cabbage and a lettuce $6\frac{1}{4}$ cents a head. Everything is very high. Claret $14 a dozen; this is a luxury rather too expensive to be indulged in, when the necessaries of life are so high. Bacon $18\frac{1}{4}$ cents per pound, etc. However, things will either be lower, or we will, when we get into the health region of the country, get so healthy and so stout as to be able to do without them, as we can then eat anything.

No news from the interior on which any reliance can be placed. Col. Kinney, who seems to know everything, told me this morning that peace was not talked of in the country around this place, that Santa Anna was approaching the coast with a large army. I cannot think that he has so soon forgotten the thrashing Genl. Taylor gave him at Buena Vista, and am not inclined to think that he is willing to measure his strength with the army.

I am still highly gratified at my change from Garrison to Camp; my men are in better spirits than they were: here I can hear them cracking jokes and indulging in merry laughter, in the Castle they looked like convicts. No castles for me. I have to-day another newspaper for you, the second number of the *American Eagle*, containing some of Genl. Scott's correspondence relative to the surrender. The paper is badly printed. This press will, I presume, follow us into the interior, so that you will probably receive all the numbers of it. Whether the paper established at Tampico still exists I know not. I had thought of having it sent to you regularly, but when I can write regularly, even if I can send a letter but once a week, there will be but little left uncommunicated.

Yesterday, as the papers state, was a hot day, but not hotter than I have experienced in the United States. Col. Belton is still in the Castle. I expected him and the remaining Compy. of this Regt. this morning, but his Excellency dislikes relinquishing his Governorship. No news yet of Major Wade's arrival; it *should* be a severe disappointment to him, if he is kept from advancing to Jalapa with us.

Now that I am here, for the last time in my life I trust, I am anxious to see as much of the country as I can, and would therefore be pleased, if it can be done without interfering with my leaving this land as soon as possible, to go as far as the City of Mexico. I hope that the land bounty will give us good results for our winter operations, and that the President will increase the Volunteers to a force so respectable in numbers as to sweep over the whole country. I will now bid you a good-morning, as I must examine and send off my quarterly papers. *Bonjour.*

After tattoo. I cannot retire, without having a little chat with you. My old friend, Capt. Wall, arrived to-day and has been sitting with me and talking over army, and former-day affairs. He takes command of the Compy. now commanded by Lt. Steptoe, who will, I suppose, be promoted to Capt. Vinton's Company.

In Mexico

Some of the Alvarado expedition have returned; they report having found plenty of cannon-batteries abandoned. It seems that a midshipman was ordered to precede the fleet, with orders to blockade the town. But on getting in sight of the place, he took it into his head that he would try the range of his gun; having fired a few shots, a boat pulled out from town offering a surrender. He ran in, found the batteries abandoned, took possession, and, having succeeded so admirably, he ascended the river some twenty miles to another town, where he met with no resistance. The Great Fleet and Army now arrives, and Commander Perry finds all done. The Midshipman, Mr. Hunter, he has placed under arrest for disobedience of orders, he having been sent to *blockade*, not to *take* the place. I am sorry that the Navy will not have "Alvarado" to add to their list of conquered towns. The capture of this place draws after it, almost as a matter of course, the surrender of all the other towns along the coast.

April 7th.

I have just returned from Col. Bankhead's tent; he is very desirous of getting off, and has gone to the City to ascertain if a vessel will sail to-day. He will embrace the earliest opportunity and will either sail for New Orleans or New York. If he goes to New Orleans, I will ask him to take charge of this letter. But otherwise I will keep it and add another sheet or two before sending it off. Genl. Twiggs is under orders to advance to-morrow with his Brigade. Genl. Quitman will follow with the 3rd, and we close the march with the 1st Brigade. The transportation is thus far limited to one wagon for two companies. I hope that by the time we march, the Quartermasters'

Dept. may succeed in increasing their means, so as to be a little more liberal with us.

A mail arrived, I hear, in the *Massachusetts*, last evening. I must send a man, Yawn, to enquire. I have sent him, and hope in a half hour, to enjoy the delightful pleasure of reading a letter from you. God grant that I may receive good news from my wife. As my married men may not be very punctual in wri'ing to their wives, it is time for me to make a report to enable you to comply with your promises to their wives. Corp. Devit, Privates Cramer and Howard are all slightly indisposed; nothing more, I think, than chills and fever. Many of the men are on the sick report to-day. This is always the case with new recruits; they invariably, after an arduous tour of duty, will be found on the sick report for some days. And in that Castle, the men were prevented by fleas and mosquitoes from sleeping.

Capt. Backus, 4th Infy., relieved Capt. Vinton's Compy. yesterday, so that we have the remnant of the 3rd Arty. again encamped together. Genl. Worth stopped a moment yesterday as he passed, and informed me that Mrs. Sprague had given him another granddaughter. The Genl. looks in better spirits since the reception of his Major General's commission. I have not had the pleasure of seeing Genl. Twiggs; he is too cunning to permit Genl. W. to outgeneral him. I fancy that Twiggs's friends will succeed in getting a brevet for him, bearing the same date, or an older one than Gen. W. I *must* wait till Yawn returns.

Afternoon. Yawn returned without bringing me a letter. Perhaps I ought not to have expected one, as my dates were later than Dr. Cuyler's from Savannah, but, whenever I hear that a mail has come,

In Mexico

without reflection that, as you have but one mail per week, I cannot receive them oftener, I think that I must have a letter or two from you in *that* mail.

The order for the commencement of our march into the interior is issued. Genl. Twiggs starts to-morrow with the 2nd Division. Genl. Patterson follows the next day with two Brigades of Vols. He leaves one brigade of Vols. and the Tennessee *dismounted* Cavalry until the arrival of their horses. Genl. Twiggs and Genl. Patterson will each have forty-five wagons for their commands. Every man takes forty rounds of ammunition and five days' rations of hard bread, and bacon and pork (cooked) for two days. As this order omits all mention of us, I presume that we stand fast till some of their wagons going with their Divisions return, when we shall move honored with the presence of our gallant General.

I thought till this morning that my old friend, Dr. Harney, was to remain, but Dr. Porter now tells me that he thinks that he, Dr. P., will have to remain, as Dr. H. thinks the mountain air necessary for his health. The Dr. has not been well since he has been in this country. I am afraid that he is breaking down. If Dr. Porter leaves the 3rd Arty. I presume that Dr. Cuyler, who has been medical purveyor till recently, will take charge of us. Dr. Wright may remain; Dr. Porter says he is half inclined to do so.

Poor Col. Bankhead has relinquished command, and is to sail home to-morrow, with the cannon and flags. Genl. Scott sends, I think, twelve beautiful bronze cannon. One I selected for West Point. I do hope it will be sent there; its date is 1685, "Le Mordicant" beautifully chased, etc. Col. B.'s departure places our Brigade under the command of Col. G——,

—th. Infy., a man deservedly unpopular with his officers, notoriously setting a bad immoral example to his juniors. Genl. Scott, whom I have not seen since the surrender, looked very well when I last saw him.

If to-morrow be not too excessively hot, I propose going into the City for a short time. I have very little curiosity. Many have spoken of the marks of ruin they have seen, of the vast amount of public stores, etc., to be seen, but I care for none of these things. If I could find any little mementoes and had a favorable opportunity of sending them to you I would move as briskly about it as any of them.

I heard this morning that Major Talcott had been importuning Col. Bankhead to make special mention of his services in the trenches. I would cut my tongue out before I would allow it to commit so great an act of indelicacy. Col. B. will not, I hope, do it. He has already been induced to insert the names of two Top. Engineers, who were at one of the Batteries, mentioned because they volunteered, not because they did as much or more than others. The fact is, that at the Batteries there was but little room for individual distinction. I will now lay this down for to-night.

Night. Capt. De Hart came in at dusk, and has just left; it is now too late for me to add much to my letter. I find from the Capt. that the Govt. patronized him in the publication of his work on Courts-Martial, by taking one hundred copies! Col. Bankhead is to leave in the morning, but at what hour I cannot learn. Lt. Andrews will go to the City in the morning, and I will, unless I hear that the Col. sails either late in the day or not until the next day, give him this letter. Goodnight. May God bless and protect you. *Bonsoir.*

In Mexico

April 8th.

A friend waits for my letter. I must close it for fear of missing this mail. Nothing new, Genl. Twiggs is moving. Good-night. Love to Father and all the family.

No. 3. Camp near Vera Cruz, Mex.

April 8, 1847. Night.

My letter closed this morning. I hope was in time for the mail, though I am a little apprehensive that my old friend, Col. Bankhead, left too early. The least delay on the part of the gentleman entrusted with it must have caused it to miss a mail. I do not, however, attach as much importance to my letters now being too late for mails, as I know that your heart has been relieved of a heavy load by the reception of my letters announcing the progress and termination of the siege.

During the Siege, or at any time previous, and subsequent to my arrival, when I knew how important it was that you should hear from me regularly and frequently, I regarded the chance of missing a mail as a very serious affair. Now, you should have nothing on your mind to worry about. I am about leaving the seaboard to go to a place as notoriously healthy as any in the world. Even had I been ordered to remain here, I think by prudence I might have remained and got through the summer safely. I have not attempted a description of Vera Cruz because really I have seen nothing of it. A detail as member of a Genl. Court-Martial will take me there to-morrow and many consecutive days: so that I shall *perforce* learn something of it, and will give you such sketches as I think interesting. I had intended writing a good long letter to-night, but was interrupted by the arrival of Major Graham and two other gentlemen who spent the evening with me. I must now close, as the night is far advanced.

NOTE. The Genl. Court-Martial has been ordered to meet in our Camp.

April 9th.

Reasonably good news from Washington, as the President has, in his benevolence, condescended to give to friend Capt. Charles P. Smith, two brevets. He is now a Bvt. Lt. Col., a very slight reward for his many gallant acts.

I have been so long engaged in Court-Martial duties to-day, having finished the trial of three officers (for not very serious breaches of discipline), that I feel very little like writing and will retire very soon, hoping that we may not be so much pressed to-morrow, as I shall then make a respectable addition to my letter. I fear however that the visit contemplated in the first part of this letter must be deferred till our return from Jalapa, as I think we have cases enough to be tried to engage us during the time we are to remain here.

Before closing, to shew you the variety we have in our reports, I will give you yesterday's and to-day's reports. *Yesterday*, Jalapa and Puebla de los Angeles declared their independence of the Central Govt. and have determined to treat for peace. *To-day*, Santa Anna is at the Flat Mountain between Jalapa and Puebla with an army. Good-night, and may God bless you.

April 10th. Saturday Night.

Hearing this morning that a steamboat was to leave

for New Orleans to-day, and not having time to finish my letter, I enclosed and forwarded this morning's paper. On the Court-Martial we have made great progress to-day, as we concluded the cases of the two officers who were to make their defences this morning, and tried twelve soldiers; most of them plead guilty and their cases were so simple as to leave no room for consideration or doubt.

This afternoon I strolled into town for an hour, but by the time I searched the part where the fashionable shops are, it had become so dark that I could not see. I did not see anything curious or rare in the shops I was in, and what I priced was extravagantly high. They are determined to make us pay dearly for our whistle. I do not blame them; it will absorb all the profits of their stores for years, to repair the damage we have done them. Never, never do I wish to be one of a besieging army again. And faith, I have no great desire to be one of the army besieged!

Though much has been done to cleanse the streets, they are yet filthy. Our Surgeons are busy establishing a general hospital here. The Army moves with so little transportation, that we have to leave our sick behind. Dr. Porter says that he will send them to their companies by the earliest opportunities after we leave. In some of the companies in camp, there is a good deal of sickness—some of the cases have proved fatal. Thus far *we* have had no dangerous cases; all of my men will, I am convinced, recover as soon as I can get them into the mountainous region.

I have heard no camp news about Santa Anna since yesterday. To-morrow, we should hear from Genl. Twiggs's Brigade; we *certainly* shall if he hears of an opposing or a threatening force.

Bvt. Major Backus, commanding Ulua, has, by the working of some fifty Mexicans, succeeded in making it a much cleaner and more habitable place than it was when we were in it, but, bless him, he will be unable to remove either the fleas or the bedbugs; the latter, I find, colonized very extensively in my bedding, whilst we were there. I think of sending some of these Ulua curiosities to Washington. To-morrow being Sunday I will, if the day be not too warm and I can conveniently leave camp, go to one of the churches in the City. Good-night.

Sunday, 11th. Morning.

Yesterday a negro fellow was hung for a heinous offence, having been tried and sentenced by a Milty. Commission, composed exclusively of Vol. officers. The man was a servant to a Vol. officer. This morning two Mexicans are found, one dead and the other nearly so. This devilish deed was undoubtedly perpetrated by some scoundrels among the Volunteers as a repayment for the loss of the negro. I sincerely hope the perpetrators of this act may be brought to punishment.

The morning is so warm that I have no intention of attempting my visit to church in town to-day. I have therefore gone through with an hour Sunday routine of readings (reading my part distinctly and your part silently), and after a loll of an hour am now ready for the duties of the day.

In town yesterday I met one of Genl. Worth's A. D. C.s who said that Genl. Worth spoke of our Commands moving to-day or to-morrow, as there are not one quarter wagons enough here to move with the limitation of baggage already imposed. I do not

In Mexico

think it possible for us to march. I doubt if we can leave earlier than the 15th inst. One Brigade of Vols. and one Regt. still remain; they should march before we do, as they belong to a Division already on the road.

The Doctor has just sent six of "G" Co. to the Genl. Hospital in the City. Cramer (the husband of the pretty woman who came with the recruits) is the only married man among them. His wife has, I believe, left Tampa Bay, with Mrs. Hannel and Mrs. Devit, for Tampico. I advised Howard to tell his wife to remain where she is. Women are, as I anticipated, a great plague to their Captains in the field. So little transportation is allowed, that if permitted to accompany the troops they must purchase or steal some poor horse or ass to carry their baggage. A woman with one child can thus get on tolerably well, but when they have more, they soon find it impossible to move in that way, and are left or sent back by some return train to some large depot.

No mail yet. I fear that some of your letters are lost, as I hear that one of the vessels wrecked on the beach near our first camp, on the 26th March, contained a large mail. Lt. Thomas has stopped in to inform me that Major Wade has arrived. I hope that the change from Tampico to this place will be agreeable to the Major. I do not think that he will take a very violent liking to our Lt. Col. who is occasionally as unamiable as he sometimes shews himself in the company of his amiable spouse.

The addition of the Major's Compy. to our little battalion is very acceptable, as we were too small to be *respectable* in so large a command. I will now make my bow until this afternoon.

Night. Major Wade has arrived; his Compy. has taken its position in our Camp. Lt. Johnson is with him; he looks very well, and will, I hope, continue to think himself so. The order is out and been received by us, for our march to-morrow. The order designates twelve for the hour of march, so I presume that we will not make more than nine or ten miles.

I hear that Genl. Twiggs sends word back that Genl. Santa Anna is fortifying himself at some position this side of Jalapa. I can scarcely credit the opinion that he seriously intends giving us a fair, good fight. If he be there, it may be with the view of making a show of defence and then entering into terms with us. God grant that this may be the case, as blood enough has certainly been shed to satisfy the honor of both Nations, and a treaty formed at an early date would restore the most of us to our families very early this fall, and perhaps some Companies would be sent home at once.

Report says that Santa Anna has his cabinet with him, and that Genl. Labrega is also there. Why his Cabinet is there would be a question worthy of consideration were it certainly true.

The afternoons are sufficiently pleasant; as at St. Augustine the hottest part of the day is in the morning, say from seven till nine; after these hours by keeping out of the sun the temperature is very agreeably pleasant.

Genl. Scott will, I presume, either accompany us to-morrow, or follow us the next day. On every account it is highly important that we should move towards the mountains. One reason that we get off earlier than I anticipated is that over two hundred mules arrived to-day, thus giving us unexpected addition to our means for transportation, and again

In Mexico

our Division moves before some of the Vols. left here by Genl. Patterson's Division.

I omitted mentioning the arrival of Capt. Winder, who landed this evening with his Compy. of twenty-eight men. He finds a detachment of recruits from which he will, I hope, fill his Compy. I have not seen him—indeed our Army covers so much ground that I do not attempt visiting any one. We meet our friends occasionally on duty, or I see them as they pass my tent going to, or returning from town.

As I may have an opportunity of finishing this sheet to-morrow before the hour of starting, when there may be something of interest to add, I will only encroach further by bidding you good-night. I must look to a judicious reduction of my baggage. The allowance is, however, more liberal than was anticipated, as one wagon is allowed to each Company.

April 12th. At night.

We are now reduced to our travelling allowance of tents, etc. Our Camp presents a singularly scattered appearance, each camp, where two hours since there was a full allowance of wall and common tents, now formed with only three small tents. Our baggage will soon follow. So large an army requires a very large train for the transportation of its ordinary supplies. I have retained as many of my comforts as I could reasonably, seeing how little accommodation was allowed for the men. My camp bed, mosquito bar, and trunk, with the morning gown, old cloak, and big boots go with me. My library is not very large— my two Sunday books and one Vol. of Tactics constitute all.

Thank God I have received a letter from you dated

March 12th. But, my wife, you imagine a thousand dangers, and our Heavenly Father leads me unharmed through all to which I am really exposed. I think after having received news of our almost bloodless victory here, that you cannot but place entire confidence in that God who has so constantly heaped his blessings on both of us.

Look around us and see how many are, though laboring under heavy afflictions, bearing up cheerfully under circumstances which would seem to leave them no room for hope. They are frequently rewarded for their great faith in this world, and look, with assurance to their better reward hereafter. I would not have you conceal your feelings from me; on the contrary, I feel happier in knowing that you describe your feelings as they really are, than I would be to detect your attempt to conceal them. Think of all that has really passed, see how many dangers your love has conjured up, and despond no more.

To-morrow we leave for a healthy region, where all the invalids will rapidly recover. Be not uneasy at paragraphs you may read in the papers about the Army. You may not hear from me as frequently as you have hitherto, but I shall write by every opportunity. And now be of good cheer, and rely upon our Heavenly Father. We make a very early start to-morrow, and I must close to-night. That God will continue to guard and bless you I sincerely pray.

13th, four-thirty A.M. Packed and ready for a start. Genl. Twiggs writes word that he thinks he will reach Jalapa—this shows that there is not much to be apprehended from the expected opposition. Good morning.

Mr. Thomas and Maj. Graham beg to be remembered.

In Mexico

No. 5.[1] CAMP ABOUT SIXTEEN MILES FROM
LA PUENTE NACIONAL,
April 14th.

I believe that my No. (5) is correct, the last I wrote the morning of our departure from Vera Cruz. Yesterday (our first day's march) was a very severe one. Leaving about half past five A.M. we marched along the beach, say about two and a half miles, and then turning perpendicularly to the left marched through heavy sand hills, a deep hot road, about three and a half miles to our first watering place. The day, or rather that period of it in which we executed the latter part of our march, was excessively close and hot.

The country was a succession of cups of sand; the only redeeming thing about this part of the march, was that we heard the sweet, sometimes plaintive, sometimes cheerful notes of the birds in the recesses of the glades. Here we halted sometimes, but the men had become so much exhausted that by the time we reached our encamping ground, say eighteen miles from Santa Cruz, nearly one half of the men were absent. Some soon came up, but at tattoo, many had not yet arrived. To-day in consequence of the disordered state of the Command, we have only marched nine miles. Enough of this march for the present.

I acknowledge, with cheerful gratitude to God, the receipt of your letter of the 18th. The letter is in much better spirits than its predecessor and cheered me greatly, I assure you. I wish your letters to indicate exactly your feelings, and I can then know how you really are. You distress me much more by an attempt to conceal what I know full well you feel, than a full and frank disclosure does.

[1] No. 4 is missing.

Our camp is surrounded by some of the most beautiful flowers I ever saw. I send in this a few lilac flowers growing on a large vine which overhangs my tent. I have collected some seed. The favorite of our Florida home grows here in great variety, but I do not find any as sweet as those (opopanax) you used to collect at Tampa Bay.

The road to-day has been hilly, the hollows however not rich; we passed Genl. Santa Anna's residence about three miles back, a fine field of corn was growing near it. I merely had a glimpse of the house—a large white one with tiled roof. His Excellency owns the country on both sides the road from about nine miles this side Vera Cruz to the City of Jalapa; he owns a good deal of bad land.

We learned from some persons returning from Genl. Twiggs's Brigade, that he intended attacking Genl. Santa Anna at nine o'clock this morning. I expect that he will think better of it and wait for us to come up. Major Genl. Patterson has not yet come up, Genl. Pillow is with Genl. T. They may decide upon making a bold stroke for glory before we reach them. Genl. Scott who has gone ahead of us will probably reach the advance early to-morrow, when the decision will be made by him. I have this moment finished my dinner and tea. The twilight is so short here that I must close as it is now nearly dark. We start at early dawn in the morning. Good-night.

CAMP ABOUT 16 MILES FROM LA PUENTE NACIONAL.
EL PLAN DEL RIO.
April 15th.

Twenty minutes to five P.M. An early start with a well-conducted march brought us to our present

In Mexico

camp, at the National Bridge, before twelve o'clock. The Brigade would have advanced farther, but as no water could be obtained until we reached Genl. Twiggs's camp, sixteen miles, and as Lt. Col. Duncan stated that his horses could not go so far without water after a morning's march, it was determined to halt here.

17th. Thus far had I written day before yesterday, when I went to visit an old fortification intended to command the approaches to the bridge. The fort is an old one on a high hill, the side towards the river and our camp is inaccessible, the other side pretty well defended by musketry fires. This place we learn had been furnished with eight pieces of Arty. which were withdrawn the day before Genl. Twiggs left for Jalapa. The scenery at the bridge is beautiful, combining enough of the grand to make it interesting to all classes of admirers of scenery. The bridge is like all of the Spanish works of art constructed during their stay in this country, well executed and on a magnificent scale.

At tattoo. The Brigade received orders to march at one A.M. this morning. Reveille was beat at twelve and the men were formed at the appointed time. After some time, a Staff Officer came up with directions to allow the men to take what rest they could. Everything being packed, very little rest was taken.

At half-past four yesterday afternoon we took up our *camp* to march six miles to *camp*. We marched that distance, and were told whilst continuing our march, that as we could not get to water, the Command must march to the camp of Generals Twiggs and Pillow. We had a most fatiguing march, night marches are necessarily so, but this was rendered particularly so from the officers and men having been deprived of their rest the preceding night, and from the fact of their not having filled their canteens for a long march.

We arrived here, say eighteen miles, at twenty minutes to two this morning. At eight this morning a command was sent to occupy a hill which commands some of the enemy's batteries. The hill was found occupied by the enemy, but they were driven from it by Col. Harney; three officers were wounded—Major Sumner, 2nd Dragoons, slightly in the head, Lt. Maury left arm with bones broken below the elbow, Lt. May and another officer are also wounded.

To-morrow morning we are under orders to advance. As our men will have, I hope, a good night's rest, I feel confident of their doing good duty. I shall write you the earliest moment, if by the continued blessing of God, my life be spared. I place as ever all my trust in Him who has thus far saved me in numberless dangers. As I must be fresh I will now retire to rest, praying our Heavenly Father to protect and guard my wife and that He will soon receive you into the little select flock constituting His church elect upon this earth. The name of our camp is "Camp near El Plan del Rio."

FORTALEZA NACIONAL DE SAN CARLOS DE PEROTE.

Thursday, April 22nd.

Since the preceding was written I have been so constantly and sometimes so fatiguingly engaged that I did not have an opportunity of sending my letter immediately after the fight of the eighteenth, and this is the first mail of the departure of which we have been notified, and now I shall be so pressed for time that I shall have but half an opportunity of scribbling a few lines.

The newspapers will, I fear, long since have informed you of the heavy losses sustained by us at the battle of Cerro Gordo. The number of killed and wounded is probably not far from 500. One of my young friends, Lt. Dana, 7th Infy., is, I fear, dangerously wounded. I was not in the engagement, as by some mismanagement we were delayed, and work intended for us was done by the 2nd and 7th Infys. The enemy was completely routed, leaving in our possession thirty-five pieces of cannon, about 6000 prisoners, small arms and ammunition of all kinds in the greatest abundance.

The position occupied by the enemy was a very strong one. I may say that had we moved along the road to the attack, their position could not have been carried by our forces; but Genl. Scott, by judiciously turning the flank of their main batteries, and carrying by assault a high battery in the rear, which commanded their advanced works, saved the lives of our men and conquered.

These works were carried, and the battle over by half-past ten. The enemy ran in such disorder as to leave behind and on the road all their muskets and even their eatables. Had Genl. Scott's orders been complied with, not one of the enemy would have escaped.

We are now in the celebrated Castle of Perote where Genl. Santa Anna and other patriots have been occasionally confined. We shall remain a few days before advancing. Every soldier had left this place, though it is a very strong one. Let us unite in thanking God with all our hearts for His continued protection. I must close as it is so dark that I can scarcely see.

No. 6. Fortress of Perote.
Friday, April 23rd.

I closed my letter so hurriedly last evening, that I fear some portions of it were illegible, if not unintelligible. I think that in this, I will go back, and take you over the parts of our road so unceremoniously run over. I mentioned, I think, that Genl. Twiggs's Division was ordered to take a height which had been found unoccupied by the enemy, and one which commanded one or two of the batteries of the enemy.

The enemy, it seems, discovered their mistake in not having fortified this hill, and were found by the Division in large force upon it. It was gallantly carried by Col. Harney, with some loss on our side, and it is now reported, a loss of 174 on the part of the enemy.

This was the engagement of the 17th which Santa Anna has the impudence to claim as a victory. The 1st Brigade received orders on the evening of the 17th to march at early dawn on the morning of the 18th (Sunday, I am sorry to say). Our Brigade, 2nd and 3rd Arty. and 4th Infy. were ordered to support the attack on the enemy's battery.

The road from Battery No. 1 to No. 3, is cut out of the solid rock. The bank on the left side of the road in the rear of this part of it is too steep in many places for a man to go down to the water's edge; the little stream runs nearly parallel to the road. This may give you some faint idea of the ground, etc. As I was so busily occupied the day of, and the day subsequent

ROUGH SKETCH OF THE BATTLE-GROUND OF CERRO GORDO—APRIL 18TH, 1847

to the engagement, that I could not inspect the positions, I have been compelled to rely for my sketch on the information of others. The sketch is perhaps wrong in some points, but may on the whole be regarded as sufficiently accurate for a non-military reader.

We left our Camp early the morning of the 18th and halted when the head of our column had reached the *ranch C*, for the Vols. under Genl. Pillow to come up. They halted a moment near us, when Col. Haskell of Tenn. gave his men a spirited address. They then filed, by heads of companies, into the woods and we resumed our advance, a portion of Lt. Col. Duncan's Battery in front of us. We turned off the main road to our right at *D*, and had proceeded but a short distance when we heard sharp musketry firing on our left; this was Pillow's Brigade engaged with the enemy.

This Brigade fell back, and Genl. Pillow sent a staff officer to Genl. Scott to request that some Regulars be sent to him. He is a brave man and was deeply mortified; he was wounded.

In a short time the road became so rough and steep that we were delayed more than half an hour in taking two of the guns up a steep hill in the road. Hearing cannon firing in our front and it being found that Duncan's battery could not be taken forward in time for us to participate in the fight, we were ordered to the front.

The enemy now discovered us and threw a few shot and shell at us. No one was injured. Staff Officers now galloped back and called on us to advance, as we were very much wanted. Now commenced the most fatiguing work I ever had. The fire become very lively in every direction, and we had to gain our position on the hill where Battery No. 5 was situated.

With men exhausted by the heat and exertion of running, we struck the base of the hill, our troops calling for us to advance and the Mexicans calling on their side for reinforcements.

Before we reached the top our colors were flying on the flag staff, the hill had been taken. Duncan's Battery had kept us out of the battle. The Brigade under Genl. Shields had divided, a few were with him in his attack on field Battery No. 6, where he was mortally wounded by a grape shot, gallantly leading; his men then fell back and received a second discharge from the Battery before they advanced again.

The troops in Batteries Nos. 2 and 3 were now summoned to surrender; they asked for the appointment of commissioners and for time. They were told that if they did not surrender in ten minutes, the attack would be made on their Battery. We had now our forces in Battery No. 5, whose fire turned on them would soon have silenced them. They surrendered five Generals and about 5000 men.

Genl. Santa Anna's equipage, and about $30,000 in his chest, were found in or near his tent; his carriage was also found, he having left the battlefield early that morning or the night before. An immense supply of ammunition for Artillery and small Arms was found in caverns, etc., near the batteries. The field was strewn with the dying and the dead. The hill of Battery No. 5 presented many horrid sights— I never want to see such again. Our men gave the poor devils what water they could spare from their nearly exhausted canteens. Our Surgeons amputated the arms and legs of some of the wounded.

The action was over by half-past ten o'clock. The remainder of the day was employed in pursuit, and in collecting the wounded. We slept that night near the base of the high hill No. 5, the Compy. in the road, and your humble servant with the Adjt. in his tent, pitched on the right of the road at the spot marked by a dot. ⊙

Early the next day we resumed the advance, halted about twelve near Genl. Santa Anna's residence—that is, *one* of his residences, called "Encerro." An Officer was stationed here by Genl. Patterson or Twiggs to protect the property. We marched about 12 miles farther and made a late and uncomfortable encampment.

The next day we reached the beautiful and celebrated City of Jalapa (only think of it, nearly all the jalap used as medicine is taken from this place). Marched our dirty and wearied troops through as if we designed making a display, halted in the outskirts of the City till three P.M., when we again took up our line of march leaving the 2nd Div. in that City.

We encamped that night near a large cotton factory; the night was intensely cold, ice formed in our basins.

Off again the next morning early, road ascending and rough; about eleven we came to a village at the entrance of a pass which they had commenced fortifying, but seized by the panic spread by the runaways from the battle of Cerro Gordo, they had abandoned it, leaving seven or eight pieces of cannon on the ground. This would have been an ugly pass, as it was in the midst of the lava of an old volcano, exceedingly rough and sharp; its rough jagged points would have impeded the advance of our troops and kept us under their fire.

Passing over this volcanic road, we soon found ourselves in the region of the pine. The scenery was exceedingly grand and picturesque. Encamped that night at Las Vegas, water excellent, night cold. The next day we entered this celebrated work early in the day, the troops having hastily abandoned it the preceding day. We are now in the region of the cedar.

PEROTE, MEX.
April 26, 1847.

As this is merely a note to inform you of our leaving this place this morning I do not number it with my regular series. I have a letter nearly finished in my trunk which I packed thinking I would have an opportunity of mailing it from our point of destination, but as a mail may leave here to-day or to-morrow, I regret not having kept that letter out, and closing it here. The drum has just beat for the assembling of the 1st Brigade. To-day we march about eleven miles, to-morrow thirteen, on the road to Puebla, then we await further orders. Genl. Scott is expected here to-day. The news from the Capital told by the diligence yesterday is cheering. Everybody was panic-struck by the reception of the news of the battle of the 18th. Genl. Santa Anna had not been heard from; those formerly most "loud for War," now talk of peace. I must now close. May God Almighty bless and protect you.

No. 6 continued. The preceding sheet I had written and it had been packed away in my trunk, when I penned so hastily a note to you from Perote this morning. I now write in my tent at our Camp about eight miles on the road towards Puebla. We must not, however, leave Perote without devoting a few lines to remarks upon the country between Jalapa and Perote and also to its celebrated Castle.

In Mexico

Until we reached Jalapa we saw very little to interest the land speculator. At Jalapa everything indicates a richer, better soil; the land is well situated also for cultivation. You see here along the roadside as well built stone fences as the Yankees boast of. The houses, too, are better built. The climate also seems, and is reputed to be, delightful.

A rapid ascent, however, soon brings you into a region rather cool to be pleasant to those who come up rapidly from the hot lands of Vera Cruz. The land is rich, both in approaching the volcanic stream mentioned in the preceding part of this letter and after leaving it. The scenery is beautiful, regularly-sloped hills rise on every side, and in the distance may be seen the snow-covered peak of Orizaba; the intervening valley as deep rich soil as to be found anywhere; corn, oats, barley, rye grow well here, peaches and cherries were seen; with them you see the *Agave Americana* and other plants we see as curiosities.

At Jalapa the coffee bush grows. When you reach the plain of Perote, the soil is evidently less rich and shews sand and clay. The town of Perote has, as far as I can ascertain in marching through one of its streets, very few respectable-looking houses.

The *Fortaleza*, or Castle as it is called, is situated on a plain, about half a mile from town. The main work is a square, surrounded by a large square, the angles of which are bastioned, the whole having a ditch around it. The walls of the inner work which form the exterior walls of the quarters are three feet thick. This place has been at various times the prison of some of Mexico's greatest men. The turn of the political wheel has taken them from the palace to this prison. There were confined the Texan prisoners.

In the Chapel we found the tomb of Mexico's first President, Genl. Victoria. Generals Morales and Landero who commanded at Vera Cruz were released from a confinement ordered by Genl. Santa Anna, by the evacuation of this place by the Mexican troops. Genl. Landero had a conversation of about an hour's length with Genl. Worth since we came here. He wished to know what our Govt. desired. He says that Santa Anna has allied himself with the *sans-culottes*, that the better instructed class desire peace, that if the United States do not press too hard upon them, and can only save Mexican honor, that all may yet be well. He says that the last battle has been fought. It is now becoming dark so rapidly that I must close. God bless my wife, etc., etc.

April 28th. Tepayahualco. Our Brigade is accompanied by Duncan's Battery and Lt. Col. Smith's Battalion of Light Troops; we are twenty-five leagues (say fifty-five miles) from Puebla, where we are, I presume, to take up summer quarters, that is if we do not go on to Mexico. For really our being here is so unexpected to me, that I know not where we are to stop. Our orders are to remain here until further orders.

I can not speak positively of the whereabouts of Genl. Scott, or of the other Divisions. One Compy. of our Division with two pieces of Arty. under Lt. H. Brown, were left at our Camp of yesterday, the remainder of our Division was left under Genl. Worth at Perote.

Genl. Scott was expected to reach Perote the day after we left. I suppose that the whole Army will gradually come on. They may halt at Perote and at some other places for the coming up of our train with provisions, and also to secure and obtain supplies from the country. Thus far everything we obtain is paid for liberally, probably at higher prices than the usual ones of the country; this is however mere conjecture. This I *do* know, that individually we pay enormously for everything we purchase.

We are now, and have been for the last forty miles, in a volcanic country. On every side you see the uneven and jagged peaks of old volcanoes, or pass along the side or over the beds formed by the lava. These volcanoes have not been extinguished long enough for the lava to become sufficiently decomposed to support vegetation, and consequently we rarely see any approach to a tree.

The cactus here and there encroaches up the jagged side of some mountain. We are beyond the growth of cedar. Orizaba still shews us his white head. I hope that our soldiers will, if permitted to rest here a few days, get well. So sudden has been our transition from the burning sands of Vera Cruz to the cold region, and this change has been accompanied by so much and continued exertion, and with so great a loss of sleep, that our Command has been sadly reduced. Ten of "G" Co. are on the sick report to-day, none seriously sick. Most of these cases have been in fact produced by a cause I have not enumerated, viz., daily change of the kind of water drunk.

You must not be astonished at not receiving letters from me as regularly as you see statements of our movements published in the papers. Look at things as they now are; you may see weekly accounts of Genl. Scott's being with the Army at such a date; now, when he sends his mails we know not. Again express men are sent back, I understand, without escorts, and I think we shall soon hear of some being killed. I fear that in that way we shall find our correspondence sadly interfered with.

If the Mexicans have any gallantry, and that they have has long been their boast, they will send all except public letters to some place whence our expresses may again take them. Though I do not know when this letter can go, I shall close it now and send it to Genl. Hd. Qrs. whence they will send it by the first man who returns to Perote. Then again it will wait for a *chance*.

I have not mentioned who our Brigade Commander was—it is Col. Garland, 4th Infy. Of our Battalion Commander I have become heartily tired. He is eternally cross, snapping and snarling at everybody and at everything. He has been messing with me, but I gave notice to-day that the mess was broken up. I will have my meals undisturbed by ill temper. Everybody is disgusted with him. Pity it is too, as when he chooses he can be an elegant gentleman.

Friend Lt. Col. W. W. Graham, 11th Infy., is with us. He pays me a short visit nearly every day. Our young friend Thomas has a very ugly cough. I had one touch of fever and ague, but two doses of quinine mastered it, and I am now feeling as bright as usual.

Santa Anna has not gone to the Capital. 'T is said that he is with a handful of troops at Orizaba. Mexico has no Army. May it please God to end this war, and to restore me to my own beloved family.

No. 7. TEPAYAHUALCO, April 29th. Morning.

Your sweet letter was received last night after I had closed and sent to Hd. Qrs. my letter No 6. I

In Mexico

cannot allow the return to Perote of an express from our Camp without acknowledging its receipt and thanking you most sincerely for so charming a letter. And so you wonder whether I thought of you on the 26th of March? My answer you have ere this received.

I pray to God that your mind may have retained the sweet tranquillity which was beaming on it when you wrote, and that you have not been unnerved by the numerous rumors with which the papers must have been filled about the battle of Cerro Gordo—a battle more valuable in its results than any which has been yet fought in Mexico.

I do not feel like underrating, nor do I intend to underrate, Genl. Taylor's glorious victories, but they differ from Genl. Scott's at Vera Cruz and Cerro Gordo in this: in Genl. T.'s actions, but few unconditional surrenders of prisoners have been made. By both of Genl. Scott's about 17,000 Mexicans have been bound not to take further part in the War. Indeed, by the surrender of their Arms, they have been incapacitated from so doing.

We hear that Genl. Santa Anna could raise a large army of the young men of the country, but that he cannot obtain Arms for them. We shall soon find out what Mexico intends doing; at present panic pervades every place. Whether it will rouse the people to great exertions, or cause them more wisely to turn their thoughts to sweet peace, no one can tell.

The policy pursued by Genl. Scott is, I think, producing a favorable result on the common people. Nothing has been forcibly taken. I think that as far as I can see the laboring Mexicans care very little about the War, and that, by a continuance of this course, after a few months they will feel more secure in their persons and property than they have ever been under their own authorities.

I fear that there are occasional violations of Genl. Scott's orders, on the part of the Volunteers, and in a small way, on the part of the Regulars, but all these combined amount to much less than they have been compelled to bear from their own soldiery.

To-day we shall receive a supply of fifteen days' rations in wagons from Vera Cruz; this neighborhood can furnish our large force with very little of any kind of provisions. We have passed over a very rich belt of land, and are now where there appear to be no large farms.

The little market in this village contains very little. I went on a foraging party this morning, and the amount of my purchases was one pork's backbone, twenty-five cents, and eight eggs, twenty-five cents. For an old hen, its monster master wanted me to pay seventy-five cents. I give you these as samples of the prices. Occasionally you can get mutton, and a few prematurely ripe tomatoes. When we get to Puebla, we shall again be in the land of plenty. I shall expect to fatten rapidly. The great article of Mexican cookery is the black bean. Frijoli and red peppers grow everywhere.

I am sorry to tell you that an application has been made by Lt. Thomas for orders to leave Mexico on account of his health. He has a very distressing cough, is unfit for duty, and, if he remains here, will, I think, be useless for a long time. Capt. Taylor has, also applied for the same indulgence: he is incapable of marching, from varicose veins. The 3rd cannot now muster an officer for duty with the companies here. Where all our officers are, 't is hard to find out—some are with the northern portion of the invading Army.

In Mexico

April 29th. Evening.

I received this evening your letter of the first, full of apprehensions and alarm. You did not express yourself as freely as you did in some of your previous letters, and I regret it because I know that you would have felt more comforted and resigned after having done so. I know what your state of mind was, but thank God, the agony is now over, and you have since felt how sweet it is to put your trust in "Him who alone can save."

I had intended keeping this, and writing a long letter, adding something to it daily, but the reception of two letters in two days is an event which deserves special notice and a prompt reply. Friend —— is, I regret to say, on a little frolic to-day. I must give him a war talk to-morrow; he is just beginning, I fear, a long spree. A word from Father in this out of the way part of the world would control him greatly. He thinks all the world of his old General.

One of our officers returns to Perote to-morrow; I shall send this letter by him, hoping that it may be rapidly forwarded to you. Fearing that the express may leave too early for me to add to my letter, I shall close it to-night. My eyes are not strong enough to write well by the light of a Mexican tallow candle, which is all we can get here.

No news of an advance. We are as quiet here among these people as if we were old friends. How thoughtful of you to keep my old Mother informed of her stray son. Thank you. I ought to write to the family, but, when I take up my pen, it seems that the lines must be addressed to you.

An Artillery Officer

No. 8. Tepeyahualco, Mex.
May, 1, '47.

Word has just been sent me that a mail would leave in half an hour so that I shall have time to write you a very few lines. Of news there is nothing, except that this morning a messenger from the British Minister at Mexico passed through this place. He says that the Mexican Congress is divided equally, one half for making and the other for opposing a peace. He says that there will be no more fighting, that there are no troops at Puebla, and that in the City no resistance will be made. God grant that we may soon have peace and that his predictions about no more fighting may be verified.

Genl. Scott has not come up, indeed we have no news from the rear. The climate is here so cold, particularly at night, as to be most unpleasant. Yesterday, as I informed you, one of our officers was sent back to Perote on duty; he will be up to-morrow, and will bring us information from Hd. Qrs. I am tired of remaining in this miserable place. Nothing is raised here, that I can see, but the Maguey plant, from which *pulque,* the cider of the country, is obtained. Everything is brought on the backs of donkeys.

To-morrow, Sunday, is the great market day. We shall see what the neighbors will bring in for our money. These people are the veriest Jews I have ever met. Regarding us as enemies 't is natural that they should make us pay dearly for everything, but it seems to me that our commanders, on arriving at a town, should demand from the Alcalde the customary prices, and arrange a tariff accordingly.

Orizaba is in distinct view. I do wish you could enjoy with me some of the grand views we occasionally have on our marches. Not a day passes that I do not regret that I have not cultivated the little talent I have for sketching. Fearing that the mail may go suddenly, I must now close.

TEPEYAHUALCO, MEXICO.
May 1st.

(The priest spells this word TEPE.) The note sent off this morning was written so hurriedly that you see that I do not count it as *one* of my letters. That yours of the 1st April about the desponding tone of which I wrote in mine (number 6) should have been written at that time is not at all surprising, as you had just heard of the immense loss of life attending Genl. Taylor's great battle at Buena Vista. But the reports of Genl. Scott's victories at Vera Cruz and Cerro Gordo will, long ere you receive this, shew you that matters are managed here differently.

There is not a better soldier or braver man than Genl. Z. Taylor, and he will gain victories, but those who fight under him must incur with their Genl., who is nearly always in the front of the battle (where he should not be), the full dangers of an open direct attack. Genl. Scott has his battle-fields well reconnoitred, and avails himself of all the advantages which science or skill may suggest. Maj. Wade, whose tent is next to mine, has come in and commenced talking to me so that I have to stop writing for to-night. Good-night.

Sunday, May 2nd. 11 o'clock.

I have just finished my morning's readings in which I always try to make myself think you take your part, and resume my pleasant labor of writing to you. 'T is a labor of love.

152   An Artillery Officer

Genl. Scott has, we hear, ordered two of the new Regiments to join our Army; the 11th Infy. is one; which the other is, I have not heard. I would like very much to have Duncan in our Brigade, but the chances are that the 13th has been ordered to Point Isabel; if so, he will be with Genl. Taylor, an excellent friend of Father's. Lt. Andrews states that at Perote, whence he returned yesterday, there are no rumors about our advance; indeed, it is there said that Genl. Worth has received orders from Genl. Scott to make no movement until he receives orders.

Genl. Santa Anna, report says, is trying to organize an Army at Orizaba which is said to be a very pretty village in a fertile region of country. We may be ordered to take summer quarters there, instead of at Puebla. I should prefer the latter place as it is a large city and one where our men might be made more comfortable than in a smaller place. Here, the majority of the population (evidently nearly full-blooded Indians) live in houses made by driving a few posts in the ground and thatching the sides and tops with a species of palm-leaf. Some few live in houses built of rough stones forming very thick walls, plastered inside and outside, having tiled roofs; the best floors are formed of large bricks about fifteen inches square, or made firm and hard with a kind of cement. The buildings are of one story; those I have been in, have very little furniture, and that of the rudest kind; around the walls you find almost invariably, pictures of saints, occasionally a painting, generally coarse, colored engravings.

The other morning I was offered, seemingly as a great treat, one of their dishes, a little pork cut in fine pieces, rolled in cornmeal dough, and boiled,

In Mexico

well covered by a corn shuck. It tasted pretty well, and I answered their enquiries by telling them it was *muy bueno*. Perhaps I went to market this morning too early. I saw nothing there but some chickens, a few eggs (three cents apiece), and onions one cent apiece.

I hear that our Brigade Commander saw Lt. Johnson (you saw him at Ft. Moultrie) going to church this morning and that he expressed dissatisfaction at his going alone—fears that officers may be murdered in church! What next? Lt. Thomas is not improving; indeed, I think that if he be not sent off very soon, that he will die; he is a very sick man, and has never been well since he had an attack of brain fever at Monterey. He ought to have left the country then, but could not be induced to do so. I will now put away this letter till after dinner.

Having mentioned that I would stop writing till after dinner, I may as well state what our dinner was, particularly as it was a very respectable dinner and very well cooked for a camp. First course, vermicelli soup, rice; second, midlings and greens, and fricassee (beef, bacon, and onions), pickles; third course, Mamé pear and musk melon, sauce, sherry wine and sugar. The melon was a present. Thus you see that I am not starving here. The *we* composing our Mess embraces Wade and myself. Lt. Thomas is a third, but is too sick to join us at table. Here is where we live; the area is surrounded by a rough stone wall about twelve feet high; it was formerly a room, but the rafters and roof having decayed, it is now exposed to the light of the stars; the floor is of cement.

Genl. Scott's order for the troops to hold themselves in readiness to advance as soon as our expected supply train reaches Jalapa with provisions from Vera Cruz, was received this morning. He says that as it will soon be impossible to keep up the communication with Vera Cruz, it will be necessary for the Army to look to the country for its means of subsistence. He therefore urges the necessity of conciliation and kind treatment towards the countrymen. States that nothing must be taken from them without payment being made, denounces those who act differently, as enemies of their Country, etc. So I presume that we shall soon leave this place. This all of us will rejoice at, as the water is so bad here that our sick lists are daily increasing. If this be a fair sample of the water in volcanic countries, I prefer almost any other. The parade drum is now beating, so that I must stop again, resuming, if I can, tonight.

Monday, May 3rd.

Lt. Totten, son of Col. Totten, Engineers, one of the new appointments, has just joined us. He came up the day before yesterday from Vera Cruz. I am sorry to learn that Genl. Scott was indisposed, when he, Lt. T., passed through Jalapa. He says that the Genl. was writing when he called to see him but that he had been suffering from chills and fever. This is certainly, to persons coming from the seacoast, a sickly climate. The people of the country look well and hearty, but our sick list is still increasing daily.

Lt. T. informs me that some companies of the new Regts. had already arrived at Vera Cruz, that there were many cases of dysentery among the men, as with us, but no yellow fever. Col. Wilson is, I believe, a very good police officer, and will do all in his power to keep the City clean.

I omitted mentioning that my right bower, Derr, had been unwell; he is now nearly well and will, I hope, continue so. Old Wilson is with us—he was unwilling to be left behind. Most of the "G's" left in the Hospital at Vera Cruz are now, I learn by a note from Dr. Porter, on their way to join me. I regret not finding Cramer's name among them. As he is a handy man and pretty good clerk, Dr. P. may have kept him, though well enough to have been sent with the rest. I hope, for the sake of his poor wife, that my surmise may be correct. Capt. Lee, Engineers, thinks that we shall leave this place in a few days.

Our Surgeons have urged Genl. Worth in the strongest manner to remove the troops from here as soon as possible. Genl. Worth still remains at Perote, and as such representations have been made to him about our unhealthiness, I fancy we shall not see him until we are to resume our advance.

At Perote the Ord. Officers are engaged in breaking up the small arms found in the Castle and in collecting and preparing the powder for transportation. The number of muskets collected at Cerro Gordo and at Perote must have been very great. As they were of no use to us, it was perhaps wise to order them to be destroyed.

Mr. Thomas says that he feels somewhat better to-day. Dr. Satterlee came to see him yesterday; he says that he is not dangerously ill, but that if his disease be not soon checked he will become so. An answer to his application to be ordered to the United States may be received to-morrow.

May 4th.

The return train which has, I learn, just arrived is to take a mail back, and I regret most deeply to say that we have been notified that it will be our last opportunity for some time for writing home. I hope that this will not be so, but at present it has the sanction of the highest in authority here, as our Brigade Commander told one of our officers this morning that after this mail was despatched, it would be a long time before another would be sent. Should you therefore fail to receive letters as regularly as you have hitherto, you will know the cause and not be uneasy.

We expect to leave for Puebla in two or three days, and no resistance will be made. The inhabitants, we hear, are preparing for our reception—cleaning and whitewashing their barracks, baking bread, etc. I hope that when the citizens of Mexico find our army established in our summer quarters there, they will feel the inutility of resistance, and to save themselves the disgrace of having to surrender their Capital, they will make peace. God grant that this may be soon accomplished; of one thing you may be well assured, that I will eagerly embrace every opportunity of writing to you.

We are now so far in, that I presume if peace be made soon after we reach Puebla, we can hardly hope to be able to leave the country until late in the Fall; so that I must make up my mind to abandon all idea and hope of seeing you for many a weary month.

Seven of the men left at Vera Cruz arrived this morning. I am sorry to learn from them that Cramer was very sick when they left. There had been no cases of yellow fever in the Hospital where my men were. I was afraid that our Doctor would send some of the Company to the Hospital at Perote or Jalapa.

I have been overlooking your letters and find that commencing with the one of Jany. 7th I have them for each week to the 1st of April. Can it be that after one or two mails more we are to be cut off from our communication with Vera Cruz, and to be deprived of the invaluable blessing of hearing from our families? I cannot think that Genl. Scott will not, soon after reaching Puebla, make some arrangement for receiving and forwarding mails.

Mr. Thomas, who since he has had a hope of leaving the country has gradually improved, will leave tomorrow morning. Capt. Taylor will probably start with him. They do not know whether they will be allowed to go directly to the United States or have to stop at Perote or Jalapa. Perote, except the superiority of its water, is not much better than this place. I envy the gentlemen the happiness which awaits them on their return home, but would dislike to be sent there on account of ill-health.

I send in this letter some seed of the most beautiful yellow tomato I ever saw. We may have the same kind in the United States, but I have never seen them. I have several other kinds of seed, but as some of them cannot well be sent in letters I have them stowed away in the top of my old trunk. The corn is, in this region, very small in its grain, which is very long. There is a very pretty variety of small black corn, some of which I will bring home. Barley is cultivated here in greater abundance than any of the small grains; the grain and straw is the principal food for horses. I may not have time in the morning to write any more; if I can I will cross-write a little, and will therefore close my letter now.

Do not be over-anxious at not hearing from me; believe no newspaper stories from the Army. I cannot resist giving you here one or two instances of misstatements to shew you how much we who are in the Army are deceived by false statements. Genl. Shields and Lt. Dana have both been reported dead—information positive—the last news is that they are both at Jalapa and with favorable chances of recovery. Fortunately, I did not write to Lt. Dana's mother, as I was near doing. Placing with me your whole confidence in God, let us hope that it may soon be His pleasure to restore me in good health to you.

May 5th. Before breakfast. The express goes early this morning, so that I shall barely have time to bid you good-morning. Dr. Satterlee has decided that Capt. Taylor is not to go. Lt. Thomas leaves with the express. Good-bye, etc. Shall write to my dear Mother by this mail.

No. 9. Tepeyahualco, Mexico.

Wednesday, May 5th.

Although I wrote this morning, and warned you that I might not have an opportunity again of soon forwarding a letter to you, I cannot refrain from pursuing my old and pleasant task of writing to you. This day one month ago, I left Vera Cruz. One month before that, I reached Anton Lizards. What important events have taken place since the last mentioned dates! How different might have been my fate, but for the all-sustaining power and mercy of God! I pray that I may become daily more and more fervently thankful for His mercies, and may feel my entire dependence on Him more fully than I have hitherto.

In Mexico

Preparations are being made here for the reception of the remainder of the Army, but I have not heard that any information had been received as to the time they might be expected. I presume that as the accommodations are very insufficient here, even for our present force (about 1500 men) we shall advance as soon as another portion of the Army arrives. As Puebla is a large city, containing between sixty and seventy thousand inhabitants, I suppose the Army, or the larger portion of it, will make a display by entering it in one body.

We hear that a large mail is on its way, but why it does not come as rapidly as rumor, which reports its slow movement, I cannot tell. I hope it will soon arrive, as I am very anxious to hear from you. Your next letter will give me news of you up to the eighth of April and may perhaps inform me when you will leave for Habersham. I fear that I may have changed the direction of my letters too soon. But anxious that a letter should reach Clarkesville about the time you did, I changed my direction, hoping to give you an agreeable surprise.

I have just seen Genl. Scott's order, dated Japala, May 3rd, announcing that Genl. Patterson's Division was to commence its march by brigade on the next day. Genl. Worth also announces to his Division that it is to resume the march in the advance of the Army.

His order alludes to the cowardly conduct of the Mexicans in assassinating some of our men, perhaps some stragglers on our marches. Our men frequently lag behind the column, sometimes through fatigue, at other times for the purpose of pilfering or drinking. I am not at all astonished at their being murdered.

From the tenor of these orders I presume we shall leave here on the 7th, and I have not the least idea of seeing a *soldier enemy* between this and Puebla.

The Mexican Congress have, it is said, already adopted resolutions as to what they will do when our Army marches to their Capital. Poor deluded Nation— the people are not fit for self-government, and we are, perhaps, instruments intended to open this country to the world and finally to establish enlightened and free government in it. Education must first be spread among the masses, who are now ignorant and idle.

That our Army will be followed by active and enterprising men, who will remain in the Country, I do not doubt. They will give a stimulus which will finally produce good results and effect great changes in the people and Country. God grant that *I* may soon complete my task in this great work, and be restored to my native land and my own beloved fireside.

I have been listening this afternoon to the band of the 4th Infy. (now under command of Lt. Col. W. W. Graham, 11th Infy.) and am better pleased with its music than with that of any of the bands with the Army. The former leader of the 4th Arty. Band, Bloomfield, is at his first station, the recruiting depot, New York Harbor. Since his departure, that Band has deteriorated very much. I must now bid you good-night. *Bonsoir.*

Thursday, May 6th. Early this morning, four French gentlemen arrived from Puebla. They report that no opposition will be made, that the inhabitants of Puebla expect us, and do not know what to think about our not going on. They do not appear to be men of consequence, but may be intended to learn what our

In Mexico

expectations and plans are. They speak of going to Jalapa, and say that a pledge given by Genl. Scott to the Church Party will have a good effect, that the War Party are circulating reports that we are inimical to their Church, and that we will not respect their persons, or protect them in their rights and property. As this pledge is no more than the Genl. has already given, there will be no difficulty on that point.

The Mexican Congress is still in session and it is said to be issuing commissions to Guerrilla officers. If they commence that species of warfare, and wage it in the cruel manner their relations did in Spain, we shall be compelled to adopt a mode of warfare totally abhorrent to our feelings and wishes. God grant that I may never be engaged in so conducting a war as to be compelled to give no quarter, to take no prisoners. I do not believe that the Mexicans will attempt a game in which they are so certain of being the heaviest losers.

No mail yet. No news to-day from Genl. Hd. Qrs., though we all expect orders this evening to be ready for our forward move to-morrow or the next day. Although our men have crowded the sick lists since we arrived, the time here has not been lost, as by our daily drills we are getting our raw soldiers into some semblance of military men. "G" Co. is now on paper 100 strong, but I rarely have more than 60 on duty.

No case here of serious sickness, but cases sufficiently important to render it necessary for them to be excused from duty. What has become of my old friend Capt. Burke? The last heard of him was that he was recruiting his Compy. in North Carolina.

The provision of the Bill passed by the last Congress, granting one hundred and sixty acres of land to all who serve during the war, must, I think, have soon presented him with enough recruits to fill his Compy. If he has succeeded in completing his Compy. I suppose we shall soon have him with us. We will then have in our little Battalion the three senior Captains of the Regt.

My journeyings are all plain matter of fact joggings on. We start early in the morning, and after a certain number of halts, stop at some designated spot, where we make ourselves as comfortable as we can for the night. As it is now near Retreat, I will close for to-night.

Friday, May 7th. 4 P.M. A Command of two Companies of Infy. and one of Dragoons was sent forward this morning on the Puebla road, some fifteen miles, to bring an Alcalde, or some of his subjects, to task for preventing the inhabitants around his town from bringing provisions to our troops here. This move will, I presume, be totally unexpected, and his being brought down and probably sent to Perote may have a good effect. Our paying the Mexicans liberally for what they bring will induce them to come, our punishing those who prevent them, will shew them that we know and feel our strength, and that it will be exerted when necessity demands it.

The Command will not return till sometime tomorrow. No mail and no positive information about one. Col. Garland received, I hear, a letter from Genl. Worth last night informing him that we were not to advance as soon as had been anticipated. What important or unimportant events have caused this delay is left to prolific conjecture.

In Mexico

It is amusing to hear the various reasons assigned for everything, the object of which is not understood. Some surmise that the express, whose passing my last letter announced, had important communications from the British Minister for Genl. Scott, etc. I care very little what takes place, so that a peace be soon honorably secured.

I have said very little of the temperature and apparent climate of this place. The climate is not unlike that where you are (Habersham[1]). Exposed to the sun during the day, between nine and four it is very warm, uncomfortably so, and at night it is sufficiently cold to require at least two good blankets as covering. How our poor men are to sleep out exposed, as they must be on the march from this place to Puebla, to the chilly night wind without tents and some of them without blankets, I cannot imagine, without their being made sick.

At Major Wade's request, as he said it would gratify his wife very much, I wrote her a note the other day, informing her that we were messing together, and that we had promised to take care of each other. She is, you remember, a sister of Bvt. Major Robert C. Buchanan, and is said to be a remarkably fine woman. The Major will not, I fear, return home so as to be present at his daughter's marriage. He is an excellent-hearted, and one of the most liberal men we have with us.

I much prefer living as we now do, to being in the large Mess I had when we arrived. Now we are sociable. Then our Commander worried me at every meal by some display of petulance, or by uttering some ill-

[1] Genl. Clinch's seat in the northern part of Georgia in the mountains.

natured or ungentlemanly remark. He now enjoys his solitary meal alone. The Adjt. eats with one of the Compy. officers.

The market people are becoming much more reasonable in their prices; we now buy a dozen eggs for eighteen and three quarters cents, occasionally five cents for a pie; onions, sixteen for six and one quarter cents, and bananas, seven for six and one quarter cents. Chickens half grown, eighteen and three quarters cents *each*. These prices will do very well. The fresh meats we get are generally hog and sheep—the hogs always skinned—most funny-looking things they are with their jackets off. In this region, we scarcely ever see a cow.

I must now go out and take a look at the drill; our men get enough of it, two hours before dinner, and two in the afternoon. Our Regt. is the only one in the Brigade whose companies have to drill in the morning.

Saturday, May 8th.

Anniversary of the battle of Palo Alto, the beginning of the War. Poor Mexico, what has she not lost during the past year! The progress of our Arms has been astonishing. The Companies sent out yesterday have returned. They found within twelve miles of us a very fertile valley, where an abundance of grain, mutton, and pork can be obtained for our troops.

A fine village, San Juan de los Llanos, was visited. There they found marks of refined civilization—ice-cream, champagne, and nice candies. Barley and corn are extensively cultivated there.

The Préfeto had escaped; he is the man who is responsible to the Govt. and was the man the Command went after. The Alcalde professed friendship, and promised to send provisions in.

One man, the rich man of the valley, was stubborn and surly. The Officer in command told him that we wanted supplies, and that he would be paid well for them if he would bring them in, but that if he did not send or bring his grain, etc., in to-day, that a Command would be sent for them, and that no remuneration would be made to him. He promised to send in what he had.

Genl. Scott's order directing the discharge of the Volunteers whose terms of service are about expiring was received this morning. Major Genl. Patterson returns to the United States with them. He is complimented. Brig. Genl. Quitman, Mississippi, remains in command of four Regiments of Volunteers of the last levy. The 6th Regt. of Infy. will join us this evening. Whether this indicates an advance, we know not.

Major, I ask pardon, *Lt. Col.* Graham has just informed me that the express was to leave immediately for Perote. Fearing that I may lose the chance of this mail, and be thus thrown back for several days, I will now close.

No. 10. TEPEYAHUALCO.

Saturday, May 8, 1847.

No. 9 was despatched this morning. I hope it may be sent rapidly to its destination.

Soon after it was mailed, Col. Garland, our Brigade Commander, paid me a visit and shewed me an order from Genl. Worth directing him to send a Compy. of the 3rd Arty. back to Perote, to constitute part of its garrison and also a letter from the Genl. A. D. C. suggesting that Capt. Robert Anderson would be a proper person to send, 1st, "for his peculiar fitness," etc., etc. I immediately told the Col. that I appreciated the compliment very highly, but I was convinced that the climate of Perote would not suit me, and that I thought Dr. Satterlee, our Senior Brigadier Surgeon, would so decide. We immediately went to see the Dr. who promptly said no, it would not do to send me there.

My friend the Dr. has thus saved me from being incarcerated in that Castle for the summer. I cannot bear the place—it reminds me of a penitentiary, and the rooms even were very uncomfortable to my feelings during my stay there. A regular fever and ague place. Capt. Taylor was then ordered, and he has already left with his Company.

I am desirous of going as far into the interior as any one goes. But as our Battalion is reduced to three companies I fear we may be broken up to garrison different places along the road. The 6th Infy. will arrive here this evening, the remainder of the 1st Division will stop to-night at San Antonio, between Perote and this place; to-morrow Genl. Worth is to arrive and we are to resume the march the next day, the 10th.

We hear nothing of our long-talked-of mail, but hope that it may come with a large train. Genl. Scott's order mentions it as being on its way from Vera Cruz.

By the bye, I think I did not mention that a train bringing up about $500,000, was attacked the other day at Santa Fé, the first watering place this side of Vera Cruz. The *rancheros* followed the train about three miles, but were finally driven off. Supplies have been sent in to-day from San Juan de los Llanos. From the representations given of that place, it seems to me unfortunate that we did not send a command there soon after our arrival here; it might have added much to our comforts in the eating line.

I dined to-day at Brigade Hd. Qrs. and will, to shew you that their bill of fare was not much better than we have, tell you what our dinner was. Chicken soup with rice, pretty good; loaf corn bread (a rarity and treat) and wheat bread; second course: roast turkey, stuffed, plenty of onions—turkey not quite done—rice. Dessert, pineapple. I confess to two things that *we* cannot place on the table: claret wine and a fine glass of sherry, in drinking which we did not forget the battle of Palo Alto.

Genl. Quitman, we hear, has been promoted to a Major Generalcy, and is the only one of our recent Brigadiers who is to remain in Mexico. Generals Pillow and Shields, both wounded, will, I presume, soon return as heroes to their homes. No news from Puebla or Mexico to-day.

Sunday, May 9th.

The order is out for our march to-morrow. The Brigade takes the lead, with the Compy. of Dragoons under Capt. Sibley, Lt. Col. Duncan's Battery of Arty. and the train of Heavy Ordnance—one battering train; on the day following, the other Brigade of this Division. The remainder of the Army will, I presume, follow in the same order.

Genl. Scott must certainly soon establish some regularity in the means of transportation and transmitting intelligence to and from home. I have amused myself to-day in reading the newspaper accounts of our landing at, and investing Vera Cruz. The enemy's fortifications, possession of which was taken by our troops the day we landed, must have been *Châteaux en Espagne*, literally Castles in the air, for we never heard of them before.

My letters will appear tame, compared with the graphic accounts of our famous letter-writers. I wish that those gentlemen would stick to their desks at home. The Savannah papers appear determined to make heroes of all her sons; it will tax the ingenuity of their editors to raise the Navy as high as the paragraphs we have seen indicate their desire to do.

I presume that you have read Genl. Scott's report of the capture of Vera Cruz and also of the battle of Cerro Gordo; we shall not see them till returned to the Army by the United States papers. The Genl. has not sent us his order on the victory of Cerro Gordo. I do not know why he delays; he must, ere this, have received returns and reports from the Commanders of Divisions and Brigades, furnishing materials for an order.

Genl. Worth has not arrived yet, but he will, I presume, certainly come up this evening. We start to-morrow with five days' rations, two days' cooked, in the men's haversacks. Another of the men left at Vera Cruz came up to-day. I am sorry to hear him say that he does not think that three of those who were left behind will ever join the Compy. again. This campaign has been a very trying one on the poor soldier. The sick report of our Battalion for this morning was about sixty. I have had one man sent back to the Hospital at Perote, and regret it as I think he will not be much improved by the change.

We have not heard of or from Mr. Thomas since he left us; he will continue to improve so long as he flatters himself with the hope that he is to leave the country, and so great an influence do I think his imagination exercises over his disease, that I am satisfied, if he were stopped at Perote by a denial of his application that we should soon hear of his being a very sick man.

To-day we have had no drills, a decided improvement on the doings of last Sunday, when no respect was shewn for the day. We ought to be very particular here, as we have been represented as opposed to the religion of the Country, and being determined to put the priesthood down.

Genl. Scott has ordered a spirit of conciliation to be practised, and among other things, we should seem to evince respect for the Sabbath. I hope, without very urgent necessity, we shall have no more drills on Sunday. Hoping that I may have an opportunity of writing a few words before we leave to-morrow, I shall now close.

Monday, May 10th, seven o'clock.

Yours of 9th April was received yesterday. Thank God your anxiety was relieved by the next mail, as by letters from Savannah I find that Lt. Van Vliet, who was at the siege, arrived there on the 14th. But you must try to put your confidence more entirely on the merciful Father who has so constantly guarded us from every danger. 'T is He who rules the storm and governs its course to subserve His own wise purposes.

I will not have time to write a long letter this morning, as we start at eight, and all are now busy loading the wagons.

We will reach Puebla in about four days. No information of any hostile force on or near the road.

An Artillery Officer

No. 11. Puebla, Mexico.
May 15th, twenty minutes past one P.M.

I have this moment washed the dust of the road from my face and hands, after having made our *entrée* into the City early this morning. We were kept in the Plaza waiting for the selection of our quarters for about three hours. We are now quartered not far from the centre of Puebla, in an old barrack. So much better, however, than we have been accustomed to in Tepeyahualco, that we consider them reasonably good. Major Wade and myself have again taken a room together—this I agreed to rather than to inconvenience all the young officers by my selecting a separate room.

This is a beautiful City, well built; some of the squares or blocks must have cost immense sums. The Cathedral is a very large building, very massive, but not of as beautiful or good a style as some of the churches. I may, however, before saying anything more about the City, take up the narrative of my march from the day of our leaving Tepeyahualco, the date of my last letter, 10th inst.

That night we encamped at Virreyes, ten miles; the 11th we marched about thirteen miles, and encamped at a horridly dirty *hacienda*, called Santa Anna. We had, however, passed a very pretty little church at Ojo de Agua—the country improving in fertility and losing somewhat of its volcanic traces. Very contradictory reports of the enemy on the 12th. Passed about midday Nopolucan, the place where the road running from Vera Cruz to Mexico intersects the road we came.

The Padre met Genl. Worth before reaching the City, and was very kind and full of friendly pro-

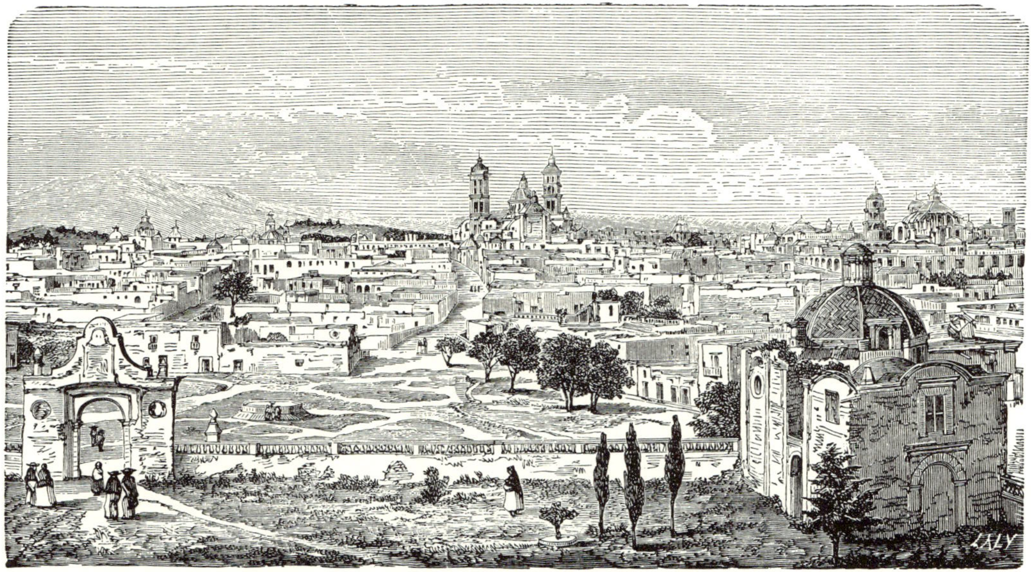

PANORAMA OF PUEBLA

fessions whilst we were there. He requested that the soldiers might be permitted to walk through the church. It has a great deal of gilding, filled with paintings; some of them, I would judge, making allowance for a miserably bad light in which they are seen, are very good. In one room, removed from the main body of the church by a side door, I saw a representation of our Saviour lying dead in a bed; the coverlid was said to be more than two hundred years old, well worn, worked with silk figures, flowers, etc. The whole affair did not produce a favorable effect on our minds. There was nothing pleasant either in the design or execution of any part of it.

Encamped this night at the Hacienda de Piñal where we were joined by the 2nd Brigade, under Col. Clarke. Rumors of Santa Anna's having gone to Puebla. Twenty pickets posted around Camp, the soldiers informed that the enemy "are said to be near," and that they must sleep on their arms. To cap the climax, and to render a false alarm inevitable, an issue of grog was made after tattoo. About two in the morning, the whole Army turned out, because some of the men on guard fired at jackasses or something else—*drink* the cause.

The valley of Nopolucan is very rich, presenting a beautiful appearance, the fields divided by hedges of Maguey.

13th. Marched through a romantic country, the first part of our route much broken, reached Amozoc, about fourteen miles, early in the afternoon. No one knows anything positive about Santa Anna. Men informed that we are to remain here one day, for the arrival of Genl. Quitman, and to enable them to clean and brush up. A quiet undisturbed night.

Sunday, 16th. Soon after breakfast, whilst the men were busy cleaning belts, guns, etc., we were startled by hearing the long roll. All were soon under arms, when we heard that the enemy was coming down from Puebla. They were seen filing along the base of a hill about three quarters of a mile to the right of the town, their line extending as far as the configuration of the country permitted us to see, say a mile. Troops, Arty., Cavalry, and Infantry were immediately dispatched to attack them. Couriers were instantly sent to inform Genl. Quitman of their presence—he was known by Genl. W. to be within four miles of the City.

Reports stated that the Mexican troops, as seen, amounted to about 5000 Cavalry. The Ord., Arty., and Col. Smith's light Battalion were stationed in the public Plaza, to guard it, and to remain there *in reserve*.

Firing of cannon was soon heard, and in a moment the men stationed on the house tops proclaimed, by a shout, that the Mexicans were running in every direction. Having but parts of two Companies of Cavalry with us, we could not avail ourselves of that, the only species of troops useful in picking up the retreating enemy, so that they got off with the loss of such men as were killed by our Arty. The Infy. brought in six prisoners, one of them an ill-looking Padre. We had not a man either killed or wounded by the enemy, who passed by the town towards the direction we came from. Genl. Quitman saw them, but as soon as he showed preparations of arrangements for a fight, they bore off.

Genl. Worth questioned the prisoners and learned that Genl. Santa Anna was with the Mexican troops. The loss of the enemy in killed was reported to be sixteen—it may have been much larger.

In Mexico

The troops were dismissed about twelve o'clock with orders for our Brigade to be ready for a march at three o'clock. We had scarcely finished a hasty meal at half past eleven when we were summoned to our Arms, and after a little delay, were told that we were not to march for one hour, and that the Command must be prepared for a night march. Left the City about the appointed time, and marched about a mile and a half; encamped under orders that we would start between eight and ten o'clock.

Symptoms of rain shewing themselves very plainly, Maj. W. and I had a small tent pitched. A few minutes afterwards, a heavy storm came on. During the rain, a Staff Officer rode up, stating that the movement was postponed till three A.M. As the Major and myself were about composing ourselves to sleep, we heard our even-tempered Colonel say "that he wished to God that he had his tent pitched." We then determined that we would ask him to come in with us. The invitation was immediately accepted, and he slept there till word came that it was nearly three o'clock and that we were to march at a quarter past. He did n't say "thankee" but "moseyed" off.

I then went to Hd. Qrs. where I saw five genteel-looking Mexicans, who Col. Garland told me were a deputation from Puebla. Whilst there, a note was received from Genl. W. stating that in consequence of the darkness of the night the troops would not leave Amozoc till daylight. Word was now sent to our Command that we would march at daylight.

We left in the morning of the 15th at half-past five. I have been thus minute, to let you into the secrets of one night of a campaign, and to shew you how *innocently* sleep may be killed.

After divers halts along the road, we made our entrance into this City about noon yesterday. Nearly all of its eighty thousand inhabitants must have shown themselves either along the sides of the streets, or in and upon the houses. It reminded me of a New York crowd on some celebration day—turning the New Yorkers into some resemblance to Florida Indians.

Having brought you into this City, I will not attempt any description of it at this time. I am not only desirous of seeing something of it first, but am apprehensive, if I delay sending this letter to Hd. Qrs. that a courier may be despatched to Genl. Scott without it. I shall only therefore now add, that I am in a room by myself, and that I visited the grandest church this morning I ever saw—the same whose front and external appearance I mentioned as not pleasing me much. Genl. Santa Anna is said to be at St. Martin, about nine leagues (thirty miles) from here, on the road to Mexico. An election for President took place yesterday; we do not know the result.

No. 12.   Puebla de los Angeles.
May 17, 1847.

I fear that our correspondence cannot be continued with the punctuality which has attended it thus far. Should any of my letters fall into the hands of His Excellency Genl. Santa Anna or any of his officers, I hope that they will do me the favor of forwarding them to you. My letters can be of no possible service to them, as I, from my position, am debarred from all knowledge of the secret plans (if they have any) of our Commanders. No. 11 was sent to Hd. Qrs. yesterday, and is, I hope, well on its way.

I have been strolling round the City but have seen

In Mexico

very little of its beauties. The style of building of the houses and of the churches is entirely different from anything I have seen. The people too, the lower class particularly, remind me, as I see them around the fountains, of the old pictures of the Egyptians. I cannot say much for the beauty of their Rebeccas, for as yet I have not seen a *tolerably* handsome face.

Genl. Worth called, with the Commanders of Regiments and Corps, on the Bishop this morning. They were very affably received; the Bishop professed that he wished to see kindly courtesies felt and exchanged between his flock and ourselves. He returned the call in about an hour.

Lt. Austine says that he never saw such splendor as was in everything connected with the Bishop's Palace; the walls were filled with the choicest paintings. The Bishop, a very old Spaniard, apparently eighty or ninety, mentioned that he was in New York in 1825. If he and his clerical brethren desire, they can bring about a peace. God grant that wisdom and not passion may prevail in their meditations on this subject, and that they may ere long deserve and receive the blessings of all good Christians for accomplishing this desirable result.

The priests must know that if the war continues much longer, there will be great danger of their churches being reduced to the level of other denominations, which will be called into existence to satisfy the wants of tens of thousands of foreigners who will be attracted from every part of Europe by the reports of the richness of their lands, the delightful temperature of their climate, presenting to the palate every delicacy of the most favored climes.

If the War be soon terminated, and the United

States will not, I presume, though in actual possession of all the seaports and of the largest and best portions of their country, ask for a peace which will not save Mexican honor, she can soon resume the ordinary functions of her Govt. and if she prefers, again close her doors to foreigners. As I shall probably spin out this letter to a more than usual length, I will not attempt any description of churches or City, till I have had more than a mere glance at them. We have not heard from Genl. Scott since our arrival. Report says that an express despatched by him to Genl. Worth has been cut off. I think it quite probable, as there is great danger, even in times of peace, in travelling along the route we came.

I may have something to say about manufactures before closing this letter, as Puebla is called by some the Lowell of Mexico.

May 18th.

In walking through the streets this morning, I saw many boys and women exposing for sale Genl. Scott's address to the Mexican people. Presuming that all these papers are as responsible as *our papers*, I will merely state that he tells them truths in such a simple style, in relation to the manner in which the people and Army have been misled, and shamefully abandoned by their Govt. and generals, that it will do much good. Foreigners here speak highly in its favor. The General tells them that he is going to Mexico, etc., etc.

I find that each day in going out, I am losing the impression of *novelty*, which the first sight of the City made on me. I had therefore better communicate this impression before it wears off. It may present some views I might not otherwise give.

PUEBLA DE LOS ANGELES

In Mexico

The streets are broad with sidewalks of flat stones, the centre paved with round stones. As you enter either of the principal streets, the first thing that attracts you as novel is a row of tin pipes (several to each house) projecting some three or four feet from the upper part of the walls of the houses; these are to throw the water into the streets, which are thus policed by every rain. Each window is closed by an iron grating, projecting sufficiently into the street to enable the *señoritas* to stand, or sit, and command a view of the street. The upper story has a corresponding balcony nearly all filled with flowers.

The walls, instead of presenting the sameness of ours with the red bricks uniformly placed, present all kinds of bright lined mathematical figures; the man of wealth shows a front formed of pieces of porcelain (generally with the figures), presenting a very handsome appearance; his neighbor, probably not quite as rich, has here and there pieces of porcelain forming detached figures, whilst another has his house painted to look like the old-fashioned calicoes. Not far off you see one painted in rectangles.

Some of the dwelling houses must have cost immense sums. The room in which I now write has its walls rudely but not unhandsomely painted to the height of five feet from the rough brick floor. If you can make anything of this attempt,[1] it is more than I can. The ceiling is formed of two arches intersecting each other, an ellipse, a circular one, with a wreath of the annexed figure running up and over the two arches.

Though ashamed of my previous attempts, I must go one step farther in letting you know something more of my room, which is about fourteen by eighteen feet. This

[1] A sketch was enclosed in letter.

table is also my mess table and my washstand. I have not much furniture to boast of; for washing I have an old tin basin, and an earthen bowl, the latter about eighteen inches across, an old brass candlestick (from home) with an enormous candle in it eighteen inches high, and an inch in diameter, a Mexican knapsack and a haversack, a canteen, Grandfather's tickler, which I have had covered with canvas to keep it from being broken; a pail, tumbler, and piece of Mexican matting complete my sum total of furniture, etc.

We find the marketing abundant and reasonable; of fruits there are fine watermelons, muskmelons of various kinds, apples (small), pears (not very good), apricots, plums (indifferent), oranges, lemons, limes, bananas (excellent, eight for six and a quarter cents), Mamaias (not certain about that spelling), and others I have forgotten. Of vegetables, tomatoes, onions, cabbage, lettuce, radishes, parsnips, potatoes—Irish and sweet (both large), parsley, corn, and peas, etc., beans of any number. Chickens, turkeys, and eggs are also abundant. As I think I have written enough of nonsense for one day, I will now close for to-night.

19th. Everything is as quiet about the City as if we were at home. It will not do to allow our men to walk about the streets singly or unarmed. The General's orders are very positive and correct; no soldiers are permitted to go out of their garrison yards in less numbers than six and under the charge of a non-commissioned officer, all to have their arms. One fourth of our men are constantly under arms. The Genl. is reported to have been very courteous in permitting about eighty of Santa Anna's Cavalry to enter the City yesterday.

In Mexico

Nothing would delight me more, save ending the war and restoring me to my family, than to see this war *civilized*, to witness interchange of civilities between the forces whenever they are not engaged in battle. At Cerro Gordo it was delightful to see our officers and men giving food and drink to the wounded, and doing all in their power to smooth the hard pillow of the dying. I noticed many of such acts which test both the valor and kind-heartedness of our Army.

The Mexican officers seemed to have forgotten that the field was strewn with their dying and dead, and left all to us. In civilized warfare actions are sometimes suspended to enable the contending armies to take care of their wounded and to bury their dead. The Mexican soldier is not regarded or taken care of as ours are.

I have been out shopping a little to-day, getting a few articles for the Compy. and for myself; the prices of hardware are enormously high—fifty cents apiece for the Britannia forks and spoons, three dollars for an old-fashioned coffee mill, and a dollar and a half for a kitchen iron dipper, smallest-sized box of matches three cents.

I may as well say something about the dress of the common people; the ladies have not become sufficiently well accustomed to the presence of the barbarians to shew themselves. The men wear jackets, pantaloons of buckskin, blue cloth of any kind or of velvet, fitting tight around the waist and open on the outer seam from the hip bone down, ornamented with buttons, or lace, embroidery, etc., the inside lined, and shewing under them the full leg of what is, I suppose, another pair of pants but not open at the seam; this under-garment is invariably white. Over the shoulders, and generally thrown over the left shoulder as a cloak, they wear the universal blanket.

Their hats have very broad brims and almost invariably ornaments at the side, a band or two of silver lace where we wear the hat band, and sometimes lace around the circumference of the brim. On horseback, their legs are protected by a large piece of skin or leather, attached in front of the stirrup leather, which covers the leg perfectly. The foot is doubly protected, first by the huge wooden stirrup, secondly by a thick flap of leather which is fastened to the upper part of the stirrup.

The common women wear the chemise (I suppose) and over it fastened around the waist some petticoats, the outer one either entirely of some fancy colored material, or, at all events, the lower part, from the first swell of the hip downwards, will be found colored. Over their heads, breasts, and shoulders, you again see the blankets, or *ribosa* which is worn by all who can afford it. These are placed on the crown of the head (sometimes fastened to the hair by a pin) crossed so as to meet about the chin, and the ends sometimes thrown over the left shoulder, as the blanket or cloak is worn by the men.

I saw a child carried by her mother, this morning, in a manner I never saw before. The woman had a basket full of some marketing, which was supported by her blanket, tied so as to form a kind of bag, the ends of the blanket *tied together*, and pressing on her forehead; between the basket and her blanket bag were seen divers kinds of vegetables, and under her left arm, its head (back downwards) dangling about the mother's hip, and one of its little feet seemingly holding to her dress behind was carried her little

Indian child. It was certainly a novel way of carrying a child.

You see them frequently carried here as the Indians do theirs in Florida, in blankets on the back. In fact the common people here resemble our Indians so strongly in their habits, it would be easy for them to assimilate at once. Education would make them good citizens. Ignorance keeps them serfs. Enough for to-day, *bonsoir*.

May 20th. I spent about an hour in the Cathedral, hoping when I left home that I might, on my return, be able to give you some description of the building and of its decorations. But without drawings it were perhaps better to say nothing, or, at all events, to speak in very general terms. In this interior chapel I saw no one, the other day during Mass, except the priests and children who were engaged in chanting.

The outer sides of this chapel are filled with paintings, some apparently very valuable; and it also has two little altars. The effect is grand beyond description, though you see much gold, silver, and gilding, still it is all in such grand style that you do not entertain the least feeling, such as I mentioned I entertained in seeing the Church ornaments at Nopolucan.

Every altar (except two) has around it pictures of various sizes, some not very good, but many very well executed. O how I wish that you could walk with me and enjoy the glorious beauty of this Cathedral. I feel that it would help to make me a better man. But behold, I am on my eighth page; I fear that if I do not reduce my daily scale of writing, the express, when he goes, will not carry my bulky epistle. I must now close for to-day.

May 21st. I have made a few corrections and additions to the sketch of the Cathedral, which I visited to-day for the purpose of verifying my work of yesterday. I shall add very little more, as I cannot describe it in terms to make you see, or delight in, its grandeur.

The arches forming the ceiling spring from sixty-four enormous stone pillars, arranged in groups of four, some of which are designated by (*) in the drawings;[1] along the side walls are seen corresponding sections, presenting one whole pillar and the two halves, from which spring the arches connecting with the walls. In another part of this same pile of buildings, we entered to-day two chapels, each containing three altars, one shewing the neatest and most beautiful rich altar-piece I have seen. It looks like rich chased gold. *Enough!*

No news from Genl. Scott; the rumor I heard yesterday that he was at Tepeyahualco, has not been confirmed to-day. Yesterday, a very heavy seizure of tobacco was made; it is worth several thousand dollars. Here, the Govt. monopolizes the tobacco trade. The rainy season seems to have commenced here, as we have rain every afternoon or night. I do hope that Genl. Twiggs's Division is provided with tents; if the men are not inside some kind of shelter at night, they must suffer very much.

Saturday, May 22nd. No mail, no rumor that a mail is on its way to us—nothing from Genl. Scott—in fact, we are without news from any part of the world. Even from Mexico, the Capital of this Republic, we hear nothing. So long as I could hear from you with the least degree of regularity, my mind was quieted from mail to mail, in hopes that the next mail would

---

[1] Sketches were enclosed in the letter.

give me good news of you, but now, when I look forward to a long summer in which I *may* hear from you very seldom if at all, it requires more philosophy than is now at my command to bear it.

I will yet hope that Genl. Scott will, when he arrives, devise some secure means for ensuring the regular and safe carriage of our letters. Thus far I have been much disappointed in not having received at least one mail since our arrival.

The Diligence came in to-day from Vera Cruz; it was robbed by some of the *rancheros*, or in other words, by some of the old established robbers, who now design legalizing their rascality by claiming to belong to the Mexican Guerrillas. The report that Genl. Scott was at Tepeyahualco two days ago, is contradicted by the passengers of the Diligence, who say that he was at Jalapa when they passed through. No one knows who tells the lie, rumor No. 1 or No. 2.

Cannon and musketry firing were said by Lt. Judd to have been distinctly heard this morning. To-morrow I presume that, if such is the fact, I shall let you know its cause. Out Dictionary hunting to-day; found a pocket edition of Nugent, old and much worn, for which the sum of five dollars was modestly asked. I need not say that the book was left on the table whence it was taken to be handed to me.

I finished to-day reading the *Prairie Bird*. I do not know whether you read it. Whether it was because it was the only book in our language which I could get, or that the work has intrinsic merit, I know not, but I was very much interested in it. Those who know anything of the localities described, might criticise the pigeon-like flight of his characters from one part of the country to another, but his characters of War Eagle, Winnegund, Ethelston, and Prairie Bird are certainly well drawn. He has, too, interwoven in a tale of fiction much true knowledge of Indian character, and many anecdotes illustrative of their habits, etc.

Dr. Holden and I think of taking lessons in Spanish if we can find a good and *reasonable* instructor. I find that I can ask for many things, but I could not attempt to ask or answer questions in conversation. Our little friend, Capt. Brooks, is very useful in interpreting, as he reads and speaks the Spanish language very well.

I must now lay this sheet by till to-morrow when I *may* have to thank you for another letter. God grant that it may be so. To His care and protection do my prayers ever consign you. Good-day.

Sunday, May 23rd. I fear that in my anxiety to give you *multum in parvo*, I may render my letter so nearly illegible as to destroy my object. Really, sometimes when I think of our position, so far into the interior of the enemy's country, and with so small a force, though I have not the least apprehension about our being able to keep our ground, still I cannot see how our communications can be kept up with our seaports. Would that Genl. Scott were here, he would soon solve all *my difficulties*.

We attended, by invitation, High Mass this morning in the Cathedral. The ceremonies were more showy then I ever saw in the United States, as the number of priests and attendants was larger than our Catholic communities *could* get together, and their dresses were also much more costly than we see in the United States. The three officiating priests wore the richest garment (I know not its name) over their backs and shoulders I ever saw; it looked like gold cloth. The music was very fine, not so sweetly pleasant to the ear as the vespers, as we heard them sung in St. Peter's Church in New York. You remember the time.

To-day during a part of the Mass, the voices were accompanied by orchestral music, some violins, a bass viol, and two or three wind instruments. This gave us delightful music. Not a female voice was in the choir—a great defect, as the voices of the boys have not the sweetness of those of females. Next Sunday, being Trinity, I presume that we shall be again invited. Nothing new, no word from General Scott. Good-night, God bless you.

Monday, 24th. Some of the quick-eared report musketry and firing having been heard again this morning, but no one believes it. Genl. Worth received a dispatch from Genl. Scott yesterday, in which he stated that he would leave Jalapa on the 23rd (yesterday). He may be expected here in about six days.

We have this morning a rumor that Genl. Bustamante is raising an army of 13,000 men in the City of Mexico, and that another Genl. is to join him with 9,000 men from the *tierras calientes*, the country beyond the mountains. Others say that old Genl. Bravo is marching down with an Army of 50,000 men. We do not believe any of these reports and feel confident of beating any Army Mexico can bring against us.

One thing I observe to-day which gives me great pleasure, viz., the ladies are making their appearance in the streets. This shows that confidence is being established. For the first four or five days after our arrival, not a lady was seen in the streets, private carriages were not seen, but few females shewed themselves at the windows. To-day we see very genteel equipages and ladies and gentlemen taking drives. I hope that in a short time the Pueblans will find that we are not as barbarous as we have been represented, and learn to regard us as good friends.

No one can tell us where Genl. Santa Anna is. I have been reading Thompson's *Recollections of Mexico*, in which he gives many instances of Santa Anna's generosity and other good qualities. I expect from the tenor of some severe articles recently published against him, that he will soon be again compelled to leave his country, for whose Independence he has fought in many an action.

I find that I am forgetting that I ought to restrict myself in my writing as I am running off into dissertations which had better be contracted or omitted. When I take up my pen to write to you, I instinctively write every thought as it enters my mind. This you see by my erratic style. But of this you are ever well assured, that you always fill the heart and soul of your own devoted husband.

Tuesday, 25th. No letters. No Genl. Scott. Ill-tongued rumor even goes so far as to say that when the Genl. arrives, no mail will be brought, as no mail has been received at Vera Cruz for one month. I will not believe the story—it cannot be true.

I had written thus far, when Maj. Wade, Dr. Holden, Lts. Judd and Austine came in; they have just left, giving me a late bed hour. I have nothing new to communicate. The reports about Bustamante's raising an Army in Mexico is contradicted to-day; it is now reported that Santa Anna was enthusiastically received in Mexico, that he is to be the next President, that he is organizing an Army and preparing the City for defence. I do not believe this tale—it is too improbable. The Genl. who lost the battle of Cerro Gordo cannot be received with enthusiasm in the Capital.

I must not close my letter without telling you of our visit to one of the Churches this morning where the railing and enclosure of the main Altar was ornamented with flowers and evergreens in pots; the effect was very pretty. The idea struck me as an original and very charming one. The padre of that Church must be a good man. That God may keep my wife under His especial care is my prayer.

May 26th. I have just returned from a walk with the Doctor, and was informed that an Express was to leave in the morning. As Col. Belton has sent his letters off (without asking for our letters), I know not but I may be foiled in my attempt at getting this into the mail. But I will leave no proper means for doing so untried.

Among the other curious sights here, I see the tails o mules put up in leather bags or pockets. The harness is made with these pockets to keep their tails from interfering with the driver's lines, of which there are *none*, as the driver rides on one of each pair of mules.

No. 13. PUEBLA.
May 28, 1847.

No. 12 was, I find, taken yesterday morning by a Mexican gentleman who has started for Vera Cruz.

He has my warmest thanks for his offer to take letters, and if, by his agency, you succeed in getting mine, I shall be under everlasting obligations to at least one of these *will be enemies*. I was prevented from writing last evening, by a visit, from an early till a late hour, of nearly all the officers of our little garrison.

Lt. Johnson was, I thought, last week about relapsing into the state in which he was represented to have been at St. Augustine—so nervous that he could attend to no duty. But something fortunately occurred, which roused him from his lethargy, in which I hope he will not again indulge.

In speaking of the City, no mention has, I believe, been made of the Alameda. This is a large lot arranged for the afternoon walks and drives of the citizens of Puebla. A double row of trees, mostly willows, shades the principal drive around its four sides; from this, several walks lead to fountains in the interior; some of these have "jets-d'eau," in others the water merely bubbles, or wells up.

All these walks and fountains are shaded by trees, among which I saw a tree resembling very closely my horror, the Lombardy poplar, but I was told it was a species of willow. Hedges of roses, sweet peas, marguerites (with here and there a dahlia) and pinks, surround and intersect this beautiful spot. Of roses I never before saw such a profusion.

All the flowers are the same we have in our gardens; not an uncommon one did I see. Looking at the flowers and trees, we might, had it not been for the operations of *fond memory*, have imagined ourselves in our own beloved land. But the delusion would have soon been dispelled by the constant presence at the fountains of some of the water-carriers. The

MEXICAN WATER CARRIERS
From a photograph

In Mexico

earthen jars here used are, I suspect, the exact pattern of those used by the Israelites. Though not famous for sketching, let's try.[1] Each carrier has two of these jars, holding, I think, ten gallons; one is carried in front, the strap crossing the man's neck, and the other behind, the strap over the upper part of the forehead.

Major Wade saw one of these carriers, who had just filled his jars and started from the fountain in front of our quarters, and was so unfortunate as to have both of them fall, and of course break to pieces. The poor fellow stood muttering something and crossed himself repeatedly, gazing at his loss. This is mentioned as an instance of their adherence to the forms of their religion.

I have frequently been in sight of the public Plaza, where the market is held, at the hour of the officiating priest's elevating the Host in the Cathedral. It is announced by the striking of a particular bell; at this sound, every Mexican throws himself on his knees and there remains till another signal gives notice that the ceremony is over, when they immediately resume their business. I have seen the market-place filled with buyers and sellers, all on their knees, and the Mexicans in the streets near by leading to the square, also kneeling.

In other parts of the City, at the sound of this bell all uncover. This last they invariably do whenever they pass the door of a church (and they are very numerous) or a priest. The respect they pay to their religion is wonderful, and to me a very pleasing sight.

Genl. Scott has arrived; he came in this morning, with an Escort of Cavalry and Mounted Rifles. I

[1] A sketch was enclosed in letter.

have not seen him, but shall call on him to-morrow. Lt. Judd states that he heard we were to advance, leaving a force here of two thousand men. I have most unlimited confidence in the judgment and discretion of the Genl. and will blindly pin my faith to any of his decisions. You know that in my journalizing, I give you sometimes daily rumors which are subsequently corrected by others which I give; this may be the case with the above rumor.

Thus far had I written when my room was filled with officers who have just left me. It is now *good* bed time, and, as I have already given you a long letter for one day's writing, I will now bid you good-night.

Saturday night, 29th. I called to see Genl. Scott this morning and was delighted to learn that a mail was coming up with Genl. Twiggs; he has arrived with his Division, but we have not been informed when or where the mail will be opened. The Genl. does not look very well; he is, I presume, merely suffering from the fatigue of a rapid march.

Most of my Army friends have arrived with him. My friend, Capt. Irwin, is, I am delighted to see, looking better than when we parted at Vera Cruz. Capt. Wayne mentioned that he had a letter from Mrs. W. dated the 24th April. I hope that my good news from you will be of as late a date.

I am sorry to hear that there is every probability that my first letter from this place has been taken, as General Scott has never received Genl. Worth's report of our entering this place, forwarded by the same express. I am now writing in the fond, and, I fear, foolish hope, that I may ere long have a safe opportunity for sending this letter. During this long, long summer I fear that we shall scarcely hear from each other. What would I not give, if the two Nations would like sensible people agree at once upon some honorable terms of peace.

We have, by the General's Staff, been favored with papers from the United States, announcing the reception of the news of the battle of Cerro Gordo. I have not read any of the accounts, but have no doubt they, as is generally the case, deviate widely from the truth. I hope that Capt. R. Lee, U. S. Engineers, will write a Military Memoir on that battle, accompanying it with correct topographical maps, indicating the position of the batteries, and showing the varied positions of the troops during the battle. The accurate description of that battle would place the science of our Army distinctly and most creditably before European Military readers.

Capt. Swift's death, though not unexpected, has filled the hearts of his friends, and all who knew him were such, with feelings of grief. He was an excellent man, and a most valuable officer. You saw him at West Point. Capt. Mason, of the Rifles, who lost a leg at Cerro Gordo, has, I am sorry to say, died from his wound. He was a favorite also with his acquaintances. Our friend Lt. Col. Bragg rises rapidly in the Military world. Genl. Taylor's encomium on him, in his report of his last battle, is good for another brevet; this will place our young Capt. among the Brevet Lt. Colonels. Enough for to-night.

Sunday night, 30th May. I had just closed my eyes last night, when I was roused by a tap at the door, and was told that there was a letter for me. My heart told me that it was from you. It was yours of the 20th. Its reception has relieved my mind of a heavy weight, as it tells me that your heart is at rest in relation to Vera Cruz. About Cerro Gordo you cannot have been kept long in suspense.

But, my wife, you are stark mad and crazy about my name's not being mentioned, or my not having been brevetted. A Capt. of the line of the Army has the least possible chance of being mentioned among the *distinguished*, however distinguished his conduct may be.

The reason why, is a very simple one. As he is *part* of a Command, whether Regt. or Battalion, whatever is done by the *Regt.* or *Battalion*, is placed to the credit of *its* commander. It is only by a captain's being detached with his Compy. on some special service that he has a chance to distinguish himself. Hence the advantage of an officer's commanding a Battery, etc. Dispel this idea from your mind, and regard me as returning plain Capt. Anderson, however well and zealously I may perform my duties.

If I should be brevetted, it will be *luck*. Genl. Scott, though my best friend, cannot designate me, unless I am reported to him—the ill-will or ill-temper of the Regtl. Commander might not, even under a highly favorable case, give him an opportunity of so doing. Let this not worry you. I hope that as long as I remain in service, I shall continue so to act as to command the favorable opinion of all those with whom I serve; as to gaining brevets, that is a lottery in which there are many blanks to the prize; though all the candidates pay the same price—most gallant deeds—but few are lucky enough to draw the prize.

I dined with Genl. S. to-day, and am sorry to say

that he was compelled to take quinine. I had hoped that he would recover without more medicine, though I knew by my own case how long a time it required for me to recover from my Perote chill. The Genl. has been as kind and affectionate as ever to me, and begs me to call whenever I can. But knowing how little time he has to spare to friendly intercourse, I cannot intrude often on him. He made many kind inquiries about the family. I hope Father has written to him.

I was in the Cathedral at Mass this morning, Trinity Sunday. The pillars through the body of the church as well as those against the walls, were entirely covered with rich damask velvet. The music was much more delightful than it was last Sunday. It was sublime. Genl. S. was there with his Staff. I regret that I did not understand the sermon, as I was pleased with the manner and voice of the preacher. Enough for to-night.

May 31st. Capt. De Hart took supper with us and remained until after Tattoo, so that I shall write you only a few lines to-night. Your letter advises that henceforth I ought to direct my letters to Clarkesville; I fear that my having changed too soon my directions to that place may have caused you much uneasiness. My previous letters have given my reasons for my having done so.

News of great (it may be) importance came last night from Mexico, that Santa Anna, to heal the political and personal dissensions in the parties of Mexico, has determined to *sacrifice* himself, and has declared that he will not accept the Presidency. Who will be the President seems to be very uncertain. Generals Bravo and Valencia have command of the Mexican Armies, the one at the Capital, the other in San Luis.

Of Genl. Taylor's movements we know nothing. Our placid Lt. Col. has been named by Genl. Worth as his successor in the Milty. and Civil Governorship of this City. A worse selection could not have been made.

This looks a little like the 3rd's being intended as part of the garrison of this Post. I shall exert all my ingenuity to prevent *my* being left. I am exceedingly desirous on many accounts to go as far into the Country as any one. *Nous verrons.*

Friend Capt. Knowlton sent me a package of New York papers; if I can find a safe opportunity I must return him my thanks. My anxiety that you should hear from me will cause me to embrace every opportunity of sending a letter whether it be considered safe or not; if any one reaches you it is a point gained.

June 1st. Nothing new to-day. In fact, as I am Officer of the Day, I have not been outside of our quarters. I have read Genl. Santa Anna's resignation of the Presidency; the latter part is as pretty a piece of egotism as I have met with for a long time.

Yesterday the Municipal authorities of this City retired from their offices. Genl. Worth has, in the exercise of his authority as Governor, directed an election to be held to fill their places and has ordered those officials to return to their duties till their places are filled. I have not been to see Genl. Scott since Sunday, but must call to-morrow to enquire how he is.

My wife, you have either mistaken the purport of one of the sentences in a letter from Vera Cruz, or it states what I did not mean. I did *not* receive the

In Mexico 195

white flag whilst in the trenches; the parley (as we believed it to be) was sounded and the firing suspended for the bearer of the flag to approach, but as we had no bugle to answer their call, we missed the opportunity of receiving the flag, which without the enemy's firing another shot, went to Genl. Scott early the next morning, that is, the *same morning* we were relieved in the trenches.

Col. Bankhead's report, giving only the names of the officers who were in the trenches the first day, has, I hear, been published; his excuse for not mentioning all was, that he had *forgotten* the names of the others—a pretty excuse to be sure, as it could have been so easily rectified. He promised to make a fuller report on reaching Washington when he would name all the commanders of the batteries. Enough of Vera Cruz, and enough, I must say, for to-night.

Tuesday, June 2nd. As Major Wade was absent from the garrison all the morning I could not go out till late this afternoon. My first visit was to Maj. Kirby, and whilst he was engaged in business, I went into another room to see Capt. Myers. The Capt. has, by a fall, I fear, injured himself so that he will walk lame for the rest of his life; the knee-pan seems to be detached from its proper position.

The Major and I sallied out sight-seeing and we saw what were great curiosities to me, *viz.*, figures of Mexican Indians made of prepared linen; the countenances were very expressive. One was a group of three figures—a drunken man, his neck too limber to support his head; next is his mother perfectly enraged at him, and intent upon administering chastisement on her foolishly good-humored son, which she is prevented from doing by her daughter-in-law who holds her arm.

A second group is an Alcalde, administering a lecture to a man whose wife is in tears on the other side of the Alcalde, who is seated between the other figures who are standing. Should we ever have peace I must bring you some of the curiosities of these singular people—many of them I shall have to abandon an attempt to carry, from the difficulty of packing them safely for so long a journey.

Col. Pierce Butler informed me this afternoon that one of his Captains was about returning home, and that if I would send any letters to his quarters he would with pleasure give them in charge of his Captain. I thanked him from the bottom of my heart and will hand this letter to him.

Thus far no means have been devised to secure the safe transmission of our letters, and we catch eagerly at any opportunity which seems to offer a chance delivery of them. We may get another mail by some nine hundred recruits who are expected from the United States *via* Vera Cruz, but with that exception, we see no prospect of any other, till the President sends us an addition to our small but invincible band.

Had we 30,000 men and Genl. Taylor 20,000, the War might soon be closed. Our Govt. should remember and act vigorously upon the advice given by Father[1] to it before the breaking out of the Florida War. I must leave a little clear space for to-morrow.

Genl. Scott's Office, June 3rd. Being on guard at the General's Hd. Qrs., I must close my letter to-night for the mail which leaves to-morrow, without being

[1] Genl. Clinch.

In Mexico

able to add as much to it as I had designed. As Capt. Huger and some others are waiting to avail themselves of the candle-light which I am using, courtesy and fellow-feeling prompt me to close at as short a time as possible.

I have no other news to give. Col. B. has left our quarters, much to our satisfaction, and taken up his abode in a corner of the Palace. Col. Butler has again urged me to confide my letter to his "Captain," who hopes to raise a party at Jalapa sufficiently large to march with safety to Vera Cruz. We shall have in a few days an addition of 2000 men to our present command in addition to those you see mentioned as coming from the United States.

No. 14. Puebla.
June 4th. Friday night.

Although very tired and sleepy from my necessary wakefulness last night, I cannot retire without having a little chat with you. All were disappointed in not witnessing yesterday the great ceremonies usually performed in Catholic communities on that, Corpus Christi, day. Fearful that they might be insulted by our soldiery, they limited themselves in the observance of their ceremonies to the walls of their churches.

Many years have passed since I saw these ceremonies, and I regret very much, from my recollection of what I then witnessed in Bogota, South America that the grand procession was not made in all its splendor through the streets here. The streets through which the procession passed were hung with the richest cloths and satins. Everybody, priests and laity, was dressed as splendidly as *their own*, or the means of their friends would enable them. The consecrated wafer, the Host, was carried from church to church and then returned to the Cathedral.

Yesterday, I was told that the ceremonies in the Cathedral where the Host was taken round, were not remarkably imposing. I heard this morning, that had the assurances made to the Clergy night before last, that they would neither be insulted nor molested in any way by our men, been given the night before, the procession would have taken place, but after the notices there was not time for the necessary preparations.

The rumor of to-day is that the Mexican Congress have declined accepting Santa Anna's resignation. They are determined to thrust the Presidency upon him. One thing looks unpromising for the Mexican Nation in this, that it seems they look to him and him alone, it may be said, for their salvation from our power. From the reputation Santa Anna purchased by his bravery, zeal, and skill in their internal broils, the Mexicans ought to regard him as one of their greatest men.

In his controversies with the Texans and his battles with us, the splendor of his star has been somewhat tarnished. He may now make desperate efforts to regain his lost brilliancy. *Nous verrons.* He has a very prudent, brave, and skilful adversary to cope with. Enough for to-night.

Saturday night, June 5th. Rumor says that Santa Anna insists upon his resignation being accepted, and that he has asked for his passports to enable him to leave the country. As I have a long report to make to-night to present to Genl. Worth in the morning, in relation to the case of a Mexican sabred by a soldier, I must be very brief. I am on duty to-day, as Division Officer of the Day, having been thus honored in consequence of my being placed on duty, as Acting Major of the Regt. ! ! ! A great honor, Acting Major to three companies. To-morrow I will make amends for this brevity.

Sunday night, June 6th. As soon as I heard of the arrival of the mail this afternoon, I hastened to the Quartermaster's office and was there presented with a letter from the Pennsylvanian who was with me at Vera Cruz. You may judge of my disappointment!

My friend, Dr. Cuyler, has just sent me a most welcome contribution—your letter of the 26th April. To-night I can do no more than thank you for it.

Monday night, June 7th. Let me now give answers to certain queries in your last letter. Our arrangement in Genl. Worth's Divison is permanent, and would only be altered by a re-organization of the Command, or by our being left in garrison. You need not send your letters under cover to Col. Hunt—if directed to me as "belonging to the Army" under Genl. Scott in Mexico they will come safely. Our friend Lt. Brown is here with Capt. Wells' Co., the one formerly commanded by Lt. Steptoe. He left me a few minutes since; his manner is always kind and affectionate. He always enquires about you.

Two officers are now attached temporarily to "G" Co., Lt. Andrews and Lt. Shields; the former performs the duties of Asst. Q. M. and Asst. Commissary of Subsistence, the latter, who attends to Compy. duty, has applied to be permanently attached to the Compy. Our cousin, Lt. A., speaks in very high terms of Lt. S. and says that he is a gentleman. Lt. A.'s wife is with her father's family on Governor's Island; they have no child, having been unfortunate.

I am rejoiced that your dear grandmother is well again after her dangerous attack. Of our friend Lt. Sherman we have not heard, except through the newspaper which announces his arrival in California.

Tuesday 8th. I hear that when the Regts., etc., now under orders for our Army reach us, our force will amount to twenty thousand men. Had it been half that on our arrival here, we might have been long since in the City of Mexico, and that without having to shed another drop of blood. Report says that Genl. Bravo is now raising an army of 35,000 men, and that the Mexicans are fortifying some points on the road. We have had so many Mexican stories about their positions, strength, etc., that I pay no attention to any that I hear.

Yesterday the Brigade was inspected by the Inspector General, Col. Hitchcock, and made a very respectable display for troops in the field. Genl. Worth speaks of commencing Division drills next week. With his energy and thorough knowledge, we will soon bear the palm from all competitors. Genl. Twiggs, not understanding evolutions of the Line himself, cannot instruct others. I may do him an injustice; my remark is based upon what I have heard. I never saw him drilling.

I suppose it certain that we will not leave this place till our reinforcements arrive. We are *now* strong enough to whip any army the Mexicans can raise. You remember Lt. Johnson. He had not, before the arrival of the last mail, received a line from his wife since he left her, and that mail brought him information

In Mexico

of the loss of his little boy. As he is a Christian, he bears it well. Feeling confident that his child is now a happy angel in the presence of God, he grieves not for it. He says that preceding letters, giving an account of the illness, etc., must have been miscarried, as his wife writes of it as an event some time past. He says that her letter is what it ought to be—that she is very pious, and sets him a good example. We all sympathize very sincerely with him.

A letter from Tampico informs us that Mrs. Gates has presented the Col. with a little Mexican daughter. It has raised him a couple of inches higher. Capt. Burke is under orders for our Army; he ought to be at Vera Cruz now, as his orders are dated April 27th. Think of the Capt. as Commander of the 3rd!

Among the oddities of the Mexicans, I have not mentioned that small pieces of *soap* are current *coin*, instead of the smallest copper coin, *clico*, worth half a cent. In market I frequently see the soap given as change.

Wednesday, 9th. A little fatigued from a day's hard work. I was congratulating myself about 9 o'clock this morning that I would have a quiet day in which I could write a few letters to Larz and to two or three others to whom letters are due, when my designs were suddenly crushed by an order to march the Regt. to the exercise ground and there to drill at battalion drill till Col. Garland's arrival. Major Wade was absent on Court-Martial, so that I had to play Colonel.

I had been drilling but a few minutes when Genl. Worth and the Inspector Genl. Hitchcock showed themselves among the spectators. The remaining Regiments of the Brigade soon came on the ground, and we took our positions in Line. Col. Garland now took command and kept us on the field until half past one o'clock—a pretty good day's work.

On Saturday the Division will be reviewed, manœuvred by Genl. Worth. We are already cautioned to take our canteens filled with water and lunch in the haversacks; we shall have no child's play then. Of news we have not heard a word to-day. To-morrow we may, probably, hear from Genl. Child's Command mentioned in my last letter.

Mr. N. P. Trist, the special and most Extraordinary Minister of President Polk, is in the city. I have not heard him mentioned. Everybody thinks he is here on a fool's errand, and that he had better go home as soon as possible.

By the way, I was very much astonished at meeting our Tampa Bay Sutler in the streets here a day or two since. He left his wife at Tampa, and has come out to see if he can collect some money due him by some of the 8th Infy. Companies. I asked him if he had sold the articles left by me with him. He said that he sold nearly everything at excellent prices, and that he had directed Mr. Ferris to sell the remainder at auction on some court day, and to remit you the amount.

Poor Mr. Clark has, I fear, come on a wild goose chase, as no one knows when the men will be paid off. The Captains of Companies are generally anxious that the men should not be paid whilst in a large city, as drunkenness and broils will take place, and we shall have Mexican soldiers murdered.

What do you think of an American Theatrical Company opening in the City of Puebla!! I saw to-day a notice that the Theatre would be opened in a day or two by Messrs. Wells and Hart. Enough for to-night.

June 10th. I have been here so long that I feel that I have seen enough of the people to describe some of their peculiarities. They exhibit a greater fondness for children than any people I ever saw. I do not think you can point out any article used by grown persons of which I can not shew you its miniature among the playthings. Of dolls—wax, wood, and rag—there are thousands, from the very smallest to our common sizes. The Indians bring in the rudest and most ludicrous representations of animals you can conceive of. Of saint and of soldier you may purchase a collection not very flattering to the vanity of either.

In preserves (this word does not embrace the infinite variety of articles prepared with sugar we find here), the Spanish people, I presume, excel all other people. The common sponge-cake sold in the streets is generally excellent; then you find figs, dates, and various kinds of rinds, exceedingly well preserved; again you find other sweetmeats, of which milk is a component part. Their candied fruit is very good. I hope that on our return I may find transportation for a box or two of these articles for you.

The toys and *dulces* are exhibited for sale under the arcades of the large houses separated by streets from the Plaza where the market is held. The market is to strangers a great curiosity, being held in a large open square. On examining closely you will find that in the seeming disorder and confusion there is much method.

Along the outer side of the square, and indeed *out-*

side of the square, and encroaching on the sidewalks, you find Mexican crockery, plates, dishes, cups, bowls, water jars, baskets (willow) of sizes from large, three and a half feet in diameter, flat ones, to those three inches in diameter, and matting from coarse to quite pretty.

The first row inside is corn, spread out in large piles on matting; next to this you find onions, large and white as snow, tomatoes, generally of the wild kind, green and about an inch in diameter, and some coarse kind of greens, parsley, etc.

Next are some women who have their charcoal furnaces at work cooking and selling various Mexican stews, etc.; here you may buy from this girl, who removes a dirty cloth from the top of the basket near her, tortillas made of corn soaked in lime mashed by a roller on a large flat stone prepared for that purpose, and then baked. She is too dirty, or at all events the cloth which keeps her tortillas hot is too dirty—let us pass on.

On the next row among the onions, cabbages, tomatoes, large and small (I have not seen any of the beautiful golden tomatoes here), radishes (very large, and good), turnips, squashes, peas, carrots, you may perchance see some of your old acquaintances, but so disguised that you will scarce recognize them; those shining sleek objects are sweet potatoes, boiled and sweetened by some sugaring process, and those *crooked*, mammoth pods, six and eight inches long, are said to be ochre. I have not seen an uncooked one in market.

In the next row, you find fruits, baskets of pears, mostly green, indifferent peaches, apples and cherries, Mamaias in abundance, small apricots, sapotes both green and blue (neither good for anything), alligator

SCENE IN A MEXICAN MARKET

pear, and, for a rarity, here is a woman who has some mushrooms.

Under that awning, you find oranges, limes, muskmelons, watermelons (six cents a slice), goat's cheese, eggs, chocolate makers, coarse wooden spoons, etc., and pears and apricots which you can buy cheaper from the market women farther back.

Passing a little higher up in this row, and around the fountain in the centre of the square, you find cooking utensils, *earthen and iron*, and near by, the chickens, turkeys, and pigeons. Those piles of white chalky-looking substance are lime, used in cooking, etc. On Thursday, the great market day, you find piles of beans of all colors and sizes. Flowers are also seen frequently in Market—pinks appear to be favorites. I have omitted bananas and plantains, cocoanuts and pineapples. The cocoanut is very fine, but I think the plantain the best fruit I have seen. I have also omitted the fruit of the cactus, two kinds, green and purple. Peppers abound always. These are in little piles on matting—the women sitting by them in a way peculiarly Mexican, on their legs doubled under them; all sit in that way.

Friday, 11th. I am truly thankful that there is a prospect of our having another mail. Genl. T., I hear, received information from Genl. Childs to-day, that Genl. Cadwalader was on his way from Vera Cruz, and that he would come up with him. Genl. Cadwalader must certainly bring a mail, and that mail must certainly bring a letter from you. When this poor scrawl is to start on it's way to you I cannot say. As yet, I see not the glimmer of a chance.

Genl. Santa Anna, finding that the Mexican Congress

kept his resignation under consideration four days, and that they did not promptly urge him to remain in power, on the end of this month withdraws his resignation. The plea he gives is twofold; first, that the American Army may be expected to advance on the Capital at any moment, and that it would endanger the Country for us to do so, whilst the Congress is either organizing a new Govt. or before the new President has had time to make necessary arrangements for defence; secondly, that he has received from all sides the most urgent entreaties to remain in power, etc., etc. The document, his resignation, and the reports of his conduct at Cerro Gordo and Amozoc have done him no good. They have lowered him very much in my estimation.

To-morrow is to be Genl. Worth's big day. He is to inspect, review, and drill our Division. I saw him this afternoon, and told him that I had heard of better ground—he said that it was better, but not so *public*. So he flatters himself that we will make a good show. I hope that he may not be disappointed. I will write the result. As we have to rise very early to-morrow to prepare, I must retire to bed early, and will now take my leave for the night.

Saturday evening, 12th. Our *field day*, as the English call it, is passed. The Division made very pretty display, while halted. But I cannot say much that is favorable for their marching—but allowance must be made; how can it be otherwise, with troops who have never been properly instructed. Muskets placed in their hands as soon as they join the Compy., and probably placed on guard the next week, these men at once fancy that they are soldiers, and that they know everything about their duties. Such a course would ruin any recruits. The crowd of spectators was very large, embracing, I was glad to hear, some of the best families of the City; among them was the Lt. Gov. of this State. Genl. Worth did not inspect and he kept us out but a short time. This was in consequence of his not feeling well enough to take the Division through many manœuvres.

I see by some of the papers received by the last mail, that Duncan's[1] Regt. is not among those ordered to join Genl. Scott's Army. Duncan will therefore be with your brave old Zach. Where he is, or what he is doing, I know not. I presume that they are much better informed upon these points in the Cities of Mexico and Washington, than we are here.

I have not, I think, told you of the fate of my letter No. 11. It was given to a Mexican who has been attached to Genl. Worth for several months; this man returned last week very much emaciated, the Genl. says, and reports that he was taken prisoner, carried to some place off the main road, and that he secreted the mail where no one could get it. He was thoughtful enough to return to the Genl. a letter he had written to Mrs. W. Now, how my trusty Mexican could abstract that letter from the others without his being seen, I cannot conceive, unless he was very badly guarded, in which case he might have escaped sooner. At all events No. 11 is destined to remain in Mexico.

I do not remember any incidents of much interest contained in that letter, but the foolish Donquixotish march of Santa Anna to the neighborhood of Amozoc the day we lay there (15th May) and his retreat back again. With the usual mendacity of his reports, he says that he bantered us to fight in the open field

[1] Mrs. Anderson's brother.

which we declined. What fools he must take Mexicans to be—they know that he had a large body of Cavalry, and as we had only two squadrons, if he had desired an engagement, he must have attacked our Infantry. He took precious good care to keep out of the way of our Infy. and his Cavalry rapidly dispersed on receiving a few shells in their midst from Col. Duncan's Battery. The less his biographers say of "Amozoc" the better for his Milty. reputation. His coming down was a silly and unmilitary proceeding.

Another statement he makes is also false—that a train of two hundred wagons was coming towards Amozoc with a very light escort, and that it was his intention to cut it off, but the train, instead of marching at the usual hour, broke up its last camp very early in the night, and thus got into a secure position before he reached them. No train of wagons came up but the one accompanying Genl. Quitman's Brigade, which was amply strong to have whipped the General's Cavalry. But enough of correction—I am not engaged in writing a history of the War, but merely make these corrections, to let you see how untrue will be the Mexican Official documents on this War.

I hope that our historians will give us the truth, even were it to make us feel a little sore—but thus far, we have nothing to fear. Our course has been plain— very few acts have been committed, even by the Volunteers, which have required and received chastisement. But I am devoting too much space to my evening's speculations and must now bid you good-night.

Sunday, 13th.

My kind friend Major Wade, having nothing to do, has been polite enough to devote all the evening to me,

In Mexico

and leaves me now at an hour so late that I am deprived of the pleasure of a long chat with you to-night.

I have not been in the City to-day, and have, besides attending to my proper duties, written letters; one to Larz partly on business, one to Mr. Austen, another to a Mr. Oliphant, both of Uniontown, Pa. Mr. A.'s letter to me was full of thanks for my "kind attentions" to him at Vera Cruz, and urging me to pay him a visit with my family. Mr. Oliphant wrote to ask me whether Mr. A. had been with me at the siege, and in what capacity he served.

The news is to-day that a party of 3000 horsemen have gone on the road towards Vera Cruz for the purpose of procuring subsistence and also to intercept the train of wagons, sent from this place a week since. They will catch a tartar.

The Mexican papers publish a letter from Mrs. Col. Childs to her husband which contains some political remarks which her husband would rather not see in print. She speaks of President Polk and says that his course is driving many of his old friends to the support of Genl. Taylor. This letter was taken from the saddle-bags of a Col.——— who was coming on as a bearer of despatches, and who rode with the advance guard, instead of remaining with the main body of his escort. I hope that he had none of your letters. I shall know in a few days. The Mexican paper states that they have a large bundle of letters. The vandals should send all private letters to the Army—no civilized soldiery should violate the sanctity of family correspondence. At Cerro Gordo I saw a letter addressed to Genl. Santa Anna, the seal of which had not been broken. Enough for to-night. May God continue to protect and guard you.

Monday, 14th.

My birthday. How can I better commence this day's letter than by thanking our Heavenly Father for all His mercies towards me and mine, and praying Him that He may continue to guard and protect us, and long before another year passes, that it may please Him to unite us together. What would I not give to have had you with me to-day! This afternoon, I accidentally went to my old friend's, Capt. Irwin, and there found another classmate, Capt. Huger, and a party. Some one mentioned that it was my birthday, and my good friend, contrary to my entreaties, brought out a bottle of good old Madeira, to drink to my health. And as far as friendship could go, all was well and happy.

But what was this to me, when I thought of those who were far, far away. This is peculiarly to me a day for home thoughts and home feelings. Think not, my wife, that those thoughts make me feel sad and lonely. That it is in a measure so, is true; but still it is not a sadness without a light of pleasure. Hope tells me that we cannot be much longer separated, and that then my joy will be so great that I will count as nothing all the little discomforts, etc., during our separation. God grant that I may very soon be restored to you. As I shall probably close this letter to-morrow, that it may be ready for any mail that may go out, and that I may commence another, I shall close for to-night. No news from the Mexican Army to-day—the fact is they can't keep up an Army.

Tuesday, 15th.

The report alluded to in my scribblings of the 14th has been contradicted, and then re-asserted.

To-day 't is said that Genl. Valencia has a rabble of badly armed and undisciplined men in the City of Mexico awaiting us, about 16,000—that their boasted fortifications along the route will be easily mastered.

My opinion about reports taken even to Hd. Qrs. is that they are frequently carried by men out of employment, who hope by their pretended assiduity and zeal to secure employment in some capacity with the Army. Other reports are doubtless fabricated in the Mexican Camp and sent out to produce an effect on their countrymen, or to attempt to deceive us. I therefore rarely think it necessary to report the rumors of the day, and then hear, a day or two after I have heard them, *the latest news* from Mexico, or from the Mexican Army.

I am rejoiced that I can say that I now daily witness the verification of my prediction about the change of feeling which Genl. Scott's course would work in the Army. I hear every day the strongest expressions of admiration and implicit confidence expressed towards, and in him, by men who a few short weeks since received a toast alluding to his gallant services during the last war with chilling coldness.

Dr. Tripler, who has just left me, says that he heard Genl. Twiggs (not notorious for speaking well of his superiors) say that he considered Genl. S. one of the greatest generals of the age, that Genl. Taylor ought not to be mentioned in the same day with him.

I am thus particular in dwelling on this subject because I know how much pleasure and satisfaction these facts will give you. Father knows the Genl. as well, indeed much better than I do, and he will not be astonished that at every battle, and by every important movement, he gains warm friends.

Genl. Worth is, I am sorry to say, not well. He looks very badly, and told me this morning that he had no appetite, and could scarcely bear the sight of food. When we get into active motion again, the Genl. will brighten up again, but were we to remain inactive, he would, I fear, soon break down.

Genl. Cadwalader and Genl. Shields will be up in a few days. I do not see what can be done with Genl. Shields—should he be sufficiently restored—as it seems to me that his commission as an officer of the Army expired with the term of service of the Volunteers who were called out last year.

I do not see as much of some of the Vols. as I ought, and as would be agreeable to me. But on returning from our morning drills, I feel so tired, that I generally, instead of visiting after dinner, indulge in a siesta.

Col. Butler has been remarkably kind in making frequent calls, and I have been to see him but once. I will call to-morrow to see him. He informs me that Genl. Butler was most anxious to have me with him, but I am almost certain that I mentioned this subject in a previous letter.

The Editors have followed us to this place, and issued on the 12th inst. the first number of *American Star*—No. 2. If anything of interest should be treated of in the papers, I will send them. This first number is filled with an order publishing the Military laws passed by the last Congress, and by late news from the United States, and would furnish you with not one line of interesting reading.

An anecdote is told of Genl. Scott which should be mentioned. As he was coming to this place with an escort of only four Companies of Cavalry, the advance guard sent a messenger to report to the Genl. that the

In Mexico

Mexicans were approaching in large force. The Genl. was, when the messenger came up, engaged in conversation with some officers, and simply directed the messenger to report to Col. Harney. Those present say that he evinced not the least concern, and having sent the man to the Commanding Officer, he resumed his conversation as if nothing had occurred.

And now in fact No. 14 must be closed. **No. 15** will be commenced to-morrow, and will, I fear, be finished also before this goes.

June 18th. I have just heard that a mail will be sent to-morrow. Nothing of much interest since the last date of this letter. No. 15 is not sufficiently advanced to commence its journey.

No. 15. PUEBLA, MEX.
Wednesday, June 16, 1847.

This has been an interesting rumor-day. We hear that Col. McIntosh, on his way up with seven hundred men, was repeatedly attacked, and that at the National Bridge, affairs were so serious, that he halted and sent back to Genl. Cadwalader, whom he was preceding, for reinforcements. The two commands, Cadwalader's and McIntosh's, would arrive last night, report says, at Jalapa.

If the report, of Col. M.'s being compelled to wait for relief, be true, I fear it will raise the spirits of the guerrilla parties, and will cause us a great deal of annoyance. It is said, too, that the Mexicans have become so daring in Vera Cruz, that they take mules from the pens. Col. Wilson should give them one or two shells from the Castle, if the City authorities do not put a stop to such proceedings.

Last night, too, was not to be devoid of interest. One Alcalde deserted, taking with him half the City guard. These are small affairs, and will have no effect on our Military operations. Genl. Scott strikes at higher game, and will not harass his troops by sending out marauding parties. He will, I presume, quietly and steadily make his preparations, and, at the proper moment, strike a blow at the great City.

I give you all the rumors reported to me. I have not sifted them to find out *how little* of truth there is in them. Subsequent parts of this letter will tell how well the false and the true are blended together.

Last night, just as I had finished No. 14, I received a long note from Lt. Judd, requesting my approval of an accompanying application for a transfer to Bragg's Compy. I returned the application with a polite note, wishing him distinction, etc., and declining to have anything to do with it. Although I do not care about having him in the Compy., he has, as I think, been so long engaged in various schemes to keep away from it, that his transfer shall come without my sanction, if he get it at all.

I saw our "innocent friend," Lt. Hall, to-day. He does not look in good health. I enquired about his mother, from whom, he tells me, he has not heard for a long time.

I have looked in nearly all the principal stores in Puebla, and I cannot find a fine Mexican blanket as small as I wish. If I cannot get one in the City of Mexico, you shall have a large one I bought a day or two since. It is a very neat pattern, much prettier than the gaudy ones I frequently see here.

In describing the dress of the Mexicans, I find, by further observation, I have not noticed one style of female attire worn by some of the "tortilla" sellers, who, instead of wearing petticoats, wrap around their waists a piece of blanket, which sometimes appears to be scant of going once and a half around them. Their black hair is passed in a coil around the largest part of the head, and is frequently interwoven with red cotton. I have not seen a bonnet in Puebla—all, rich and poor, wear shawls, or ribosas on the head.

Of beggars, this place has a large supply, and they are the most importunate scamps I ever saw. Some repeat something like a petition urging the gift of alms for some Saint's sake, which they commence before you get to them, and continue with after you pass. Others are silent, and merely extend the hand. There are very few who cannot support themselves, were they inclined to do anything, but they find it easier to beg than to labor for the little money they need to purchase what will clothe and feed them.

Thursday, 17th. The correction of yesterday's rumor is—that Col. McIntosh's command has dwindled from seven to three hundred. It seems that he, instead of being kept at bay by the enemy, drove them back every time—that a few of his men were wounded and that he lost a few mules. He parked his train and sent back for reinforcements, because he did not know what force might be brought against him.

Genl. Scott is reported, by Mr. Judd, to have said to-day, that he had promised some of the gentlemen another fight, but that as the news to-day was more favorable, he was afraid there would not be another.

We had another Brigade drill to-day, under Col. Garland. Major Wade not being very well, threw the command of the Regt. on me *again*. About a mile and a half from the City, we have a very good open space for our manœuvres. To-day, at the time we were there, Lt. Col. Duncan's Battery and Genl. Twiggs's Division were on the same plain.

Genl. Worth complains a good deal. He has not been well since he has joined our Army. With his imprudence in eating, and in improperly exposing himself, I see but little chance of his getting well. We are very much in want of his instruction. He has only been in the field in command of his Division once. Genl. Twiggs drills his Division six days in the week. Good-night.

Friday 18th. Two very interesting visitors have been in my room all the evening, and have just left me. Their conversation has been so animated, that now that they have left, so strong a reaction has taken place, that I am almost ready to fall asleep with the pen in my hand. No *news* of consequence to-day.

I read this afternoon an address to the Mexican Nation by "An officer of the United States Army" (Col. Hitchcock) which some think will produce good results. He traces, in a very simple and clear manner, the origin of the independence of Texas—shews that it was actually achieved by Texans themselves, that the cause of our citizens' taking such lively and active interest in the difficulties between Mexico and Texas was the cruel and inhuman butchery of Col. Fannin's party, who surrendered under a promise that they should be sent to the United States.

States that Texas had been independent of Mexico for the period of ten years, when the United States acknowledged her independence, which we had previously refused to acknowledge. That Texas, being

In Mexico

independent, had a right to act as she pleased on the question of Annexation, and that we had a right to receive her.

Throws the origin of the War on the Mexicans, in their actual attack on Genl. Taylor. Traces the progress of the War, and in giving their reverses, very modestly points out the great disparity of our numbers, and gives instances of the false reports of Santa Anna.

States our anxiety for peace, and in contradiction of our hostility to their religion, states that our Comdg. Genl. lost an accomplished and lovely daughter who died in a Convent, receiving all the rights of the Catholic religion, and asks whether he can be inimical to that Church, etc., etc.

I will send you one of the papers containing this address and hope you may receive it, as, in my synopsis, I have omitted several important points. I would have left out a few sentences, but, as a whole, I hope good results may spring from it.

I saw the Genl. a moment this morning; he was very kind, but so much engaged that I sat only a moment with him.

Saturday 19th. I was startled this afternoon, by an annunciation by one of the officers that a mail was to be sent to Vera Cruz. No. 14 was rapidly closed, after adding a line or two of this day's date, and I hurried down to the Post Office with it. Much to my regret the Postmaster knew nothing of the mail's reported leaving. I then went to Genl. Hd. Qrs. and there ascertained that there was no prospect of a mail's being sent for an indefinite period. My poor letter now rests quietly amid the leaves of my old *portefeuille*: and I, with scarce a hope of your seeing for many long months my daily scribblings, return, because it makes me happier to do so, to my evening chat with you.

To-day I have been trying a Mexican pony, which, if he had pleased me, the Quarter-Master's Dept. would have paid for—I being entitled to a horse, as Acting Major. I did not like him,—indeed, I do not fancy the gait of any of these horses. They are ridden with very severe bits, which, by little more than the pressure of the little finger on the rein, will bring the horse upon his haunches from a gallop. As the Mexicans use enormous spurs, between them and the bit, the horse moves as if ready at any moment to come to a dead halt, producing a kind of gait perfectly enchanting to the Mexican dandy.

No news to-day from any quarter. Last evening orders were sent to all our commands, that patrols should be kept out constantly during the night. This is intended to pick up our men who may remain out of their quarters. One, a Volunteer, was murdered last night. He had no right to be out at night. These patrols may also catch any re-enforcements who desire to join the Alcalde. I wonder if he was not driven away by being compelled to transact business with our Lt. Col. If he treated him as uncivilly and insultingly as he did some of our Regt. whilst under his dynasty—he will not conciliate a single Mexican who transacts business with him.

My Sub-Lt. Andrews has just left me. I was glad to see him, as he is unwell and feels homesick and lonely. His disease, jaundice, always prostrates the energy and spirits of a man. The whole Army seems to be *acclimating*, as the sick lists of all our commands are

In Mexico

large—that of "G" Co. is slowly, I hope permanently, decreasing.

Sunday, June 20th. Another week has passed, and God has been pleased to return me to my Sunday evening's chat with you, in the enjoyment of excellent health. My implicit confidence in Him renders me much less dissatisfied with my lot than I would otherwise be. I feel and thank Him for it daily, that He guards and protects my treasures—that that protection is as certain and continued during my absence as whilst I am with you. May our hearts be ever full of gratitude and thanks to Him, and may He soon lead us into His fold. I did not go to church to-day, though I ought to have gone this afternoon, as there was preaching at Genl. Hd. Qrs. by a Chaplain appointed to the 8th Regt. Infy. under the last law.

Army reports are to-day important, and in some instances conflicting; for instance, one report states that Genl. Taylor has been captured by Genl. Bravo, near Saltillo; another, that having withdrawn all his force from the upper part of the Rio Grande, he is now with his Army at Brazos Santiago—his destination, probably, Vera Cruz. The first report is not credited by any American, and probably by no Mexican of common-sense; the latter may be partly true. We want all the force we can get; the larger the strength of our Army, the more important will be the results of our operations and the sooner will a peace be made.

Another rumor says that Genl. Urea arrived last night at Nopolucan (about forty-five miles hence) on his way to meet Genl. Cadwalader and Lt. Col. Childs. He is said to have 5000 men, Infy. and Cavalry, with two pieces of Arty. 'T is also said that we have lost another mail and that Mr. N. P. Trist has been writing informally to the British Minister in Mexico, and that he is now about communicating officially with him. I may even think with some little patience of his acts, if they lead to an honorable peace—though I shall always entertain and express my opinion of the wrong done to Genl. Scott in this affair, of a Special Minister being with an Army in the field, the Genl. being at its head.

Have I not given you Army rumors enough for one day? I think so, and I shall therefore omit some of smaller calibre which have been thrown into our midst. As my letters will probably, by the time they are sent off, fill a good-sized octavo, I think I must write less daily than has been my habit. Good-night.

Monday, 21st. Our soldiers, under the influence of liquor, forget they are in an enemy's city, occasionally stay out of their quarters all night, and are found in the morning either killed or badly wounded—the latter is the case with one of the Germans who joined me at Tampa Bay. I hope it may prove a good lesson to the other men.

The Mexicans have been tampering with our soldiers. A Milty. Commission is in session to-day investigating the case of a German and a Mexican, who are accused of enticing our men to desert. The German is stated to have been a Capt. in the Mexican Army at Cerro Gordo and was arrested by a Sergeant of the 8th Infy., who had been told by some privates that the German had given them handbills printed in German, addressed to the Germans in our Army, and urging them to desert with their horses and arms. If the fact be proved and he is condemned by the Court, he dies.

Yesterday, Genl. Alvares appeared in the plain,

some miles from the City, with a large body of Cavalry. We are so poor in Cavalry, that we can use that Arm for few other purposes than reconnoissances and in pursuit after battle. We cannot send out a force to meet one of any respectability. Where we are with such an Army as we ought to have, say of 20,000, we should have about 2000 excellent Cavalry.

I paid Col. Butler, South Carolina, a visit yesterday afternoon; he introduced again the subject of Genl. W. O. Butler's conversation with him relative to my joining him; he is very much worried that the Adjt. Genl. did not make me the offer. I cannot see why Genl. Jones did not. I fear that Genl. Butler will think that I received his request, and that I have treated him discourteously in not having, at least, thanked him for the honor he did me by having made me so kind an offer. If I knew where he was, I should at once, that is to say, by the first mail, write to him.

Genl. Scott with Col. Hitchcock and one of his Aide-de-Camps came in whilst we were at the Colonel's. The Genl. is pretty well, but says he is dying for want of exercise.

Yesterday a party of eight gamblers went about fourteen miles into the country to buy mules; this morning two returned wounded, and reported that they were attacked by about eighty Mexican soldiers and that the others they supposed were killed, or taken prisoners. Their going so far with so few men, was an act of suicidal madness and folly.

I drilled the Regt. this morning. Major W. went out as a looker-on. He says that he has not drilled a battalion for twenty years and that he is too nervous to undertake it now. I am anxious for him to take command, as comments will be made if he does not.

Certainly, Genl. Cadwalader will arrive in two days and then I shall hear from you. God grant that you will continue to cheer me with a continuation of good news. Good-night.

Tuesday, 22nd. Blessings come and rest upon the head of our Genl.! I heard this afternoon, confidentially (of course I may tell you), that the Genl. is about making arrangements for having our mails carried and brought. He is, I hear, afraid that he will have to pay more than may be agreeable to the Govt. But it cannot be that to save a few thousands a month, our Govt. would be willing to have all communication with our Army cut off. Certain it is that no one who has relatives or friends in our Army, will object to any sum Genl. Scott may find himself compelled to pay. Humanity demands this measure, as peace *may* be declared without our knowing anything of it.

Genl. C. has not arrived. The Milty. Commission have sent their proceedings to Genl. Scott in the case of the German but the Genl. has not acted on them. We have had no rumors of any consequence to-day. In your letter after you receive this, I wish you to send me the size of your hand and foot, as I may find some gloves, etc., in Mexico, that would be curiosities. The gold embroidery of Puebla is richer and more beautiful than any I ever saw, but it is said that the embroidery of the City of Mexico surpasses this.

As the Pay Dept. will probably have no more funds, whilst we are in this country, than to supply us only occasionally with a month's pay, I may be compelled to be more economical than I otherwise would be. But I intend, as far as my means may permit, to bring you specimens of curiosity and of interest from this country.

Do urge the American peace party to receive with warm hearts the first whisperings of peace from these deluded people, who seem not to think that each month adds to our strength and weakens theirs. Every emigrant who follows our Army comes as no friend of Spanish supremacy in this Country. I have a faint hope that in my letter to-morrow night, I may thank you for a letter, or letters. I will at all events retire with that delightful expectation. Good-night, God bless and protect you.

Wednesday, 23rd. Vain hope—no mail—no news of the approach of Genl. Cadwalader. A command has been sent to meet him, and to bring the mail, but it has not returned. To-day I have been pretty constantly engaged in attending to my duties of Division Officer of the Day, an honor to which I am elevated by my useless assignment as Acting Major. I left my quarters at nine this morning to report to Genl. Worth; from his quarters, I proceeded on horseback to visit the different regiments and guards of the Division, and did not return till about two.

This is very different from the daily routine of duty I used to attend to at Tampa Bay. At eight I visit such parts of the Command as I think proper. But instead of being Officer of the Day every other day, I am here every tenth day.

One of the Guerrilla captains was recognized and taken in the City to-day. It would have been well if he had been shot in the act of being taken, but I do not see that we can do otherwise with the legalized robber than to keep him in prison. I have no doubt that the City is daily visited by these men. But they can do but little more than gratify their curiosity by these visits, as our guards are so strong and our troops so well posted that they will not attempt to commit any depredations on our property or persons.

Lt. Judd has been transferred to Briggs's Compy.—thus have the "G.'s" lost his valuable services for ever. I shall probably get Lt. Burton in his place. As Lt. B. is in California I am not likely to see him for a long time; this I do not regret, as Lt. Shields, the 2nd Lieut. of the Compy., is efficient and active.

The men are now nearly all well—the poor little drummer boy is, and has been for several days, very ill. He is better to-day than he was yesterday, and will, I hope, recover. The wounded man is also doing well; his injuries were not very grievous. Good-night, etc.

Thursday, 24th. This is the anniversary of the birth of one of my brothers. 'T is a great day with the Catholics—birthday of John the Baptist—and especially charming to children. Nearly all the boys I have seen in the streets to-day are attired as officers or soldiers—hats, caps, coats, flags (Mexican and a few American), wooden guns, pikes, and swords are found everywhere on the little strutting heroes. It is delightful to see the joy of the little ones. How you would enjoy seeing them!

This morning a note was received from Genl. Crittenden, stating that he had met with serious opposition all the way from Vera Cruz, and that he would leave Perote this day. He cannot reach us sooner than the 29th or 30th. The note gave no particulars; it was written on a very small piece of paper, and was brought by a Mexican, concealed in some part of his dress. We are nearly as much in doubt as before. We do not know whether he has lost any of his men, whether he brings a mail. And, on a very important point, we also long for information, whether he brings a very large sum of money.

The Pay Dept., instead of using its funds in paying the men, is letting the Commissary and Quartermaster's Depts. use them in procuring food for man and beast. Genl. Worth is, I am happy to say, much better than he was when I mentioned him a few days ago. He says that one or two days in the saddle will make him as well as ever. Something may have occurred this morning, peculiarly agreeable to him—he is a man of powerful impulses.

To-morrow I will be engaged in some serious matters, I presume, as I am a member of a Council of War to convene early in the morning. Capt. W. C. De Hart is our Recorder—we could not have a better. Lt. Col. Garland is the President, Capt. F. Taylor is a member. I do not know of what number the Council is composed, as I have not been furnished with the order. More of this hereafter.

Since I have recovered from the Perote chill, I find the temperature here very agreeable. The night is cool enough to sleep under a blanket and in the daytime you are but little incommoded by the heat of the sun, and you always find it pleasantly cool, either in the shade of the street or in the house.

It rains now daily, either between three and five P.M. or at night. The Mexicans tell me that the rainy season continues till October. But this is spoken of as the rainy month. The muskmelons have disappeared from the market; I find nothing new but a fruit called *mango*, which I have not tasted. Goodnight.

Friday, 25th. The Council of War, Col. Clarke (in place of Col. Garland, sick), Bvt. Lt. Col. C. F. Smith, Maj. Bainbridge, Captains Anderson and F. Taylor, were in session this morning. The case before us is that of a Mexican attempting to get one of our men to desert. The evidence does not seem, thus far, to be conclusive.

The session of another Court near us has been of greater interest than our own. A Court of Inquiry, composed of Maj. Genl. Quitman, Brig. Generals Twiggs and Persifer Smith, met this morning on the application of Bvt. Maj. Genl. Worth to investigate his conduct in some particulars of his command here, for which he had been censured by his old patron and most steadfast friend, Genl. Scott. As we were necessarily engaged in our own duties, I was not in the Court of Inquiry long enough to hear the points of the case; but, from some of Genl. Worth's remarks, I infer that Genl. Scott disapproved of certain Articles of Agreement with the City Authorities under which Genl. Scott thinks we entered this City, by which the cases of some Mexicans were tried before their own authorities for murdering a soldier.

Genl. Scott having, in his order declaring Martial Law to govern in all the places occupied by our troops in Mexico, decided that all similar cases should come before Military Commissions. These Articles of Agreement, if sanctioned by Genl. W., necessarily and of course rescinded Genl. Scott's orders.

Another case is, I hear, of more recent occurrence. While I was *Officer of the Day* on the 14th inst. an Irishman came into our quarters to warn us against allowing our men to buy articles from the Mexican women, who have their little market in front of our quarters, stating that he had been informed by a very respectable Mexican lady, that the women put something poisonous in what they cooked.

I did not credit the story, as none of our men had complained of being made sick, and I had never seen any of the women selling any cooked articles to the soldiers—and again the whole story seemed improbable, that a parcel of poor women, trying to make a little money by selling their fruits, etc., should make such an attempt, the detection of which would be certain and easy and the punishment of which must be so severe. Of so little consequence did I think the man's story that I did not allude to it in reporting to Genl. Worth the next morning—thinking it unnecessary to trouble him with an idle tale.

Three days after, we received a circular from Genl. W. stating that he had received information from a source entitled to full credit, that certain Mexicans were mixing poison with the food sold to our soldiers, and urging the soldiers to confine themselves to their rations and not to purchase any articles of food from the Mexicans.

Two or three days after the receipt of this circular, an order came from Genl. Worth, stating that in obedience to instructions from the Genl. in Chief all copies of his previous circular should be withdrawn and returned to his office. This is, I believe, Article of Investigation No. 2. How many others there are, or whether I am right in the above, I do not now positively know. But I will give you further particulars as I learn them.

This difficulty is deeply to be regretted, but that Genl. Scott is right in the matter, I do not doubt. The Mexicans may try to make capital of it, but they will find, that though Genl. W. may be disposed to kick at the traces, he will draw like a true horse when work is to be done. Enough for to-night. Good-night. God be with you.

Saturday, the 26th. We finished the Mexican's case to-day. In the Court of Inquiry, I hear that Genl. Worth proposed a question, which after deliberation the Court refused to put to the witness. The Genl. then stated he had no further questions, whereupon the Court adjourned till nine to-morrow. Major Kirby says that there is so much bitterness between the parties that this split is for ever. All regret, *deeply* regret it.

No news from Mexico. Though for the last two or three days we have had rumors here that Mr. N. P. Trist is in correspondence with Mexican Commissioners; doubtful.

Genl. S. received a letter from Genl. Cadwalader informing him that he had received instructions from Genl. Pillow to remain at Perote till Genl. Pillow's arrival—the reasons for these instructions, Genl. P. states, "he cannot now give." Thus is the arrival of Genl. Cadwalader with the long desired mail indefinitely postponed. We are truly unfortunate, and have only one source of consolation in this affair, which is, that Genl. Pillow may bring us a later mail from the United States than Genl. Cadwalader has.

I ought to receive a letter from you up to the 20th of May informing me of your arrival and domestication in your summer quarters. I feel some anxiety to hear what arrangements your Grandmother makes for the summer, who is to remain with her, etc. Your letters will have answered all my surmises long before you receive this.

The weather here is very pleasant for us who are housed, but with these daily or nightly rains, must be exceedingly disagreeable for those who are in tents.

Sunday, 27th. I sat two or three hours this afternoon with my most kind friend Genl. S. and though the news communicated to me was strictly confidential, you may without breach of confidence be made my confidante of the heads of it. The Secy. Br. Legation left here night before last. Mr. N. P. Trist has entered upon his duties as Commissioner—his letter has been received by the Govt. Congress is not now in session, but Genl. Santa Anna is attempting to reassemble them in order to refer the question to them.

He has expressed himself in favor of having a Commissioner appointed to meet Mr. Trist but will not assume (indeed he is expressly forbidden by an Act of Congress to do so) the responsibility of making such appointment. Mr. Trist having forwarded in a *proper* letter the documents presenting him in his official capacity, Genl. S. immediately acknowledges their receipt, and recognizing him as deputed with high powers states that he is willing to confer with Mr. Trist, either by writing or orally, on all questions entrusted to him. Of course until this offer is disposed of, or at all events, for a reasonable time, we are fast here. God in His infinite wisdom incline the hearts of both Nations to peace. With what gratitude shall I receive the joyful news that the war is over, and that orders are out for my return to my blessed home. I am not, however, sanguine; a commenced negotiation does not necessarily end in peace.

I hope that the United States will be generous and liberal in her terms—she may well be so. Much care must be taken to soothe Mexican pride, which has been sorely wounded. We *should* be, we CAN be magnanimous, without our motives being misunderstood. I also read Genl. S.'s reply to a very impertinent letter from Mr. T. (alluded to in a previous letter); it is cruelly severe—I do not see how Mr. T. can ever look the Genl. in the face. He closes by telling him never again to *dare* to write to him in that manner, etc.

The proceedings of our Council in the Mexican's case are published—he was acquitted. To-morrow, we have a Belgian before us—the proof will, I fear, be very direct, in his case—persuading to desert and offering to buy all horses, arms, etc., which might be brought by deserters. This letter will probably tell the result of his trial.

No information of the South Carolinian (Capt. Kirshaw) who took charge of No. 13, sent on the 4th inst. You may have received it by this time. I pray God that the day may soon come when we may at last have regular mails giving good news from home. Good-night, etc., etc.

Monday, 28th. I hear to-day that the mail which left on the 4th is on its way back to us. How deeply do I regret this, as I know that you will be exceedingly anxious and uneasy at not hearing from me. You will not be able, I know, to banish your apprehensions.

Here I am in excellent health, and almost free from the annoyances of the rumors of war, and yet I cannot get a letter to you, nor can I receive one from you as soon as it ought to come. But as yet they *do* come, and I am most truly grateful for that blessing.

In Mexico

We did not commence the trial of the Belgian this morning, but propose taking his case up to-morrow. I have been amused to-day in listening to the various rumors about the negotiations. Everybody seems to believe that something is in the wind, and all are so deeply interested that it seems cruel to withhold light from them, when I find them standing in the dark— but I cannot say a word which will let them think I know anything about the true state of facts.

The Court of Inquiry in Genl. Worth's case adjourned this morning. Their opinion has not yet been published. With our mail of the 4th inst. went Genl. Scott's application to be relieved from the command of this Army. As it is rumored that we are to receive large re-inforcements and a large remittance of money, the Genl. may think proper to suspend his application for the present. He has good cause of complaint.

Tuesday, 29th. We tried the Belgian to-day. We meet again to-morrow morning but hope that we may not have to take up a new case. I omitted to mention the fate of the two, German and Mexican, tried before the first Council: the German was condemned to be shot, but Genl. Scott, on the recommendation of the majority of the Court, founded on a belief of the partial insanity of the man, remitted the sentence. The Mexican was acquitted.

I have heard nothing more of the mail arrangement. 'T is said that a large train will be sent to Vera Cruz soon after the arrival of Genl. Pillow. Rumor states to-day that the Mexican Congress is in session. I hope that this may be true, though I expected that a longer time would be necessary to reassemble them.

Genl. S. told me that he had received very kind messages from Mr. and Mrs. Bankhead, the Br. Minister and his wife. The Secy. of Legation seemed to feel, on the questions of our relations with Mexico, more like an American than an Englishman. Genl. S. also received a very kind and complimentary letter from the Commander of the British fleet off Vera Cruz, and from a son of Sir Robert Peel, on board one of the vessels. The fact is, that when anything great and glorious is effected by our Arms, John Bull cannot help feeling that we are flesh of his flesh; jealousy, for the moment, is conquered by pride.

We find here some Englishmen, but, as far as I know, they claim to be American citizens, having first stopped in the United States. The drummer boy is better— the Dr. thinks that he will recover. Good-night, good-night. May Angels watch and guard your sleep.

Wednesday, June 30th. Nothing of interest to-day. The courier of the Br. Minister passed through to-day on his bi-weekly trip to Vera Cruz, but I did not hear of his having brought any news. The Council of War met, and no other case being presented, adjourned.

To enable you to *see* me as I now live, I will give you a detail of one day's doings; here, we are little more than machines—one is a fair sample of all. Rising at reveille, I take my usual time and means for preparing for breakfast. As soon as I complete my toilette, about half-past six, I leave my room, and walk for half an hour till breakfast, which consists ordinarily of toast, coffee, and eggs (eighteen and three quarters or twenty-five cents per dozen), *butter* (one dollar per lb.), *hogshead cheese* (fifty cents per lb.), Bologna sausage (fifty cents per lb.), or soused pigs' feet are sometimes added. The first three of the last articles—decided luxuries.

For drills or other duties, I go out at nine o'clock, returning to dinner which is generally about one o'clock. It consists of soup, a small piece of salt or fresh meat, cabbage, rice or squash, and a salad of lettuce, tomatoes, and onions. I omitted to mention a bad habit I am contracting by order of my Dr., that of taking a toddy about eleven o'clock.

After dinner, I take the *Tactics*, and generally awaken from a pleasant nap about three o'clock. Before throwing myself on my old camp bed, I usually eat a pear, peach, a few apricots, or a little of some of their numerous *dulces*. I have now some peaches, and what I think are crab-apples, prepared differently from any I ever saw with us; they are dry and well flavored; they seem to have been preserved and then dried.

Afternoon drill takes place at four, but as this is Compy. or Squad drill, I have nothing to do with it. At five, Major Wade generally proposes a stroll, when we go through the market, and do what shopping our messing requires. We thus pass an hour or so, and return, taking coffee (tea) at candle-light. Our tea is frugal, a cup of coffee, toast, and a taste of hogshead cheese, sausage, and butter. I take a little milk after my coffee. I then retire to my room, and after a few moments, seat myself at my table to chat with you.

This I continue until I think I have used as much space as can be spared for that day's letter, when I return my letter to my old trunk and sit down to the study, till bed time, of the only Milty. work I have, a treatise on *La petite guerre*, translated into French from the German of Decker; or if I have found any Spanish proclamations, etc., I borrow a dictionary and read them, and then to bed, when I always say our evening prayers, and a special one for you and my return to you. Good-night.

Thursday, July 1st. Reports somewhat important came to-day. One is that three Commissioners, Genl. Tornel, ex-Secy. War, at the head, were appointed to confer with Mr. Trist; another that the troops at Atlixco under Genl. Alvares and Canalizo have dispersed, broken up in a row in consequence of a quarrel between these Generals.

Genl. Scott received this morning, a letter from Genl. Cadwalader stating that Genl. Pillow had not arrived at Perote on the 29th. Genl. C. writes that Genl. Pillow has about 1600 men with him, Infy. he thinks. As Genl. Pillow left Jalapa on the 25th he should have reached Perote on the day of Genl. Cadwalader's report. I cannot indulge sanguinely yet in the hope of peace being soon proclaimed. Were the idea once to take full possession of my soul, its failure of accomplishment would be a very severe trial of all my philosophy. I will therefore try and await patiently the progress of the Negotiation, hoping tranquilly that it may lead to peace.

Received this afternoon a visit from Capt. Danl. Ruggles, U. S. A., who requested information about the positions and deeds of "G" Co. during the siege of Vera Cruz: he told me that he was engaged on a History of the War, and that he intended being very particular and minute in the detail of the operations of the siege. I have copied for Adjt. Austine some incidents and dates from my note-book. His work will not be as valuable or interesting as Capt. De Hart's—if he writes one. Adjt. Austine has just left my room, having sat

In Mexico 235

pretty late with me, obtaining information for Capt. Ruggles. I will now retire, leaving a little corner for to-morrow's news. Good-night.

July 2nd. Friend Kirby called to see me this forenoon. I regret to hear that Mr. Trist is seriously sick, so much so, that he can attend to no business. This is very unfortunate, just at this time when he was about entering upon his delicate and important duties. Mr. T. has no funds, it appears, contrary to our expectation. Genl. S. has offered to place $250,000 in the City of Mexico, in twenty-four hours, subject to Mr. T.'s order.

News comes from Mexico, that they learn by way of New Orleans that Genl. Scott has been ordered to suspend all further Military operations till the arrival of his successor. Can it be possible that Genl. Pillow is to be that successor, that the fate of our gallant Army, the honor of our Nation is to be taken from the safe guardianship of our great Genl. and intrusted to him or to any other untried man! I *cannot* believe it. The President may send Genl. Pillow (his neighbor, friend, and partner) as one of the Commissioners—that would be honor enough. I cannot think any higher can be intended. I must close No. 15 and let it wait for a mail, commencing No. 16 to-morrow.

No. 16. Puebla.
Saturday, July 3, 1847.

Rank, sometimes, presents its possessor advantages the subordinates cannot secure. I feel this to-day in all its force. Genl. Worth availed himself of his position, in getting a letter or two taken by the British Courier to Vera Cruz; we knew nothing of the possibility of such a thing being done, till *the day too late.* Per contra, I hear that the opinion of the Court of Inquiry has been published at Division and Brigade Headquarters, and that it bears very heavily on Genl. Worth, censuring him for the concessions made to the City Authorities on our entry here, inasmuch as some of the provisions were in contradiction of, and actually repealed, Genl. Scott's order, and also finding him at fault in issuing his anti-poison Circular.

I reported to the Genl. this morning as Div. Officer of the Day, but did not take a seat, as I was afraid he might allude to the subject. I would rather not converse at all about the matters of investigation, at all events, I would prefer postponing it until the *rough edge* has well worn down.

Some Mexicans report that there is great commotion and trouble in the City of Mexico; but, whether it be favorable or unfavorable in its results to the cause of peace, we must wait a day or two before we can learn.

The newsboys are now crying through town a sheet containing (1) the letter of the Mexican Secy. of Foreign Affairs, transmitting it to the Secretaries of Congress; (2) Mr. Secretary Buchanan's letter informing the Mexican Govt. of the appointment of Mr. Trist as Commissioner with full powers to conclude a treaty of peace; and also (3) the Mexican Secretary's letter to Mr. Buchanan, acknowledging the receipt of his letter.

As the American newspapers will have these letters at least as soon as you receive this, it will be useless for me to give even a synopsis of their contents. Mr. Buchanan's letter, the first part of it particularly, is written in good temper and with ability; the Mexican letters evince no bad feeling. The affair, upon the whole, I think bears a favorable aspect. I have not heard to-day from Mr. Trist. The mail is *expected* to-morrow.

I hear that the troops may be here on Monday—which we keep as the 4th. A National Salute to be fired at twelve, all the troops being under arms, and at eight P.M. a rocket to be thrown up for each of our States. Query: Will they give us rockets for each of the Mexican States we have annexed?

The sentence of our "Council of War" has been published—the Belgian is to be imprisoned in the Castle of Perote, during the continuance of the war between the United States and Mexico, to pay to the treasury of the United States $300, not being released till this fine be paid. So that you see the result of our deliberations places no spot of blood on my soul. Our friend is throwing himself to the dogs as fast as he can. I have spoken to him, but 't is useless—my taking him to task would lose me his friendship, and result in no good. I deeply, most deeply, regret it; there is nothing I would not do to stop him in his downhill career.

Sunday, July 4th. The anniversary of our glorious independence. Many, very many years must pass before the common people, the public of this miscalled Republic, will be sufficiently enlightened to enjoy the blessings of independence. Unfortunately, all attempts to better their condition, instead of being nursed into activity in the schoolhouse, and rendered effective at the polls, are christened by the bloody sword.

This day is not unimportant in *my* little history, as, six months ago, I crossed the bar leading from Tampa

Bay, our last happy home. Will Echo tell whether the expiration of another six will find us united? God grant that the action of the Mexican Congress may be of such character as to bring peace among its other blessings.

The day has passed off pretty well, at least I have heard of no casualties among our soldiers. The news from Vera Cruz this morning is highly important—as we heard of the landing there of Maj. Genl. F. Pierce, with 2000 men, and that he is to be followed by 6000 more. These additions to our forces will give us a respectable Army, such as we should have had to commence our march into the interior—not large enough, however, if the Mexican Congress should decline our offer of peace. We must, in that unfortunate event, act with most decided energy, and exercise all our skill.

I have not seen Genl. Scott since the receipt of this news, which I learned this morning from Genl. Worth. I would go to see him this evening, were it not both damp and chilly. To-night, I must also make up for the last night's loss of sleep.

Genl. W. stated that he heard Mr. Trist's situation was more than critical. No news from the Capital to-day, and worst of all, no mail in. Would it not be too bad if the arrival of Genl. Pierce should still longer delay Genl. Cadwalader! I will still, though it would seem hoping against hope, try and hope to-morrow will bring letters from you. Good-night.

Tuesday, July 6th. A slight chill succeeded by some fever kept me in bed all day yesterday, and prevented my writing to you last night. A letter was received yesterday from Vera Cruz informing us that Genl.

In Mexico

Pierce was encamped near there with 2500 men, that he would march in a day or two. My friend Maj. Galt comes with him. Rumor says that the bands of guerrillas along the road have fallen out with their chiefs, whom they want to hang, and that their quarrels will probably disperse them.

From Mexico, we have no news. A day or two should give us important items as Congress may be now in session, and their decision in answer to the application of our Govt. will probably be made very soon after their meeting. The news of the landing of Genl. P. and of the expected arrival of other troops *may* quicken their deliberations.

'Tis a pity that so many of our countrymen have passed through Vera Cruz and the unhealthy region thence to Jalapa at this season; I fear that we shall lose many of the men. Although I have had no chill or fever to-day, yet having been up nearly all day, I feel a little weakened by yesterday's attack, and think I had better retire early. I will then wish you good-night, praying God to guard and guide you.

Wednesday, 7th. This, which I expected would be my sick day, has passed without my having had a return of my chill, so that I hope that I may consider myself well. My friends have been very kind. Capt. R. Lee called yesterday, and to-day my old friends, Maj. Irwin, Col. Smith, Maj. Turnbull, Dr. Lawson, etc.—have all, with others, called to see how I was. Dr. Tripler, who does not belong to our Division, happened to call the day I was taken sick, and as our Dr. was not then in, I asked Dr. T. to prescribe for me, and thus became his patient; he has been very attentive. I hope I may have an opportunity of shewing my friends that I never forget kindnesses.

Genl. Pillow is in the City with the mail, which will be delivered early in the morning, when we shall have a new Commander, an old acquaintance, Capt. Martin Burke.

Our present Commander is too mild, and his kindness and forbearance are imposed upon by the young officers. The Capt. will, I think, keep a little tighter rein.

From Mexico, we have news; it is surmised that the true original peace party wish to prevent Santa Anna from having anything to do with making the treaty. They hope that some event may occur which will put him down. He is now having the Army under his influence, and holding the strong places in and near the City, too powerful for them. His friends are resolved not to have the ballot-boxes opened until September or the new President inaugurated until December, until which time they intend he shall have the power in his own hands. If they fail in their designs, Santa Anna's fall will be certain and perhaps terminate fatally for him, as he has many very bitter enemies. A few days may unravel these new knotty points.

Mr. Trist called to see Genl. Scott yesterday; his case is considered critical, as he has some affection of the lungs, and this climate is decidedly unfavorable to all persons with weak lungs.

Derr has just come in to tell me that McDonough has come. I am rejoiced to see him (he has just left me) as he was left sick, and I was afraid that he would never join us again. You do not know how attentive and kind Derr was to me in my little sickness—had I been his own son his manner could not have been

In Mexico

kinder. He was very highly flattered with the messages in your last letter. I cannot write any more till I receive your letters. God grant that they bring me good news from you. Good-night.

Thursday morning, 8th. A thousand, thousand thanks to God, and blessings on you for your letters of the 7th, 11th, and 21st May. I regret to hear of the severe attack of poor Grandmother. I only took up my pen to make my early acknowledgments of your letters.

The troops arrived this morning, so that now we have our new Commander. Lt. Thomas, who returned sick from Tepeyahualco to Jalapa, also came up; he is looking pretty well but has not recovered his strength. Maj. Buchanan is with Genl. Pillow; whether he will remain with him as A.D.C. or rejoin his Regt., I do not think he has yet determined. Col. Andrews of the Voltigeurs is here. Four Compys. of Lt. Col. W. W. Graham's Regt. also arrived. I had a good opportunity, two days since, of speaking to my old friend, and could not avoid making a last attempt. I fear it will do no good.

I am very anxious to hear from you again, as I feel very great anxiety about Father, who was, when you wrote, I fear, far from being well. Poor old grandmother, from so many and such violent attacks, so rapidly succeeding, will not, I fear, last much longer.

You ask my opinion about your paying my family a visit. I wish exceedingly that you would do so. But you will hardly be able to do it now, as, long before this letter reaches you (indeed it is perhaps at this moment too late), Maj. Sanders will have returned. He was as good a person as you could have seen to make you understand all about the positions of the batteries, etc., at Vera Cruz. I do not doubt that if he returned to Savannah in the boat with you, that his conversation interested Father very much. I hope he did so for your sake, as your agitation, you state, prevented your understanding much of his first conversation. He might have made everything more intelligible by a little sketch.

From what Genl. Pillow told me to-day, I think it is probable that Duncan's Regt. may be ordered here. I shall most joyfully welcome him though I am still sorry that he chose the profession of arms. He might have done much better. But we must now stimulate him to render himself accomplished and distinguished as a soldier.

I heard to-day, *confidentially*, that Genl. Scott had *not* received any order from the President complimentary to the troops and himself, but that the Secretary had written a very severe letter. How dare he address in terms other than courteous and approbatory (and what is his approbation in such a case) a man so far his superior in every respect! I hope that there is some mistake in this matter; if so I will gladly make the *amende honorable*, for I have always had a regard for the Secretary. Enough for one night.

Friday, 9th. Feeling a little chilly this evening, in consequence of a change of weather, I shall not write much. In speaking of this place, I have not mentioned that these changes are not uncommon. The wind shifting round to the W. and SW. brings chills on its wings from the eternal snows which cover the tops of Popocatepetl and Iztaccihuatl, which are plainly in sight in that direction.

VIEW OF MOUNT IZTACCIHUATL FROM THE EAST
From an old photograph

In Mexico

The snow-capped mountains are visible from this place—the two above mentioned—and in the distance, towards the East, lies our old friend *Orizaba*, whose familiar outline is plainly visible at an early hour of a cloudless morning. As we stand on our drill ground, we see at the left of Popocatepetl, the renowned pyramid of Cholula, where a Catholic Chapel now stands, on the spot where, probably, the Indians had their temples in which thousands of human beings were sacrificed.

Cholula was, in the days of Cortez, a magnificent city; not a trace of the ancient city now remains. You there find ruins of a large Spanish City, built since the destruction of that of the Indians.

In the old Cholula, Cortez, in consequence of discovering a plot to cut his army to pieces, inflicted most exemplary and savage punishment on its poor inhabitants. In their temples they had large cages full of men and women whom they were fattening to sacrifice or to eat. The ruins of the renowned City of Tlascala lie to the right of our road to Mexico. I should like very much to visit both these cities, but fear that I shall not be able to do so.

Rumor states that Genl. Santa Anna has ordered all the troops and all the arms to the City of Mexico—he may fear a *pronunciamiento* (*a declaration against him, preceding a revolutionary movement*), and is perhaps preparing to put it down by the strong arm of power.

I have been engaged all day in preparing my quarterly papers for the functionaries at Washington, but when or how will they go? Had I not been thus busily engaged, I would have called to see the Genl. 'T is too bad, he did not receive a line from his family. It will distress me, knowing this, to meet him.

Rain, rain, rain—this is indeed the rainy season.

It is now raining for the third spell within the last twenty-four hours. I feel so uncomfortable (you know our rooms have no glass windows, with their conveniences and comforts) that I must retire.

Sunday, 11th. As I was a little apprehensive, when the above was written, I had last night a regular chill, and remained in bed all day yesterday, having taken twenty grains of quinine in the morning. To-day I have been up since about eight o'clock, taking two grain pills every two hours, and feel so well now that I hope I may have no return of the chill.

I heard to-day through Dr. Cuyler of your having passed through Savannah. Mrs. Locke was kind enough to send me word that she had seen you and that you were looking well. The Dr. also said that you had passed through Charleston. I hope to receive at least one letter from you, by the train which accompanies Genl. Pierce.

For the past two days the City has been filled with rumors from Mexico. I have not been well enough to go to Genl. Hd. Qrs., where I will learn the truth. The general impression, however, is, that we are to have a fight, and a very severe one.

Some think, that on our approach, Santa Anna's enemies will compel him to come to terms, or others think that they will take advantage of our presence to attempt to remove him from his usurped office. So strangely do these people act, that I pretend to form no idea of what they will do. Half of the time they leave undone things they ought to have done. Certain it is that messengers have arrived from Mexico, yesterday and the day before.

The Mexican Congress have not yet succeeded in

getting a quorum. I will not commence another page to-night, but close by a good-night—good-night.

Monday, 12th. A most unwelcome visitor this morning, in a threatened chill. Dr. Tripler happened to be sitting by me, and checked it by giving me quinine and making me take a pretty good grog of "Catalan," being well covered in bed. As it was not succeeded by fever, I shall not count it a chill.

Dr. Cuyler was kind enough to send me the latest Savannah *Georgian*. In that of the 28th of May, I see the arrival on the 27th of Mrs. Anderson, and maid, and the rest of your family party. This relieves my apprehensions about Father's health, which might not, I feared, permit of his going on in that trip of the boat. I put down your arrival in Clarkesville about the 1st of June, and feel certain that Genl. Pierce will bring me a letter from you dated at Clarkesville.

Capt. Johnson Lee started with a flag of truce for the City of Mexico this morning; what his mission is, I know not; some say that he bears a message relative to the prisoners now in that City, *viz.*, Maj. Gaines and his party. No organization has yet taken place of their Congress.

To-morrow, our Brigade goes back, probably as far as Nopolucan, on a *foraging expedition*, it is said. This attack of chills keeps me here, as the Dr. will not permit me to go. Were the march towards Mexico, I would regret separation from the Command very much, but as they go over the beaten ground, and when they will only see a few guerrillas, who will avoid them, I do not care very much about it. They will be absent five days, and will probably return about the time Genl. Pierce comes up.

The impression gains ground daily that we shall advance very soon after we receive the augmentation of our force. We may find near Mexico about twenty thousand men—we shall have about half that number. Lieut. Johnston is now busy hanging up his pictures (Catholic) in my room preparatory to his going in the morning, so I will bid good-night.

Tuesday, 13th. No chill to-day, and feeling pretty well to-night; if I escape to-morrow night, I shall again hope it is broken. The Command left this morning under Capt. Burke, Col. Garland commanding the Brigade. I fear that they had an unpleasant afternoon, as we had a very heavy rain about three o'clock. I called this morning to see Genl. Scott, but as he was engaged with Mr. Trist, I did not go to his room, but sat a few moments with his Staff. Genl. Scott reviews our Army on the 15th, 17th, and 19th inst. and report says that we are to leave on the 21st. Hardly as soon, I think.

Genl. Scott has so entirely won the confidence of the Army by the prudence and bravery which combine so beautifully in his character, that they, like myself, will, when he orders us to advance, determine at once that 't is the time to do so. That he is well informed of every measure of any importance I am confident, and he will not order an advance until he is well assured that it is necessary and important for us to do so. Never were the interests of a country in the keeping of a safer chief.

There are some reasons, and of importance too, why we should remain here till the rainy season is over, and all these the Genl. well knows, and has deliberately weighed. We shall have a very fatiguing march, and

In Mexico

one atttended with great suffering and succeeded by a great deal of sickness.

We have not heard what Division will take the lead. Genl. Twiggs pretends to be very desirous of leading—saying that it is his turn as we were in the advance from Jalapa—but here no one expected to meet with resistance. But why speculate upon a question the decision of which will in all probability be given either in this or a letter you will receive by the same mail? I am sorry that Capt. Saunders did not go to Savannah on the boat with you as I fear you did not see him but once. Good-night, etc.

Wednesday, July 14th. I passed the night and this day very comfortably, no chill. This morning I called to see Genl. Scott, and found him so busily engaged writing that I did not sit down; he was very affectionate. Capt. Lee *did not* go with a flag of truce to Mexico, "escorted by two Compys. of Dragoons." Capt. Kearney, with his Compy., went as an escort to a flag of truce borne by Capt. Symmes, U.S. Navy. He returned this evening; with what news I will report to-morrow evening. Finding that I have been so grossly deceived in the report, so positively asserted by many, of Capt. Lee's mission to the City, I will be a little more cautious in crediting camp stories than I have been.

I find that preparations are making in the different staff corps of the Army for an advance, which all seem to think will be made in this month. I am exceedingly desirous of hearing what report Capt. Kearney makes of the state of the roads. I fear that we shall find them very heavy, or at all events they will be rendered so before one half of our long train passes over them.

I hear that a private express is about starting for Vera Cruz. I will enquire to-morrow about the probabilities in favor of, and against its reaching that place, and if the chances are favorable, I will despatch one or more of the volumes on hand. No one, who has not been situated similarly to ourselves, can conceive of the blessings they enjoy in the luxury of regular daily, or even weekly mails. I hope that I may never again be placed out of hearing of the "Postboy's horn."

On meeting an officer of the 2nd Arty. to-day, I learn that many of their officers were as unfortunate as myself in being left by their Regt. in consequence of indisposition. Among the number I regret naming Capt. De Hart and Cousin Samuel; the former has been ill, the latter too unwell to accompany his Regt., but not confined seriously. I have not mentioned poor Saffern the drummer boy's case for several days; he is slowly recovering.

Lt. Judd is more of an invalid than any of the officers of your acquaintance. He has been unwell for several weeks and now looks very badly—I fear that he will be an invalid for several weeks. He appears to have one of those lingering, undecided kinds of fever, a species of typhoid. Capt. Wall of the 3rd is severely afflicted with an ugly cough, which may lead to something worse. When we reach Mexico we shall have time to recruit—the climate will prove more congenial to us, I hope, than that of this place.

I have not told you that Derr is now my cook; he is highly delighted at every meal by the praises I bestow on his skill. The fact is, he looks to me for *instruction*, and I am not entirely disinterested in the bestowal of encomiums on *our* cooking.

In Mexico

Thursday, 15th. I saw the Genl. this morning, returning from the review of the 2nd Twiggs Division. He looked remarkably well. In consequence of the absence of our Brigadier, the review of the 1st Division will take place on Monday; the Division of Vols., Genl. Pillow, will be on the 17th.

Capt. Kearney went as far as Rio Frio, twelve leagues (say thirty miles) from Mexico. He then overtook (having dispatched an Indian after him to check his progress) Genl. Canalizo, who was hastening, with about seventy Dragoons, towards Mexico, to announce, undoubtedly, the approach of the whole American Army. Genl. Canalizo received the General's despatches, and would not allow either of our Officers to convey them to the City. Capt. Kearney, I learn, reports that the road is not in a bad state, and that there are no obstructions on it.

The Mexican Congress is reported to be in session—a quorum having been finally obtained. We may soon learn their determination. God grant that it may be pacific—though I fear that it will not be. If they reject our overtures I think that we shall advance upon, and probably, after a bloody struggle, take the City, there to remain till fall, or for further advices and reinforcements from the United States.

This being the great market day, I walked through the City this morning, and find a few changes since I last mentioned visiting it. The peaches and pears are much improved, some of them are quite good—there is a very large pear, very juicy, which I never saw in the United States and which I shall attempt to introduce. The seed of a large snowy white onion I wish also to procure. Pineapples and oranges were more abundant to-day than they have been for some weeks.

Of the infinite variety of beans, I have already secured several.

I experimented to-day by putting some of the young leaves of one of the varieties of the cactus in my soup; it is a tolerably good substitute for the ochre. There were some fine large citron, and a few figs in market, the first I have seen. Green corn has occasionally been seen for the past three weeks, it is small with black grains. Snap beans and green peas I must not omit, nor squashes, etc.

Of their curiosities, I have not mentioned, I think, one among the horse-trappings; it is a piece of heavy leather running back from the saddle, and fitting the form of the horse hangs about half way down his thighs; the lower part is cut into seven strips, the ends of which are ornamented with chains, or pieces of iron; the whole surface of the leather is pressed or stamped and variously ornamented.

The Spanish carriage is a very heavy thing hung by strong leather straps, which pass over heavy wooden braces, about two feet above the axletrees; the fore wheels about one third as large as the hind ones—they are drawn by two mules in the City, but when travelling you sometimes see three or four hitched abreast before the two "wheel-mules" and again two more in the lead. Each set of mules has generally its driver; the traces are generally rope made of twisted raw hide.

As I am describing, I must not forget an "Arriéro" who serenades us twice a week with his drove of mules, each of which has around its neck one large and two smaller-sized bells, giving the most discordant sounds bells ever gave.

These men are the greatest packers in the world—these poor animals look like pigmies under the immense loads they bear. The common Mexican is nearly the equal, however, of his patient ass, as he carries weights we would never dream of placing on the backs of our slaves. Their mode of carrying burthens I described in a letter from Tampico,—a strap over the forehead; the women place the strap over the upper part of the chest.

Saturday, 17th. Last night I dined with Col. Butler, S.C., and returned at so late an hour that I did not think it prudent to sit up later. When I received an invitation in the morning, I thought it was to make one of a little party, which would separate at an early hour, or I would have taken my evening's chat with you before going, and was very much surprised to find a long table arranged for a regular dinner party. Genl. Scott was invited, but did not attend.

Among my friends at the table I mention Maj. Smith, Engineers, Dr. Lawson, Capts. Irwin and Huger, Capts. Screven and Myers. We had a very pleasant party, having a respectable sitting of five hours—eating and drinking was interspersed with songs and toasts. Genl. Clinch was enthusiastically toasted, also Genl. Scott. The evening passed as pleasantly as it could with those who were far from wife, children, and home. The supper or dinner was a plain one—turkeys, chickens, ham, rice, corn bread, chicken salad, sardines, fruit, pie, oranges, peanuts, *cacahuate*, sherry and claret wines, with a bottle of brandy, and I believe I have named the articles on the table. But as we have been sufficiently long at the table, let us leave it, and come to the details of to-day.

By appointment of last night, I breakfasted with Lt. Col. Dickerson, S. C., and about eight o'clock started with a party of S. C. Officers for Cholula. After a ride of about one hour and a half, as pleasant as a ride on a sorry scrub of a horse permitted, we rode to the top of the celebrated pyramid of Cholula.

Humboldt (according to Thompson) states the base of this pyramid to be 1440 feet (square), its height 177 feet, and the area of the top to be 45,210 square feet. You see distinctly the separations of the strata of the large earthen cakes (sunburnt bricks, Thompson calls them) of which it was built, and find in them an infinite number of pieces of broken earthen ware.

Grotesque, rudely formed stone images are found in the plain; some of them I will try to procure to take home. The view of the church, which crowns the pyramid, as you approach it, at about the distance of a mile from it, is very fine; on the left you see the snow-covered peak of the highest mountain in Mexico, Popocatepetl, and the background to the church and pyramid is the mountain of Iztaccihuatl.

The view from the top of this church is exceedingly beautiful—on every side extends a very rich plain, regularly laid out in fields now under cultivation in corn, which is in various stages, from the tender stock to that now in roasting ears; the eye tracing through the plain the meandering course of a small river running between us and Puebla; whilst in the distance, on one side you see the lofty steeples of the Cathedral of Puebla, the Church of Guadalupe, the hill beyond it like a watch tower, and a little to the right rises Malinche, where stood the Capital of the Republic of Tlascala, which, Cortes says, contained five hundred thousand freeholders.

Smaller and nameless (as far as I know) mountains form the limits to your view in other directions, till

THE PYRAMID OF CHOLULA
Redrawn from an old print

you cast your eyes towards the snowy mountains above mentioned, where around the base of the pyramid on that side stand the immense ruins of the large City of Cholula built by the Spaniards. Among the huge walls still standing, you see several churches, some now open for worship, others closed. The City covered more ground than Puebla now does.

The present City of Cholula is close to the base of the pyramid, and is not seen till you rise the hill formed by the cutting of the road through the base of the pyramid. Beyond the ruins, and much nearer than the mountains, projects a volcanic mountain, the crater of which is distinctly marked.

Would that I could give you such a description as would present these views plainly to your mind's eye—you would be delighted—but I cannot. The pyramid is ascended by a good road which winds along two sides of its faces, to the top; the sides are now closely covered with bushes and small shrubs.

I brought two specimens of Indian embroidery from the Church of the Pyramid—rude enough, but they will be interesting as being made there by an Indian woman.

On my return I found Capt. Burke in Barracks with his Command. By the bye, Maj. Harvey Brown, who commanded the Escort (4th Arty.), to-day requested to be particularly remembered to Mrs. Clinch, your father, and yourself.

News to-day from Mexico is of great importance. Genl. Santa Anna's Govt. is pursuing vigorous measures towards some of his Generals. Genl. Ampudia has been sent under an escort to Cuernavaca; Genl. Almonte has been ordered to march to Tulancingo in twenty-four hours, and has been refused the assistance necessary for the journey, and Genl. Avista has been violently carried to the fortress of Acapulco. Enough for to-night. Good-night.

Sunday, 18th. No news to-day—but a rumor that Genl. Pierce left, or was to have left Vera Cruz on last Wednesday. Mr. Hargous, an American merchant, who has been residing several years in this country, offers to bet any amount of money that peace will be proclaimed in two months. I wish, in this case, that my losing a few hundred dollars would secure that result, and I would most willingly *lose* a year's pay to secure so great a *gain*. What Mr. Hargous founds his hopes upon, I know not, but I fear that he is too sanguine.

Among the sights of yesterday, I did not include the Mexican ploughman. The plough is a simple block, shod with iron, terminating in a point, having a single handle which the man holds with his right hand, his left hand guiding and urging his two oxen by means of a *goad*, a long reed, having an iron spike four or five inches long on its small end. I also saw a party of Mexicans spading up some ground; the spade is made of wood, the blade having merely a border of iron. Everything here is of fashions centuries old. The mules are generally hitched, or rather harnessed to the carts as our oxen are, supporting the weight of the tongue by means of a bar and collars or bows.

I went this morning to see some of my sick friends. I found Lt. Anderson quite indisposed, several others of the 2nd Arty. are more or less unwell. Capt. De Hart has been taken to the house occupied by Genl. Worth—he will there be closely and well attended by Dr. Satterlee.

I have not mentioned my own health, it is because I have had no more chills to report; to-morrow morning, will be seven days since my last *attempt* to have one; if I escape it then, I shall feel pretty safe. I have a grand appetite, and am ready to eat my allowance at every meal, but I must restrain, as I am convinced that we do not require here as much food as is necessary in colder climates. I met the two Doctors Steiner day before yesterday—the older has been very ill, but is now convalescing; they came up with Genl. Pillow's Command.

Yesterday, I had the pleasure of Dr. Suter's company on my return from Cholula. He is very well; his last letters from Mrs. Suter were from Washington, where she was with his father's family—the Doctor's son, Charley, had consented to go with her. I did not ask the Dr. but presume that she is on her way to her mother's.

Howard has just told me that an express expected to start in a short time for Vera Cruz, so that I will write a *short* note—they take none others—to-morrow, merely to tell you that I am well. My regular series I will retain till I find a sure and safe conveyance. You would have (could I now send what I have written) enough reading for a month, as I find I cannot follow the rule I prescribed for myself, of writing a *few lines* every night. I will, at all events, close for this night, praying that God may continue the guard and guide of my wife. Good-night.

Monday, 19th. I wrote a note to you very hastily this morning, to take its chance by an express, when one goes. Under the fear, I may say expectation, of its being intercepted by the Mexicans, it was filled with commonplace expressions. I am unwilling that they should read in it anything they could laugh and jeer over. This writing to you, every night, ruins my style as an ordinary letter writer, for now I make no attempt at condensation, writing whatever occurs to me, and not digesting the sentences. To a wife, this is perhaps excusable, but not so with any one else.

Genl. Scott reviewed our Division to-day—I did not attend, because this being the seventh day since my chill, I was advised by the Dr. not to go out. As I anticipated, the Division did not make as fine a display as Genl. Twiggs's did. Our Genl. has not had us in the field as frequently as he ought.

Two rumors from Mexico to-day—one that they are fighting in the City, where a pronunciamiento has been made against Santa Anna, and the other that the Congress has adjourned, having given Santa Anna power to make a treaty. A day or two will enlighten us as to the credibility either report is entitled to.

I may mention, though, that we are endeavoring to organize a monthly express to Vera Cruz, the men to take a certain number of letters, each written on half a sheet of fine paper. As soon as the arrangement is made, I shall, without discontinuing this series, commence a new one. I fear that in my attempt to get a great deal on my half sheet, I may compel you to put spectacles on, to decipher my writing.

I called to see Dr. Harney this morning, and was pleased to see him looking well. His slight wound gives him some trouble, and will do so for a long time; the ball struck one of the bones just above the ankle joint. His general health appears to be perfectly restored. He advises me to take a pill of quinine daily; I followed his advice to-day, and it has passed without a chill. Mr. Judd still looks badly, but slowly improves, I think. The drummer boy is nearly well.

Tuesday, 20th, after tattoo. I have just sent to Genl. Worth's Hd. Qrs. another letter to take its chance by an express, which starts to-night. Good luck attend our messenger; we know that the chances are against us, but still, should only one in twenty reach you, I shall be richly repaid by learning that you have again heard from me. Regarding that letter as part of my *evening's talk with you*, I shall say but a few words more.

Report tells to-day, that Santa Anna has appointed Commissioners—*Nous verrons*. The Q. M. has at last furnished me with a horse; he is very showy, but too high-spirited for an Officer whose duties at drill take him among the soldiers. I shall have to exchange him for another. I called at Genl. Scott's Quarters to see Capt. De Hart; he is there, instead of being at Genl. Worth's; he looks very badly, but is convalescent. Good-night, and happy dreams to you.

Wednesday, 21st. Thus far, no chill. To-day I have accomplished a duty to which I should have attended some days ago, that of making some calls on my brother Kentuckians—Capt. Pope, Rifles, was the only one at home. He was formerly a lawyer of Louisville, who found it more agreeable to spend his time pleasantly with his friends than to attend to the dry business of the Court rooms, and consequently his clients looked elsewhere for a business man.

Captain —— is, I am sorry to say it, under arrest, and will be arraigned for trial to-morrow morning, charged with indulging too freely and frequently in the social glass, and in some instances when *on duty*.

I fear that his case is a very bad one. I will attend his trial for the sake of his father, whom I esteem most dearly. His counsel is Lt. Col. Tom Moore, 2nd Dragoons.

I called on Col. Andrews of the Voltigeurs; he is, I fancy, sorry that he left his comfortable berth in Washington for this service. In his Regt. there is one Kentucky Capt. whose family I know, and I think that I know *him*, Capt. Churchill; he was on drill. I then called on Col. Butler, and some other South Carolina Vols. Thus, you see that I have accomplished a good deal.

Every person is on the *qui vive* this afternoon, as it is expected, with what reason I do not hear, that we either move in two days, or not until the fall. Capt. R. Lee, Engineers, expressed his fears last evening that he would not have an opportunity of visiting the City of Mexico. He is no idle prattler, and speaks not without reflection.

No. 17. PUEBLA, MEXICO.
Thursday, July 22, '47.

I went to the Court room this morning, and was very much pleased to learn that Genl. Scott had permitted the charges against Capt. —— to be withdrawn. I hope the clemency now shewn him may not be without good results.

A flag came to Genl. Scott this morning, from Mexico, in answer to his application, or demand, for the return of certain prisoners. The Genl. told me that the answer was favorable, that it is written in good temper.

I had a long talk with friend Kirby this morning—he thinks that chances are decidedly in favor of peace, that they are nearly equal to nine out of ten against

In Mexico 259

it. He is not apt to jump to strange or wrong conclusions; he is indeed very cautious, usually, in the expression of his opinion, and, knowing from the Genl. himself that the data on which the Major formed his opinion were obtained from the Genl., this opinion has great weight with me. But still I cannot indulge the delightful hope of peace, even when presented from such a source. I can place no confidence in the doings of this Govt. or of their constituted authorities.

To one opinion of the Major's I do fully consent, which is that if the Mexicans do not now consent to, and conclude, a treaty of peace, that the war must continue for a long and indefinite period. We cannot again offer the olive branch. Two rude rejections will bar us from making another.

Certain it is, that, as yet, neither Congress nor Santa Anna have answered Mr. Trist's letter. The officer who bore the flag embraced one of the General's aids, drank to peace, and called him his "friend." All this may well be *diplomatique*.

We must soon advance, if the Govt. comes to no decision or to an unfavorable one on Secy. Buchanan's proposal, submitted through Mr. Trist, proposing that Commissioners be appointed to confer with Mr. T. on the terms of a treaty. To-morrow, or the next day, we may hear something interesting from the City. No news of Genl. Pierce's march. Good-night.

Friday, 23rd. Genl. S. told me confidentially, to-day, that there was a slight prospect of the opening of negotiations with the Mexican Govt. The facts are these. Genl. S. A., as you know, sent Mr. Buchanan's letter to Congress; this body resolved to play a game of shuttlecock with the President: returned it to him stating that, by the Constitution, the initiatory steps in the consideration of treaties were assigned to the Executive.

Genl. Santa Anna's rejoinder has been received, in which he informs the Congress that he does not require any instructions from them in relation to his duties, that he did not send the letter to them for any further action on their part than for them to rescind the resolution passed at the close of their last Session, declaring any Mexican a traitor to his country who would listen to, or receive any proposals of peace; that he knows by the Constitution of 1824 this duty was imposed on the Executive. He tells them that the question now presented for the consideration of the Mexicans should be solemnly and wisely deliberated upon, and that it should be answered either affirmatively or negatively. It is said to be the best paper he has issued.

Some of the Members of Congress, alarmed probably at the dilemma in which they have placed themselves, have left the City. Santa Anna is preparing, in the event of Congress' adjourning without rescinding their unconstitutional resolution, to have a pronunciamiento declaring himself Dictator. The Army is not yet ready for this; but it is thought that he will, soon, as he has placed Congress so decidedly in the wrong, seize the supreme power. A few days more and all these schemes must work out results either favorable to, or destructive of Santa Anna. Genl. Santa Anna's order of the 19th inst. was received here to-day. He orders that the firing of a cannon in the *place d'armes* will be the signal of the approach of the troops, that at this all the bands shall play, and that all the military shall retire to their Quarters, and there

In Mexico

await instructions; no one to leave except on service, no carriages to pass through the streets, no horseman to be in the streets unless the military on duty, no one to leave the gates of the City, but *women* who may have brought in coal or provisions, all the shops to be closed, but those of the provision markets and where bread is sold. He prefaces this decree by a strong abuse of us, and an exhortation to the Mexican Army to restore the lost lustre of their Military fame, etc.

To-morrow I dine with the General.

Saturday, 24th. We had to-day a true Yankee dish, one I did not expect to see so far in the interior of Mexico—codfish and the usual accompaniments. Though there were meats and fowl on the table, all were good Yankees enough to take no meat after the soup—making a simple but good dinner.

Capt. N—— of Phila., ex-member of Congress, was present. He is just recovering from a severe fit of illness. His mind is as weak as his body. He was strongly disposed to deliver us a Congressional discourse upon every subject introduced—one of those men, who, when they begin to talk, cast their eyes around to catch the eyes of others, and to force attention from as many as possible to their remarks. I am very fond of modesty, and never allow such orators of the table or room to entrap me, if I can decently avoid it.

Genl. Scott confidently expects news of great interest from Mexico in two or three days. Mr. Trist has requested the Genl. to delay our advance, at least until Genl. Pierce arrives, as he thinks something favorable to peace may occur in that time.

As I occasionally mention incidents which are strange and new, I will here allude to one which attracted my attention this morning. I was lying down, and hearing the occasional tinkle of a little bell, I went to the window to see what it was. I there saw two common Mexicans at their little market, in front of my window, one having on his back a box three by two feet, the double door of which was opened and presented, turned as he rang his bell, towards the market women; as it was thus presented to each group, they advanced towards it, and, bending forward, kissed an artificial flower in front of the glass, or the glass itself. The duty of the second Mexican was to open and close the door, and to receive the contributions given by nearly every one, the fruit and vegetables, tortillas (cakes made of Indian corn) in his basket, and the money in a small tin box having a slit in the top.

The large box had an image of an angel with an infant by his side—the sides of the interior of the box ornamented with flowers. Every one gives something; one three onions, another a pear, another a banana, etc., and the tortilla sellers gave each one of their small flat cakes.

I have frequently heard this bell about eight at night, but did not know what it was rung for. The little tin money box I have frequently seen offered to the market people to kiss—mothers invariably raising their children up to kiss it also. It has a painting of the Virgin or some favorite saint of the church to which it belongs, and always gathers a few *clakos* (one and a half cents) from these poor Indians.

I think I have told you that the tortillas were made of Indian corn, soaked in lime water to remove the skin, and then ground by rubbing it by a long stone roller, or pin, on a small flat iron stone resembling a table. This appears to be the Mexican mill; the woman

MAKING TORTILLAS

sits, having the slope towards her, and with the pin in her hands, she mashes the grain, keeping it moist till she forms a fine paste, which is baked in an *earthen* dish, placed on charcoal burning in an *earthen* furnace—all Mexican utensils for cooking, carrying, or holding water, etc., are made of an excellent earthen ware.

Their spoons are either rudely made of wood, or part of a calabash, and frequently I see them using the tortilla as a spoon, bending it so as to hold a small quantity of their broths or stews, which are the ways they generally cook their food, in which they use red pepper very freely. I must confess that I have had no desire to eat what they prepare. I see daily exhibited by the market women scenes disgustingly filthy.

Sunday, 25th.

Another Sabbath, and *all* uncertainty about our movements. As late as four P.M. yesterday, Genl. S. was doubtful whether we would advance. I called at his Quarters this afternoon, but he was at church, and I did not see him. Capt. Myers' clerk told me that the Quartermasters had received orders to have everything ready for the advance of the Army in four days.

We will not, I am confident, leave this City until the arrival, or near approach of Genl. Pierce, and he will not arrive, supposing him to have left on the 16th as reported, before the 1st or 5th of August. It may well be, that Genl. Scott and Mr. Trist have received intelligence of the state of parties in the Capital, [such] as to make it expedient, or necessary, for us to approach it. A few more days of doubt, and all will probably be certainty—no half-way measures, either peace or a war changed, in its character, from that which we have been conducting upon the most civilized principles.

Genl. Pierce may, however, bring instructions from the Home Govt. altering all the schemes and plans we have been dreaming over in our quiescent state.

Capt. De Hart spent the day with us; he is improving, but as has been the case with all who have been prostrated by disease in this Country, it will be some weeks before he will be sufficiently well to attend to duty. I saw Lt. Anderson out yesterday. Genl. Worth looks badly again. The sick list of our Army is now slightly above 2000—a very considerable and important change in the strength of our force, where we are, at least, in need of all our bayonets. The spirit of our troops is, however, most excellent, and they will deserve success.

Lt. Judd has just left our Quarters, and has, I am pleased to hear, improved sufficiently to enable him to take his seat at table.

Howard tells me that my letter of the 18th was dispatched last night; success attend it. I will not commence another sheet this evening. Good-night.

Monday, 26th.

Most unreasonable and ill-timed kindness in two sets of visitors has made it so late before I could take my seat to converse with you, that I shall soon be compelled to make my bow, *very* soon. From orders issued to the different departments of the Staff, it is certainly intended that we shall leave this City as soon as Genl. Pierce gets within a few days' march of it—that is, the leading Division will start, to be followed by the others in successive days, so timed that Genl. Pierce will reach here the day before the last Division will start.

If we have a fight near the City, it will probably be the great battle of the Mexican War. Pride to save their Capital from our grasp, a desire to revenge their repeated disastrous defeats, will urge them to exert their powers to the utmost.

Our soldiery, flushed with victory, will, I am convinced, do more than mere duty calls for. Could they for one moment doubt of success, they must see that as we are situated, victory must be ours—a drawn battle even will not suffice. We *must*, we, with the blessing of God, *will* conquer.

Genl. Scott heard yesterday that the Mexican Congress would do nothing—it is not expected that they will answer Santa Anna's last message to them, in which he gives them a lecture in relation to their course in instructing him in his duties.

The news from Hd. Qrs. is still favorable—everything promises fair. If the Mexican Congress does not ruin our prospects, we may yet be home before winter.

Tuesday, 27th.

So great is the uncertainty as to Genl. Pierce's whereabouts, etc., so numerous the reports about his being harassed in his advance, that Genl. S. sent a Brigade, Genl. Persifer Smith's, with Duncan's Battery, and a squadron of Cavalry to communicate with him.

Genl. S. is one of the most prudent commanders I ever served under. Instead of wearing his troops out by issuing orders for them to hold themselves in readiness, on the circulation of every report about the enemy's approach, he has each case examined by some persons whom he can trust, and thus quietly exposes the falsity, or verifies the truth, of the rumor.

I heard him, a few days since, on Col. Hitchcock's mentioning a report that has been made of the arrival of some troops at Atlixco, say that he must get the Capt. of his Bandits to enquire into it—that twenty false reports might be made about the enemy, and that if we failed to enquire into the twenty-first, which afterwards proved true, as military men we would richly deserve censure.

We have in our pay a Compy. of Mexicans who are called the Forty Thieves; they are, I expect some of the gentlemen robbers Thompson mentions. They were asked, the other day, if they would not be afraid of being murdered by their countrymen for acting with us, after we left the Country, and their Captain's answer was: "That is our business, we will take care of ourselves." They are very useful in getting information, etc., and are used individually or collectively, as their services are required. The Capt. says he can increase his band to 1500 or 2000, if a greater number be wanted than he now has.

This afternoon, I went with Lt. Johnson to an "Old Curiosity Shop," where I purchased a Catholic Bible, 1742 A.D., for Brother William. Mr. J. purchased a similar one for himself; he says that it is a present which William will prize very highly. Do not think that my old mania of purchasing books and pictures has again beset me—you would admire the cool nonchalance with which I examine choice old books, etc., which can be purchased very cheap here, and cannot be procured in the United States. I must, on leaving this Country, purchase some curiosities for you.

A party leaves the City at seven in the morning, to visit Cholula, but, as I have been there, I will remain, so that Capt. Burke may go. Since the payments were made, our sick list has increased; we have now 2200 on the sick report.

One word about the customs of the Country, before stopping. The market and common women address us as *niño* (child); whether this is a term of endearment or not, I cannot say. I did not understand them as calling me so, until I found it was usually done. You refuse to give the price asked, and walk off, when you are frequently called back by that word, to take the article at your own price. Good-night.

Wednesday, 28th.

Unfortunately, I have been placed on a Court of Enquiry, demanded by Col. Riley, who avers that injustice has been done his Brigade in Genl. Twiggs's report, and in those of some of the sub-commanders in Genl. Twiggs's Division.

I fear that the personal feelings of Col. Harney have become interested in this matter, as he claims the storming and carrying of the height called by us Cerro Gordo, by Santa Anna, Telegraph Hill—whereas Riley states that his Command charged the hill in reverse, at the same time Harney charged it in front; both may be right, and I hope that this may be so decided by the evidence.

The other points are easily established, or contradicted; one is that Genl. Twiggs gives to Col. Baker, Ill. Vols., the credit of taking a Battery Col. Riley avers was won by his own Regt. His Court are Maj. Genl. Pillow, Brig. Genl. Cadwalader, Col. Clarke, 5th Infy., and Capt. Anderson, Recorder.

I care very little about the labor of writing as much as I will have to do, did I not fear that it will materially interfere with my evenings' conversations with you.

No one who is not as regular in his habits as I am can conceive of the pleasure with which I nightly resume my daily scrawls to you.

I have advised many of my friends who are homesick, and, to kill time, resort to rather expensive habits, to pursue the same plan, assuring them that they would soon derive benefit and gratification from it. It brings me, as it were, near to and in communion regularly with you, before retiring to bed. Writing to you is always, when I am well and not prevented by urgent business, the last work of the day, and is generally finished on retiring for the night.

I may be so much exhausted by my duties as Recorder of this Court, as to shorten our discourses very considerably. This may be advantageous, as I find that I write now a great deal about nothing. Not a report in them to-day from Mexico.

Thursday, 29th.

Though the time for retiring has passed, and I have not yet finished my labors, I must have a short chat. I am happy to report that the misunderstanding between Colonels Harney and Riley is, I think, from the testimony of to-day, likely to be solved by the Court in a manner probably grateful to the feelings of both. Col. Riley's report alludes to carrying a *crest* of the Telegraph Hill, lower than the principal crest carried by Col. Harney, not at all the same point, but at some distance from it. And again it appears that Col. Riley's Command took three guns of one of the enemy's Batteries simultaneously with the carrying of two of the same Battery (but at a distance of some sixty yards) by some Vols. to whom Genl. Twiggs ascribes the credit of taking *the Battery*.

Should there be no conflicting evidence, we shall soon finish, and I shall rejoice at there being no just grounds for finding serious fault with either Harney's or Riley's reports.

I dined with the Genl. to-day, no news. A messenger is to be despatched towards Mexico to-morrow, with what communication I know not.

Friday, 30th.

The Court has proceeded very well to-day. Why other evidence is desired unless it be intended to collect under oath material for a history of the battles, I know not. I see the points made by Col. Riley already clearly settled by the evidence. I fear that we may be drawn into other matters. I must keep a good lookout to guard against this.

It would seem from the rumors from Mexico, that the prospect of peace which began to lighten up a few days since, has disappeared, and that over the lovely landscape we thought we could get a glimpse of, now hangs the dark and threatening cloud of War.

The Mexican Congress of the 13th inst. sent what they called their ultimatum, on the question of peace or war, which we received in print to-day. This must be the paper alluded to in my date of the 24th inst. It is quite learned in constitutional law; they characterize our invasion as the most unjust of all aggressions, and say, "The people are resolved not to consent to an ignominious treaty, which will secure to our neighbors the possession of usurped territory and with it the dominion of the Continent, closing at the same time our political life in such manner that we shall not deserve even the compassion of other people;—that the Congress has always resisted everything which seemed to open the door of peace, which would now be, in every way, disgraceful, and has not omitted zeal or precaution to prevent even the remotest danger of that disaster."

Pretty strong language—but the very men who adopted that language by a vote of fifty-two to twenty-two, might the next day consent to a treaty of peace. Heavy bribes would, I have no doubt, if our Govt. would stoop so low as to offer them, buy a majority of these patriots. I wish I could witness the regeneration of the Mexicans proper. But alas, they bend their necks to the yoke of the Spanish dons, without thinking of their miserably degraded state. It will take a century to rouse them from their torpor, and to make them feel that they are free—'t is mockery to speak of Mexico as a Republic. The common laborers of the Country are slaves more lost in every point of view than our negroes; these are the men who would be among the voters. Alas, alas! Having finished my homily, I will bid you good-night, as you must be sleepy after reading it.

Saturday night, July 31st.

I cannot retire without saying a few, they must be a very few, words, as I have been busily engaged, to-night, in bringing up my papers, so that I may have a holiday to-morrow. I fear we shall be engaged a day or two longer, as Col. Riley insists upon introducing a good deal of unimportant matter, and it is hard to check him. Genl. Scott visited Cholula to-day. Genl. Pierce has been heard from; he was at Jalapa.

Sunday, August 1st.

Another month has passed, and another Sabbath

In Mexico

has come, finding me by the mercy of God still sensible of His great mercies.

The news from Mexico, as derived from the papers, is not in the least degree favorable to peace. On the 27th they mention Genl. Santa Anna consulting his principal officers as to the question whether our propositions relative to effecting peace ought to be considered or not; placing their Govt. at once "in a position the most hostile." Genl. Valencia asked permission "to take 12,000 men and dislodge Genl. Scott from Puebla." What a pity the Council did not let him come! The middle of the month will probably decide how much the gallant Genl. can accomplish in contending with our Army.

'T is strange that Santa Anna, if he has any thoughts of peace, propounded the alternative of peace or war to his Army Officers. They, of course, desire the War to continue—little care they for their bleeding soldiery, their nearly exhausted Treasury, if they can be kept in office and well paid; the latter they will attend to themselves.

The laborers, the merchants, the men of wealth, and lastly, but not the least interesting in my eyes, the poor and oppressed peasantry may one and all ardently desire to taste again the sweets of peace, but long will be the time ere their wishes are gratified, if Genl. Santa Anna and his Army are to decide when the War is to end.

The more I think of our position, so far into the enemy's country, operating against them with Armies on so many points, and with forces so exceedingly small; when the results accomplished by them are considered, and thus far, without a serious reverse, I begin to liken our position to that of some of the

Armies whose exploits are recorded in the Bible, and hope that our operations are blessed by God, whose instruments we may be, to effect some wise scheme of His providence.

Why is this Nation now so stubborn? Never was a war conducted before in a manner so little abhorrent to all man's finer feelings. We have been now in this large City since May 15th, with a soldiery gathered from many Nations, many of them undisciplined, and yet, I will venture the assertion, without fear of contradiction, that, in no City of the same size, either in our own blessed Country or in any other, is private property, or are private rights, more secure and better guarded than here.

And our Courts, before which all offences of a nature in the least serious, against persons, property, or good morals, pretty surely come, will show that they have not been engaged in trying higher offences. Not an instance, I am certain, has been elicited, or brought to light, of one of our soldiers killing a Mexican.

And since pay day, though we have many men daily drunk in the streets, and they are frequently insulting, only one case of a man's being killed in the street has occurred—and that might have been by some of his comrades. 'T is truly wonderful, I cannot understand it.

We hear of the movement of no more troops. Can it be that the Govt. thinks that Genl. Scott can conquer all Mexico with 8500 men; for we cannot leave this place with a larger force even after being joined by Genl. Pierce, as a heavy garrison must be left here with our sick.

Genl. S. has written another bitter, truth-telling letter to the Secy. of War, giving vent to his just indignation in terms that will excite strong feelings among the little men in Washington. He asks no favor. Enough for to-night. God be with you.

Monday night, August 2nd.

Only one word, for really I am so tired of writing that I cannot write. We had an afternoon session to-day, and though the Court give me no additional time to bring up proceedings, I am determined they shall find all right when we meet. Not a word of news, but that Midshipman Rogers, so long in the hands of the Mexicans, is now here. What news he brings, I know not. I hope that we shall finish in one day more, to enable me to resume my chat with you. Good-night.

Tuesday, August 3rd.

Thank God, I have received letters from you. They tell of your apprehensions about me. Oh, my wife, how full is my heart of gratitude to our Heavenly Father. He stayed, and, I hope, has dissipated, your burning fever, and over me He has always His protecting shield. What can we do without Him? Oh! let us never cease to praise His holy name.

The mail came in very unexpectedly bringing me your letters of the 10th, 18th, and 20th, the latter giving me news to the 24th. I can write no more to-night. That Almighty God will continue to guard and protect you is my earnest prayer, and ever with me, an abiding, a soothing, happy hope and belief. Good-night.

Wednesday, 4th.

Having finished the proceedings of our Court, I took them to Genl. Scott, and, on his invitation, remained to sup with him. Supper was followed, about ten o'clock, by some hot whiskey punch. I knew that the punch would be *excellent*, and the company was good; my most esteemed host, Genl. Quitinda (a gentleman), Cadwalader (whom your Father knows), Mr. Trist, Captains Huger and Drum, and Maj. Kirby and I remained till punch time.

The Army is to commence its advance upon Mexico this week. Genl. Pierce will arrive early the 6th inst. Major Gaines arrived this evening, having effected his escape from the enemy. Good-night.

Thursday, 5th.

The order for our advance is issued. Genl. Twiggs's Division marches Saturday, 7th; Quitman's Sunday; Worth's Monday; and Pillow's Tuesday, 10th, Col. Childs remaining here as Governor, and Capt. De Hart, just convalescent, as Lt. Governor. Every Officer and man incapable of performing three days' march, to be left, and organized into Companies, Regiments, etc., as they may be reported fit for garrison duty; the permanent garrison is not yet named.

This order, will, I presume, send our very amiable Lt. Col. to us again. God knows what the result of this movement may be. The Govt. has left us without funds, and our Staff Depts. are deeply in debt. In Mexico it is said that drafts on New York, etc., can be readily converted into cash. We must then perforce go there, and raise the wind, though we may have to pass through a heavy storm ere we can get at the cash.

Lt. Thom, Genl. Pierce's A.D.C., says that they received information, after their being some days in march, that six vessels had arrived at Vera Cruz, subsequent to their departure, so that we may soon have

In Mexico

another re-enforcement. Genl. P. brings us about 2500, including 300 Marines—the latter are very acceptable, as they are always good troops.

I fear that two of my notes to you have been lost, as I learn that two carriers, taking letters to Vera Cruz, have been taken, one hung, and the other's throat cut. I will continue to try all who venture, as one may be lucky enough to escape, and thus give you a line from me.

Lt. Welch, 3rd Arty., will join to-morrow, with some recruits of Capt. Bunker's Compy. Lt. Thom tells us that my old friend Maj. Galt looks badly. I shall be most happy to take him by the hand, and regret that he comes not in good health, as his merry laugh is refreshing. We have not many good laughers among us now; thoughts of home, and the dreadful uncertainty of when we shall return to all we love on earth, are silvering many a head. God's will be done. He knows best all things.

Father is right about ———; he came into Genl. S.'s Quarters last night, fully two-thirds drunk. I was vexed and mortified to death.

Friday, 6th.

Genl. Pierce arrived with his Command, and I am happy in being able to say that friend Major Galt looks better than I expected to see him. I called, this afternoon, to see some of the Marines. Their Commander, Lt. Col. Watson, I knew some years since at Portsmouth, N. H., and two of the Captains, Reynolds and Baker, are former acquaintances. I hoped that they would be assigned to our Division but they have been attached to Genl. Quitman's Brigade.

Ours is, I believe, now the strongest Brigade in the

Army,—it would therefore have been unreasonable to have added to our strength.

By the bye, I heard to-day that Genl. Worth had written to Genl. Scott a half apologetic letter, upon which Genl. Scott, as he always does, jumped over all that had passed, and they are again reconciled. I hope it may be sincere, but Genl. W. is a little too impatient of control by his old Milty. Commander, who taught him the alphabet of war, and has taken him through all the classes, even to the highest in that school.

We have another report from Mexico. That Valencia has fortified his position at Guadalupe, and declared against Santa Anna. That cannot be true—the enemy is too near the door to render justifiable such a step. All agree in the opinion that if we have a battle, it will be a hard fought one.

Lt. Welch called this afternoon and delivered me your letter from Savannah dated May 29th. Among the newcomers, I see a son of Col. De Russey's. You saw him once or twice, I think, at West Point. Dismissal and rejection from the Military Academy have proved very fortunate events for several young men, who are placed far above the heads of their more *fortunate* classmates, "who were fools enough to graduate." One man is Col. whose classmates are second Lieuts., and some of them very low down in that grade. Oh! the sweets, the beauties of democracy. West Point is too aristocratic to have any attention paid to laws intended to protect the rights of those who plod through that institution. But thank God, every battlefield attests the steady valor of her pupils: there has been no faltering, no wavering among them. Though I have in my previous letters written enough about the sights of Puebla, I ought not to leave it

In Mexico

without saying something about the night market. Many scenes are worthy of Mr. Weir's pencil—those beautiful and rich contrasts of light and shade we so often admired in looking at our campfires. The principal market presents a more variegated view than does the little one in front of my window.

I will say a few words about our house scene. Directly in front of my window is the stall of two women who sell all kinds of fruit, disposed in piles or pieces of matting. This stall is covered with long shingles, and is closed behind by a piece of matting, but open on the sides and in front; the two are seated back, near a blazing fire of lightwood, giving a picturesque effect, as you see customers approach, and by change of position see them now in strong light, now mostly in deep shade.

Next you find a different and the most ordinary, kind of stall,—it is a piece of matting fastened upon the top of a stake, by being tied to the ends of five or more cross-pieces, the pole sticking into a hole a few inches deep. These look, at a distance, like the umbrella we see on the old china plates; the arrangement for light is different here from the other, as he has a tripod about three feet high, with a blazing torch of lightwood on top, and the effect of the light from this is very fine; in the next you may perhaps see a candle, but this looks too poor by the side of its neighbors.

The groups around these stalls, the figures passing in front of them, with now and then one suddenly emerging from, or disappearing into the darkness of the background, with the effect of light on the piles of fruits, varying in colors from the snowy white of the onion to the yellow of the orange, or the dark hue of the sapote, form rich pictures. But bless me, I must close! Good-night. God guard you.

Saturday, 7th.

Genl. Twiggs has moved with his Division—the head of his column marched about ten miles, the rear, not more than half that distance. I presume that the object will be to accomplish the day's march before the rain commences, which is usually after three o'clock. Short marches will therefore be made all the way.

The Genl. is very much worried to-day, at a report from Col. Childs, the newly appointed Civil and Milty. Governor, remonstrating against the inadequacy of the garrison proposed to be left here—the first Regt. Penna. Vols. and two Companies of Regulars, with the sick and all who are unable to perform three days' march, would, Genl. S. thought, afford a sufficient protection. What he will decide upon, I know not, but he is very uneasy.

He dines to-day with Genl. Pierce, at Genl. Worth's. I was with him from his dinner hour, dining there, till he went out to dinner. Genl. P. introduced the Col. and Officers of the 9th New England Regt. to the Genl. They presented some fine faces and heads among the group.

Genl. S. hopes, that instead of the Governor's chair, your Father will consent to be run for the Senate. I told him of the position in which Father is now placed—that he would be told by the Whigs, "If you do not run for Governor, we shall lose the State elections and consequently the United States Senator—you run, we carry everything—and this election is all important to us and our party." Strong points these may be, in Father's opinion; and if so, as a politician, he cannot refuse.

In Mexico

Maj. Wade is worried to death by a letter he received the other day from his wife; he has alluded to it several times, but I never ask any questions, particularly about family affairs, and again, I am tired of throwing away counsel and advice, and have resolved henceforth to be very discreet if I can.

Our Lt. Col. assumed the command of the Regt. this afternoon—this cuts short the reign of Capt. Burke. Capt. Kendrick of the 2nd Arty. is to remain here. I regret that exceedingly, as the Capt. is very anxious to go on, and he would collect a mass of matter of the geology, etc., of the Country between this place and Mexico and in the suburbs of the City, which would be valuable.

I will now retire. I intend devoting to-morrow to finishing this and some other letters I have commenced. No. 18 will then give the beginning of our advance to the Capital.

Sunday, 8th.

We have received our orders to march at 6 o'clock in the morning; to prepare for that start, our reveille is to be beat *at 3 o'clock*. Why three hours are required to prepare for starting, I could never yet see. The men would march much better by not being aroused so unnecessarily early.

I had intended, when I finished writing last night, to have devoted some two or three hours of to-day to writing, but I have had enough to occupy me, attending to Compy. and private matters. I saw Col. Childs in the City this morning, riding through one of its streets with half a dozen Dragoons as an escort. He is capable of making as much out of a trifle as any man I ever saw. He must be a good soldier, or he never could have gained the reputation he had in the Army.

I leave thirteen men, invalids, here, but many of them are capable of performing light garrison duty. All the married men are well, and accompany me. Of poor Cramer, left sick at Vera Cruz, I have not heard for a very long time. I feel very uneasy about him. Suffern, the drummer, is rapidly improving, but is yet too weak to march with the Compy. to-morrow. Poor little fellow, he is very anxious to go on.

One of the young Georgia officers dined with us to-day—Lt. Forsyth; he is not very brisk in his appearance. He is from Macon, I think he said. We hear that other troops are at Vera Cruz. Can Duncan be among those? We hope that the most dangerous part of the yellow fever season has passed. Genl. Pierce, I think, did not lose a man by the vomit, after he got into Camp.

I will now close this letter, the last from Puebla, commencing another the first evening I have leisure. I leave Puebla with some regret, as I have had many delightful chats with you and have had several of your letters, in my snug room here. That our Heavenly Father will, in his wisdom, so order events as soon to restore me to you, and that He will continue to pour upon us His choicest blessings, crowning, in each of us, all with pure faith in Him, is my earnest and constant prayer.

No. 18. RIO PRIETO (Black River).
Monday, August 9th.

Four leagues (eleven miles) on the road to Mexico. We are, at last, off for the far famed City of Mexico. Our march has been a very unpleasant one, in consequence of having eyes, nose, mouth, and ears filled with dust; luckily for us, the day's march was so short, that we reached our bivouac by 12 o'clock.

To let you into some of the discomforts sometimes resulting from want of rank, or rank not well defined, I will give you an anecdote, the principal sufferers by which are Major Wade and myself. The Major and Capt. A. were both, during the absence of Col. Belton from the Regiment, assigned to duty as Field Officers. Lt. Col. B. having reported for duty with the Regt. relieved Capt. Burke from its command, and gives us as the orders now stand, four Field Officers, one per Compy.

Anticipating something of what has happened, I took command of the Compy. the day before Col. Belton joined. Yesterday, when we were having our mess furniture packed, Major W. asked if I could take the mess articles in "G" Co. wagon. I told him I feared it would be impossible, as the wagon would be very full, but I would have as many articles carried as was possible.

I accordingly this morning had one of the boxes put in my wagon, and after we were out of the City, Derr astonished me by saying that the box containing all our provisions, tea, coffee, and most of the cooking articles and table furniture was left behind.

It seems that the Major made a fruitless attempt to have it placed in the field staff wagon. Not being in command of the Compy. he could not *order* it to be put with the Company's property. Thus has the Major verified the truth of the fable of the ass between two bales of hay.

My position is pretty good, as friend Derr will easily manage to supply me with coffee from the Compy., and my old soup-digester is in the box that came. I am glad it is safe. We have sent back, and in a day or two the error will have been rectified.

Genl. Scott and Staff are probably now with the advance, as he left yesterday morning with Genl. Quitman's Division—intending to leave it, under an escort of Cavalry, and overtake Genl. Twiggs.

The dust was so very unpleasant to-day that I could not enjoy the scenery. One road, sufficiently undulating for good marching, passed through an almost continued succession of corn fields, from that receiving its first, and perhaps only ploughing, to that in which the corn is ripe, and acres of beans. The two snowy mountains, so often mentioned in my letters from Puebla, are on the left and in front of us. As we advance, the old crater near the top of Popocatepetl begins to shew its ragged lip distinctly.[1] Why can I not sketch? I would give anything for a good daguerreotype apparatus, which would enable me to present you with accurate representations of scenes which please me here.

I was going to say that I never would again go into foreign parts, without having one, but with my present feelings, I willingly ask you to terminate that sentence, as the little grammarian would say, with a full stop after the word "parts." Several Mexicans accompanied us and I noticed that they ate the stock of the corn as we do the sugar cane.

The men have stood the march pretty well. I started Derr on the pony placed at my disposal by Major W., but the poor fellow could n't stand it longer than about four miles, when I saw him leading him, saying that he was tired of riding.

We bivouac on a road, leading perpendicularly to

[1] A sketch was enclosed in letter.

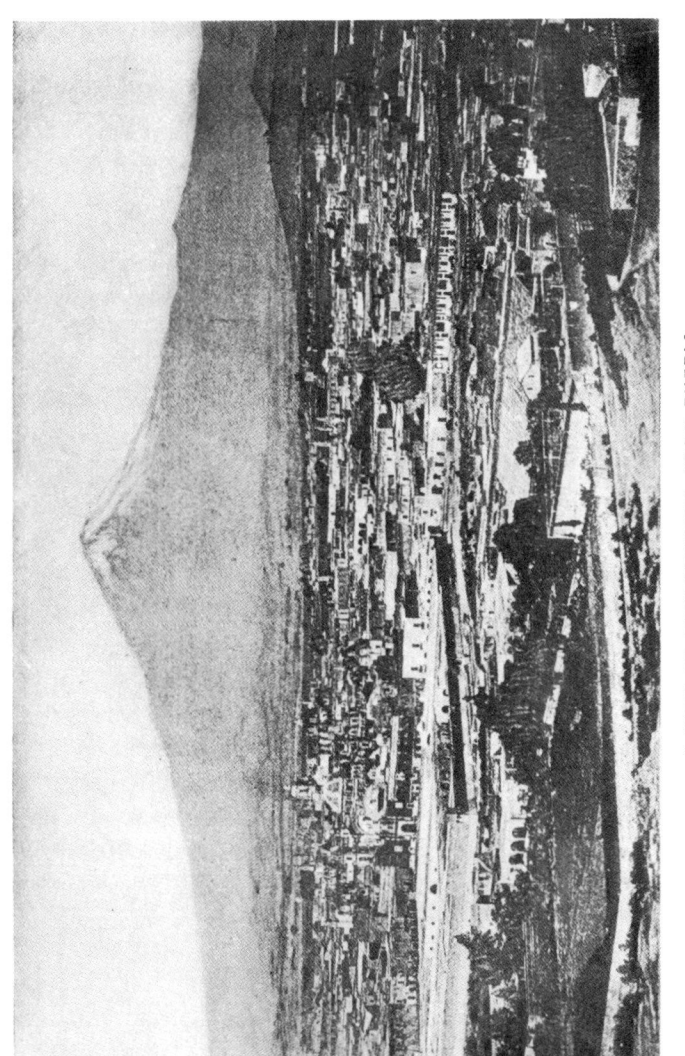

A VIEW OF POPOCATEPETL FROM PUEBLA
From an old photograph

the right from the main road, just giving room for the Officers' tents, and a passway between them and the stacks of arms, a broad ditch separating us, on either side, from a corn field in which our men, in despite of orders, will collect some fine roasting ears for their supper. Enough for one night's journal. Good-night, etc., etc.

SAN MARTIN EL GRANDE, ABOUT ELEVEN MILES FROM RIO PRIETO.
Tuesday, 10th.

After another dusty march, not quite so bad as yesterday, because of our not having as much wind, we reached this place at half-past twelve. The country, to be more particular, the land along the road, is very rich, the corn being higher and of richer growth than any I have seen in Mexico. The corn fields extend for miles along the road, which passes through them, separated by a ditch, the earth of which forms on the corn field side a tolerably steep embankment. The divisions between the fields appear to be mere lanes, or wide roads.

You see at the distance of a mile from the road, as you approach San Martin, a small piece enclosed by a post and rail fence, nearly the only one I have seen in this Country, and in the suburbs the fields of pepper and beans are enclosed by a fence of clay—unburnt brick, I suppose the book-makers would call it. I saw some Mexicans repairing a dam; this is secured by large pieces of sod, placed on each other, the grassy side up, rammed or beaten down by a large maul. You would have been amused to see them work—one man digs the sod, using for this a Mexican spade of wood, shod with iron; another man carries the sods on his back, using for this purpose the strap passing over his shoulders, as so often described.

In one field, I counted twenty-three ploughs at work, each drawn by two oxen, managed by means of the long goad, described in my letter about Cholula. By the bye, we see along the road constantly, pieces of pottery, giving the land the appearance of having been a huge potter's yard, "*à la Trollope.*"

About two hours after we halted, all were called to arms by the beating of the *generale*. A few lancers, it is said, were seen on some eminence around the town, which caused this *stampede*, as such false alarms are called; all expect another to-night. We are very unfortunate, as we have more in our Division than they have in either of the others. The love plant and the four o'clocks, with the morning glory, we saw apparently growing wild.

The first view, just as day was dawning this morning, of the top of Popocatepetl was more beautiful than any I have had. As you chanced to look in its direction, your attention might be caught by an exceedingly delicate white pyramid in the heavens; as the eye rests on it, it gradually assumes a more distinct and better marked outline and finally, at sunrise, the snow-clad mountain stands perfectly defined before you.

Early in the morning the snow is tinted with a beautiful tint of light blue. But the mountain, as first seen, just as the earliest rays of the rising sun kiss it, had to me the appearance of a dream: I can express the effect on me in no better manner. I wish I could so describe it to Mr. Weir, as to have it painted. 'T is said that the Indians called this mountain the "Blazing Star." As we must prepare for a stampede, I will now retire. Good-night, etc., etc.

In Mexico

CHALCO, Friday, 13th.

We were agreeably disappointed, in not being disturbed in our rest, what little the fleas did not deprive us of, at San Martin. That day's march was not very interesting—a few miles of the rich plain was passed, and we commenced the gradual ascent of the mountains separating the plains of Puebla, etc., from that of Mexico.

The road was pretty good for a mountain one; pine and oak, with an occasional undergrowth of laurel and two or three kinds of trees that I did not recognize as American friends, skirted our course. Coarse sandstone and pudding-stone with pieces of volcanic origin, were all I noticed in mineralogy.

At ten or eleven miles we crossed the bridge of Temalucan, and about four o'clock in a cold rain halted seven or eight miles further at Rio Frio, where I passed a very uncomfortable night. Yesterday morning, we started about six o'clock to halt, as we were informed, at the Venta de Cordova, a march of only eleven miles.

The country, this day, was much more broken than that passed over yesterday—a few miles this side of Rio Frio, we passed under several hills, where the Mexicans had completed, or commenced batteries, to defend the road. Had they made a stand there, we should have lost several of our brave troops, but the Mexicans must have lost their batteries.

At ten o'clock precisely, by my watch, on reaching the top of a little hill, my eyes caught the first view of the valley of Mexico. There it lay, as seen through the narrow opening made by the road, in the overhanging trees; a quiet landscape, having in the foreground a sheet of water; the portion of the valley visible blending itself imperceptibly in distant mountains, which could scarcely be distinguished, the day being at that moment cloudy, with a gentle mist from the clouds which rested on their sides.

Every turn of the road now opened to us a new or more extensive view in which the pictures were formed; every variety of green that could be formed by the varied light and shade of passing clouds and by real difference of shade, with mountains here, nearly in the foreground, there, in the distance, and beyond, limiting the view; and *lake*, in this part, almost undistinguishable from the grass and slime, which nearly covered it, to the clear water, in which the shadows of the passing clouds were visible; the picture studded with *haciendas*, some traced out by their huge mud walls enclosing immense courtyards, like fortifications, villages with churches, etc., presented views which were charming to those who hoped that there lay the City, from which they *must* return to their beloved homes.

Indeed, independent of everything, the scenery was beautiful. The descent was rapid and the view of our Division, which could be seen distinctly by looking ahead and in rear (we were near the rear), as it wound its way down compactly and rapidly, was the most beautiful panoramic picture I ever saw; our wagon train extended two or three miles, and could be seen with their white tops passing through the trees which shaded the road.

Everything from the Rio Frio to the Venta de Cordova was wild, not a trace of a house was visible; this day's march and that of yesterday, however, told us too plainly that man with all his worst passions had been there—the cross, *here*, of large pieces of wood, with the name of the murderer's victim, the year of his death, and an appeal to the passer-by to utter a prayer for the benefit of his soul; *there*, of two simple sticks, or a single one with the branches forming that holy emblem, marks the place of murder. In some places, a little kind of altar, scooped out of the rock, had the cross and name rudely cut.

The timber on the roadside was the same as that seen on the day before, but some of the oaks and pines were about three feet in diameter—the pines beautifully straight; on this side of the mountain we saw cedar in abundance. Along the route grew beautiful flowers, some of which would form valuable additions to our garden flowers.

We are now in a dirty village at the head of Lake Chalco, whose name it bears. The lake, or rather the slime covered water of the lake, is within two hundred yards of the shoemaker's shop we inhabit. The marketing is brought in canoes, which drawing little water are paddled through the slime and weeds.

Genl. Scott, who is on the main road leading between Lakes Chalco and Texcoco, paid Genl. Worth a visit this morning. He is in fine spirits, and has his engineers engaged to-day in reconnoitring the approaches, between those lakes, to the City. He hopes to succeed in turning Peñon Grande with its strong batteries, keeping its garrison in check by holding near it a strong force and reaching the suburbs of the City without the immense sacrifice the storming of that hill now surrounded by a sheet of water would cost us.

Genl. Worth has been directed to reconnoitre the road leading from our position around Lake Chalco to the rear of the City. The reconnoissance being completed, the Genl. will decide on his plan of attack and our Division *will lead*. We are collecting boats and timber to be used as may be deemed advisable. If necessary, the City may be approached by water from this and from several other points. An order has this moment been received, asking for the number of boat-builders and caulkers in our Division.

Genl. Pillow arrived this afternoon, with his Command, which is now in this place and in some haciendas near us. We shall soon have stirring times, in which, I fear, I shall not be able to keep up my daily conversations with you. Last night I did not write because of my being directed by our Dr. to change my quarters from those selected to dryer ones, making it late before I was fixed. The night before was too damp and cold for me to open my *escritoire*. But I will not now tire you by too long a talk. Good-night.

Saturday, 14th.

Last was a memorable night; we had been in bed just long enough to get comfortably into the first nap, when we were roused by Dr. Satterlee's entering and directing our Surgeon to go about five miles into the country where he would find Lt. Hamilton, an acting aid-de-camp of Genl. Scott's, badly wounded. The Dr. kept us awake some time before he got off, and returned in about an hour, having met the Infy. sent out with Lt. H. returning; by the Comdg. officer of which he was informed that Lt. H. was well taken care of in a hacienda, and under the care of a French doctor who was there, and that he was too sick to be moved.

Two wounded men were soon brought for the Doctor's attention, and as we were separated from the hospital by only a thin partition, balmy sleep paid us a very unsatisfactory and short visit, before reveille was beat.

Lt. Hamilton is now here, having been brought in on a litter. Dr. Holden says that he is in no immediate danger; last night he had a very profuse hemorrhage, and his life was despaired of. He started about twelve yesterday with an escort of Dragoons and Infantry, to bring a gentleman named Robinson into town, who is said to be well acquainted with the routes leading to Mexico.

The Infy. halted in a small village, from which they were enabled to watch, from an eminence, the advance of the Cavalry, which proceeded with Lt. Hamilton. The Cavalry had not proceeded far before they were surrounded by a body of Lancers, say about two hundred, who made furious charges on them—the contest, though very unequal, was well maintained by our men, numbering about seventy, for half an hour, when the enemy retreated.

The Infy. soon joined the Cavalry,—Lt. Hamilton was found badly speared, one Dragoon killed, another mortally wounded, and one of the officers of the native Spy Compy. slightly wounded. Six of the Mexicans were killed. I fear that Lt. H. may not survive, as his lungs are thought to be wounded. He is a very gentlemanly Officer.

Lt. Col. Duncan returned from a reconnoitring party this afternoon along the left shore of Lake Chalco; his report is, I learn, favorable, representing the road as perfectly practicable half way to the City, as far as he went.

The Engineers also finished their reconnoissances on the other roads, those between the Lakes Texcoco and Chalco. They were permitted by the Mexicans to pass around the Peñon, at about three hundred yards distance from it, without being fired upon. Another party advanced as far as the town of Mexicalsingo; the road to within three hundred yards of that place, was clear of any obstructions, then, it was considerably narrowed, and was completely swept by the guns of several batteries.

To-morrow I expect to see Genl. Scott's order for our advance. I marched on guard this morning with the Compy. but, in consequence of a very great change in the weather, a cold, ugly rain, the Dr. advised my being retired. I have therefore turned over the guard to the subaltern on duty with me, and am now in my Quarters. I the more willingly acquiesce in this, as I am convinced were I exposed to-night, I would have another attack of chills and fever, which would keep me from the coming fight. Good-night.

Sunday morning, 15th.

Orders have just been received, half-past eleven, that we are to start at three this afternoon—our Division, followed, I presume, by the others, approach Mexico by the road which has Lake Chalco on its right. We therefore strike the Capital in rear. Ft. Chapultepec will then be our first point of attack. I hope that I may have daily some opportunity of adding a few lines to this letter. I go on with a full and unwavering faith in the mercy and kindness of our Heavenly Father. He will do what is best for us. May He bless and preserve you. Good-day.

SAN GARGGORIO, Monday evening, 16th.

We left Chalco yesterday in a little sprinkle, but with every prospect of a heavy rain; we were, however, agreeably disappointed, as we reached our encamping ground, Tetelco, and passed the night without rain.

This morning's march, a short one, say of eight miles, was quietly made, as no enemy was seen, and no obstructions met with.

Genl. Scott, who did not leave Chalco till this morning, has arrived in our Camp. We halt, after our short march, to enable the new Divisions to come up. We are now about twelve miles from Mexico, and may have something to do to-morrow. Good-night.

> Tête de Pont, three and one half miles from Mexico.
> August 24, 1847.

The last great battle has, I hope, been fought in this ill fated Country. Our Army is now quietly awaiting the result of the labors of the Commissioners who are now occupied in their labors. The mail, which takes this, will, I think, give the news of what they accomplish. I am so far from Hd. Qrs., about five miles, that I really know nothing of what is being done there; I only know that there is a suspension of hostilities, and that the Army is now employed in securing ammunition taken in large quantities from the enemy, in attending to the wounded, and in preparations for any work they may be called on to perform.

First, as to myself—you will be as deeply mortified as I was, at learning that I was not engaged in any of the series of actions which placed us in our present victorious positions.

I started on horseback with the Compy. on the morning of the 20th, having been seriously indisposed for several days, and met Dr. Satterlee, who told me that I could not go, that the road leading to the position we were to occupy was impassable for horses, and it was nonsense for me to think of attempting to go on foot.

I told him how great my anxiety was to be in the fight; he said that he did not think we would have a fight, that we were to be placed in position to await events. I then remarked that I would see Dr. Holden. He agreed with me that I might attempt to go on. We advanced about a mile or two, when Dr. Holden came up, and told me that Dr. Satterlee told him that he ought to order me back, that I could not go on with the troops.

Feeling very badly, and hoping that there would be no fight, thus was I compelled to separate myself from the Regt. I halted, taking my faithful man Derr with me to San Antonio, the Genl. Hd. Qrs., and threw myself on my friend Capt. Irvin's bed, feeling wretchedly enough. My kind friends, Drs. Harney and Lawson, soon came to see me and to have my wants supplied.

At night, Genl. Scott and his Staff returned, from whom I learned the brilliant events of the day's work. Genl. Scott was in fine spirits, and I congratulated him from the bottom of my heart. He was for a little time much affected, and spoke in most affectionate terms of Father. He makes me take my meals and a cot in his room. The next day, finding that my Regt. was to advance with the rest of the Army, and almost hoping that there would be another battle, I determined at all risks to join my Compy. and—*me voici*, I hope with a heart ready for any service, but much chastened by the accounts received of the suffering of the dying and wounded on the battlefield, and of those who have since been placed under the knives of the surgeons.

The newspapers will give you fuller and better accounts than I can, but I will give you an imperfect sketch. The Army left Puebla in successive Divisions on the 7th, 8th, 9th, and 10th days of this month, was placed in quarters and in bivouacs on the plain of Mexico on the 14th inst. On the afternoon of the 13th, Lt. S. Hamilton, aid-de-camp to Genl. Scott, was lanced near Chalco, the then position of the 1st Division.

The 2nd Division was on the main road leading to Mexico, which the Engineers had been reconnoitring. Genl. Scott, after full reconnoissances, determined to approach the City by the road leading along Lakes Chalco and Xochimilco, and the 1st Division leading the advance started from Chalco on Sunday afternoon, 15th inst.

By short marches, we approached, seeing nothing of the enemy till the morning of the 17th when he shewed himself in small parties along the eminences skirting the road; from these positions he was soon driven by our skirmishers. One man of our Division was wounded. We halted that night in San Augustin.

Early the next morning, 18th, a field work having been discovered on the road to Mexico, we were ordered forward, our Brigade leading, all expecting and anxious for a fight. We advanced, say a mile, when we were halted, and had been there about half an hour when we heard that Capt. Thornton, 2nd Dragoons, had been killed while covering a party of our Engineers reconnoitring the work we expected to take, San Antonio.

A diagonal movement, across a field towards a hacienda on the right, showed the knowing ones that the work was not then to be attacked in front. The Division was kept under arms, and parties of Engineers despatched in various directions, to ascertain if the work could not be turned. The reports were not made till night, when it was found that the work was too strong for a front attack, but that there was a trail which might be rendered practicable for Infy. leading to its flank.

Our troops remained on wet ground and under a succession of heavy showers of rain during most of this day. We bivouacked at night in the hacienda. The next day, 19th, the army awaited the arrival of the Divisions of Twiggs and Quitman, reported near, and the further reconnoissances of our Engineers.

Towards afternoon, Pillow was ordered to cover a road-making party, engaged in opening a road leading farther to the left than the one we were on. A fire was soon opened on this party, from a strong field-work, *contrarios*, occupied by the enemy. It was actively sustained till night without any result. Early the morning of the 20th this work was carried by Genl. P. Smith (Rifles) and our gallant friend Col. Riley.

This attack not having been made at as early an hour as was anticipated, our Brigade was ordered to the support of the troops designated for the attack. On our approach, the firing had already ceased, the work having been taken. I was ordered back.

The Brigade soon received orders to countermarch, and advancing rapidly up the road, from which we had turned off on the 18th, found the enemy, having abandoned their work, in retreat. Quick pursuit was given, and the first intimation given of proximity to another work was the reception of a fire of grape from its guns. The Division was ordered to turn into a corn field on the right of the road, and to *storm* the work.

Our Regt., the storming party nearest the road, advanced under a galling fire of grape and musketry, to the edge of the corn field, when the number of men in advance was deemed entirely inadequate to assault the strong field-work, then seen about 100 yards in front of them.

It had two four-pound guns, two heavy pieces, one an 18 pounder, and its parapets lined by perhaps 2500 men. In this field, and near the edge of it, our loss was very severe. "G" Co. lost its Orderly Sergt. Brown (an invaluable soldier, who received two mortal wounds) and three privates; Porter, the Artificer, slightly wounded, and seven privates, wounded, none I hope severely. My loss was greater in proportion to my strength than either of the other Companies.

Major Wade was the only Officer of our Regt. wounded, a ball passed through the fleshy part of his leg—the calf. We have to mourn the death of many brave friends; Captains Capron and Burke (of Tampa Bay Memory), the two youngest Capts. in the 1st Arty., were shot dead. In this, I hear I was misinformed; Capt. C. lived about half an hour. Capt. B. was first shot through the hand, fainted, and as he was being borne off the field, was killed by another ball. Poor Mrs. Capron and her children, it makes my heart bleed to think of them. Capt. P. Butler, S. C., fell at the head of his Regt. which had faltered under a deadly fire. Capt. W. Anderson, 2nd. Infy., was mortally wounded.

I have not time to mention the gallant actions fought by the other Divisions. Four distinct and hard contested works were carried that day. In the work taken by our Division, and in which in the morning there were 5000 men, I am now writing. It is the strongest field of fortification I ever saw.

Col. Butler was the highest officer in rank who fell. Col. Ward Burnett, N. Y. Regt., was wounded Aug. 20th

Col. Burnett had the *lockjaw* for two weeks, and is now out on his crutches. Capt. P. Kearney, 1st Dragoons, lost his left arm; it has been amputated above the shoulder.

The papers will give exceedingly interesting and full details of all the incidents of the day. For ourselves, let us unite in thanks to our Heavenly Father for our preservation. For His own good purpose I have been thwarted in one of my heartfelt wishes. He knows best.

I must now send this to Hd. Qrs. as an express will certainly be despatched the moment the Commissioners report. That God will continue to guard and preserve you, and soon restore me to you, is my sincere prayer. Be not alarmed about me, it is only a touch of the old Florida complaint, produced by exposure to wet, and sleeping in wet clothes. A few days' rest will soon restore me.

TACUBAYA, Friday, Aug. 27th.

This poor letter was sent and returned with a statement that there was no mail, and that it was uncertain when one would be sent. I shall, however, finish it as one of my regular series, and send it by the first opportunity.

Lieut. Johnson of our Regt. says that he must go to the United States with the first escort. On the morning of the 25th my long threatened touch of fever and chill visited me. It was produced undoubtedly by the dampness of the position in which we were bivouacked. Yesterday morning, we were marched to this place, where, having a comfortable room, I shall get well, as I can now take care of myself.

Last night we were under orders to be prepared with

sixty rounds of cartridges for a night attack, but the storm blew over. It is said to have been caused by the conduct of the Mexicans in not permitting our wagons to enter the City for supplies, as agreed upon by the terms of the Armistice. Just as night approached, however, Genl. Santa Anna sent a communication to Genl. S. that Commissioners had been appointed who would meet Mr. Trist this day. The meeting, I presume, took place, as Mr. Trist passed out of town with an Escort about the appointed time.

So I hope the good work of peace-making has been commenced. 'T is reported that our wagoners were fired upon to-day and that Santa Anna's troops fired at the mob who did it. They appear sore under the gentle thrashing they have received and have not perhaps had enough to keep them quiet.

Lt. Judd, who has improved very much since I last mentioned him, informs me that Genl. Quitman intends returning to the United States. He came out not to make political capital, but to fight, and is, I presume, disheartened at not being engaged in the last battles. He is, perhaps, the best of the appointments, and I shall regret his leaving us; he is a gentleman; his successor may, by accident, be one.

Poor Lt. Irvin, shot through the neck, just in front of the jugular vein, is, I fear, too badly wounded to recover. Of the Armistice I say nothing special, as the newspapers will present you with a copy, perhaps, some time before you receive this, as I do not doubt that Mr. Kendall sent some days ago his report of the battle, and as soon as concluded, a copy of the Articles of the Armistice.

If report be true, and in this case I cannot doubt it, the 3rd Arty. has been cruelly treated by Genl. Worth and Col. Garland. Col. Belton gave a full report, giving in detail all the operations of the 20th as far as the 3rd was an actor, and spoke in high terms of the conduct of some, perhaps all the Officers; this report was returned, with instructions.

Col. G. stated from Genl. W. that all should be omitted but the simple fact that at such an hour the Regt. entered the field-work, and 't is said that no mention is made of an Officer of the 3rd, that its Commander even is not named.[1] 'T is too strange, almost, to be true.

Col. B. is very blamable for altering his report, if he did so, to suit the fancy or whim of his superior. He is, however, Commissioner to see the terms of the Armistice complied with, and cares very little for the Regiment.

The order given to the Regt. on that day to storm a work which had not been reconnoitred, can hardly be sustained before military men, and caused the loss of many of our best soldiers. Alas, alas, what is fame, what is glory? 'T is but the soldier's dream. It haunts him in his slumbers, and shortens the long weary night with its pleasing apparition, but after passing through the maddening excitement of the morrow's battle, all his hopes are crushed by the envy, prejudice, or folly of those whose duty it is to protect and advance him, and he finds a Staff Officer who did literally nothing praised for high gallantry.

I think I had better lay down my pen for to-night as I cannot now write with patience on the subject I

[1] Capt. Anderson was, be it remembered, not in this battle, or these remarks would not have been made.

have touched. Making a few remarks about the wounded, I will close for the night.

Lt. Hamilton is doing very well. Major Wade is also rapidly improving; in ten days more, I hope he will be walking about. Lt. Kearney is also doing as well as could be hoped for. And now, my wife, accept my best prayers and wishes that we may soon meet, not to be again separated till the great summons calls us, after a happy and contented life here, to a better existence in Heaven.

28th. I have just learned that the courier of the British Minister will take this, and hasten to enclose it.

No. 19. TACUBAYA, MEXICO.
August 28, 1847.

I hastily finished and attempted to despatch by the messenger of the British Minister, who leaves to-morrow morning, a supplement to No. 18, but I fear that the letter was sent too late, as I hear that the packages were made up this morning, before I learned that he would take letters for our officers. This mischance, if it prove one, I shall regret most deeply, as I am certain that many of my friends will mourn my death instead of Capt. J. W. Anderson, 2nd Infy. You will see the name correctly reported in the *Picayune*, as I requested Mr. Kendall to be particular in his report.

Poor Lt. Irvin, whose case was mentioned in my last letter, died yesterday and was buried to-day. He was a fine gallant soldier. Major Wade and Capt. Kearney, both of whom I saw to-day, are doing well. Our loss in the actions of the 20th collectively, called the Battle of Mexico, as it extended to the gates of the City (Capt. Kearney being shot when fifty or seventy yards from its wall), amounts in killed and wounded to 1052, (I think exactly) nearly one seventh of those engaged, as I do not suppose that there were as many as 8000 in the fight.

The loss of the enemy must exceed 5000, as the ground was in places thickly strewn with their dead and wounded men. What a sacrifice of life! God grant that Victory may be crowned with Peace. We cannot stand many such victories.

The impression in high quarters is, that a treaty will be concluded, and then for home, never, no never, to leave my beloved land to fight again in foreign lands.

Our soldiers and Army followers are behaving badly, robbing and insulting the Mexicans; this has caused the assembling of a Milty. Commission, of which I am Judge Advocate, which is to meet from time to time as cases may occur.

No attention is given to the fact of my having been Recorder to the Court of Inquiry, which closed its proceedings in Capt. Riley's case just before we left Puebla. Genl. Worth said he wanted me, and presto, detail was overlooked, and out came the order. So long as there is a hope of our having peace and being permitted soon to return home, I am willing to do, double, all duty. Home, how simple the word, and yet how much does it carry to, or excite in, the heart of one who, for long and tedious months, has thought years *might* elapse ere he could see *his home*. God grant that this may prove no fond dream, but a sweet reality. I do not permit myself, even now, to indulge too sanguinely in the hope that peace may be made, as some contretemps, the folly and obstinacy of the Mexican Congress, an outbreak in the City—something may happen which would break off negotiations and plunge us again into uncertainty, and active, bloody war. Mexico is at our mercy, and falls into our hands soon after the firing of the first gun, and woe, woe to the City if our Army enter it, after a bloody resistance. I dare not think of it. The sight of a sacked City either maddens the brain, or breaks the heart of a sensitive person. Enough for to-night. God keep me from ever witnessing, or being an actor in such scenes.

Sunday, August 29th.

Our Commission met this morning in compliance with our order, but adjourned over till to-morrow morning, when we meet in the Cortina Palace. In Madame Calderon's pleasant book on Mexico, you may remember her speaking of this family, this house and its fine collection of paintings. I shall take occasion to examine the paintings. As yet, though I have seen some thousands of paintings in the Churches in this Country, I have not seen one that I would call a great work. I am anxious to visit the City, where I presume some of the best paintings may be seen.

I have not heard what progress Mr. Trist is making in his treaty-making, but was told by Capt. Scott, of the General's Staff, this morning that everything was going on well.

Whilst impressions are fresh on my mind, I may as well state the differences I observe between the Mexicans this side the mountains and those at Puebla. The race is larger than those I saw beyond the mountains. Their features, too, differ very considerably;—the face is perhaps longer, with higher forehead, and cheek bones less projecting, the complexion is lighter.

It may be wrong to generalize until I see masses in

Mexico, as I did at Puebla. This being a small place, we see but few; the women are not handsome, perhaps better looking than the Pueblans. Less use is made of earthen ware than at Puebla; here, copper vessels tinned are apparently in quite general use in the kitchens.

The water-carriers do not use the Egyptian vessels I attempted to describe in one of my letters, but one of a pitcher-like form, with one handle—two are suspended from the end of a stick, which is supported on the shoulders.[1] If these pitchers do not balance well, 't is because I am not accustomed to carrying them, because that is the way; they are frequently steadied by the hands being placed against the handles, *that* you may imagine.

Whether the descendants of the Aztecs are as remarkable for their sobriety as are their transmontane brothers, I am not prepared to say.

In our market here we have oranges, pineapples, bananas, limes, pears, apples, and peaches. The vegetables are the same I have mentioned as being in the Puebla market. I purchased a fine head of cauliflower this morning.

The scamps have raised the prices on us; in small places they always do—in Mexico we could purchase marketing much cheaper. I did not mention that at Chalco we had the guava in market and in Puebla, just before we left, I saw a few beets.

Monday, August 30th.

This has been quite a busy day; the trial before our Commission and bringing up our proceedings engaged me till nearly dark, and then, in consequence

[1] A sketch was enclosed in letter.

of Sergt. Brown's death, as there was no one who understood anything about the papers for muster tomorrow, I was compelled to take hold of them.

I will not omit, however, having a chat with you, which must be short, as I have to prepare a charge against a man whom I shall take before the Commission for trial to-morrow.

I saw Mr. Trist, this morning; he appears to be in very good spirits in relation to his duties and progress in them. Herrara, the head of the Mexican Commissioners, formerly President for a short period, is considered the most honest and honorable of their public men. His being on the Commission augurs well, I think. There may be some shuffling in the Congress, which may prevent its ratification. *Nous verrons.*

The view from the highest point of this City is magnificent: the great City of Mexico, with Ft. Chapultepec in the foreground, on the left of the picture, and beyond and around the City, a highly cultivated plain interspersed with lake and mountain, or intersected by turbulent little mountain rivers; the whole surrounded by mountains, among which, in fair weather, we still see our old friends, Popocatepetl and Iztaccihuatl, presents a view well worthy of the artist's pencil.

In the plain, among other trees, we see lines or avenues of trees resembling somewhat our Lombardy poplars, but which, whether from the vastness of the plain or the background of lofty mountains, are, however, unlike the barrenness of our broomstick tree, and really produce a pleasing effect in the landscape. Good-night.

Tuesday, August 31st.

The last day of this year's summer has gone—will

the ensuing fall months be more quiet than, or as turbulent as, those that have just passed away, or will they return me to my beloved family? Would that I could command an affirmative answer to the latter query. All at Hd. Qrs. seem to think that the last battle has been fought. I hope that they may not be deceived. From our Court-room, I stole off for a few minutes to see some of the pictures in the Palace. I only examined rapidly a few that are in a bedroom. One, a very sweet face, is a young lady asleep—modern, but very prettily colored. An old painting comes next, representing a Spanish lady, of the age perhaps of Isabella, very well executed, a valuable painting. The remarkably fine large head in front of you as you turn your back to the light, is modern; the keys in his hand designate St. Peter. This is a good picture, but does not present to my mind the characteristic expression of the features of the great Apostle.

But your eye, I see, wanders to, and is now fixed admiringly upon, that sweet picture in the corner on your left. It is a lovable picture, modern, but charming. A young mother kissing and oh, so sweetly kissed by her infant. 'T is the waking morning kiss. The mother is partially raised in bed, and holds her child, who has just waked, in her arms. (I correct here, the mother, in her night-dress, leans over her infant, as if raising her from her crib.) The little hand which seeks for the fountain of nourishment, shews that the little angel thinks of something besides the loving kiss she takes and gives. How I wish you could see this picture. There are many others in the house, but this is, I fancy, to be my favorite. If I can get a good daguerreotypist here, I will endeavor to bring you a view of this charming work. Both faces are beautiful; easy and graceful is every attitude of each.

I find that I did an injustice to Genl. Worth in my remark about the returning of Col. Belton's report,— he only wished Col. Belton to omit the tactical part of the report, and desired him to mention all Officers who had particularly distinguished themselves. Col. B. got in a pet, and struck out all mention of the Officers.

September 8th.

Though I am now engaged on another sheet to complete No. 19, I will send this as it is, reserving the other part for another opportunity. Yesterday, I sent a letter by Mr. Kendall's express. I have this morning heard that Genl. Quitman and Lt. Welsh are to leave to-morrow morning for the United States and have determined to trust my budget to them. The chances are that they will go safely through—I pray to God that they may—for their lives are of value to our Country. I must now close, as 't is time to send the messenger off. Nos. 14 to 19 inclusive are sent in three packages.

Sunday, September 26th.

I close this to send by the Minister's Express.

Wednesday, September 1st.

I am so completely wearied with my day's writing (as Judge Advocate of a Military Commission) that I can only give you my blessing, and say good-night.

Thursday, September 2nd.

The Commission, fortunately for me, adjourned this

morning, to give the prisoner, a Mexican, time to get his witnesses. I have thus had a day of rest, and am, thank God, quite fresh again. Cases multiply in about the proportion of those we try, so that we have a prospect of having occupation as long as we remain. Indeed, Genl. Worth told me that he intended keeping us as a permanent Court. One advantage may be derived from my being on this duty, as it will prevent my being put on other duty which would expose me to the changes of weather, the very thing now to be avoided.

I was so much fatigued yesterday, that I did not mention my morning's visit to Count Cortina's picture rooms; there are six, I think. It is the most valuable collection I ever saw. I was disappointed in two which were called Murillo's: two mothers with infants; they did not strike me as very remarkable. There are several in the collection, by painters unknown, I prefer to these two. The subjects are so numerous that I cannot attempt naming them, much less to describe what I think are their beauties. I passed rapidly, too rapidly, through the rooms, knowing that I had a great deal of writing to be finished by nine this morning. And again, I hope to enjoy again and again, the pleasure of entering those rooms. I went again to see the mother and infant; as a work of art, it has superiors in the collection, but not one seemed to me so sweet, so lovely. There is a playful, roguish archness in the darling, as it steals to uncover the mother's breast, inexpressibly sweet. The Count is said to be the richest man in Mexico; his heirs would not miss the picture, were he to give it to me.

At the General's Quarters this morning, I again heard that Mr. Trist was in fine spirits as to his prospects. I hope that he is not a sanguine man. I wrote hastily to you this afternoon, the letter to go by Mr. Kendall's express. I am anxious that you should receive it, or the one sent on the 29th ult. May you get one or both, as your mind will then be relieved.

September 3rd.

I was about taking my seat at my table, after dinner to-day, to bring up my day's proceedings, when Lt. Andrews came in, and said that Genl. Quitman and Lt. Welch, were to start to-morrow morning for the United States, and that if I would get my letters ready in fifteen or twenty minutes, he would send them down. Business was readily laid aside, and all my old talks, from No. 14 to 19 inclusive, were folded, sealed and directed by the time appointed. I had barely time to add a few lines to the first part of this No. 19. To Mother, I was very anxious to write, but the notice was too short. I hear since our letters were sent, that Genl. Quitman will not leave to-morrow; if so, I may still add another letter to your already large stock, and also write one to my Mother. This has been a very busy day with me, and as it is now late, and I feel much exhausted, I must to bed, and now good-night.

Saturday, September 4th.

Our Commission, like a Christian, a reasonable body of men, adjourned over till Monday, so that to-morrow I shall be necessarily engaged only a small part of the day. I have just returned from Genl. Scott, with whom I dined. He shewed me his report; it is long, but will be read with great interest by all Americans, as he gives a clear and vivid sketch of the events of the 20th.

An Artillery Officer

My poor Regiment is not, I think, named in the Report, not that it did not perform its duty, but because it performed no brilliant achievement; it was not the foremost in entering field-work before which so many of our brave men fell. I should have been mortified to death had I been with the Regt. and could not have carved some bauble of honor. They may be baubles, but they are welcome, and, generally, dearly bought prizes to us. And though no one knows more truly than the soldier how many blanks there are in the wheel of Fortune, to one prize, still, like the gambler, he ventures o'er and o'er, even health and life itself, to win that prize.

The commencement and some of the concluding paragraphs of the General's report (that of the 20th) are beautifully and forcibly worded. The sub-reports I have not read, but I have no doubt that every one who made a report looked more particularly to elevating self on the ladder, than to doing justice to those who were under his command.

Genl. Shields and Genl. P. Smith distinguished themselves greatly on that day. Genl. Smith stands as high with the Army for good sense and military qualifications as perhaps any man of his rank with us. Mr. Trist, who lives with the Genl., appeared in good spirits to-day. I asked him, however, no questions about his duties, or what I so much desire to know, what he thinks of the prospects of peace. This state of uncertainty must ere long come to an end, as the points in dispute cannot certainly occupy reasonable men longer than a couple of weeks more—and that time, to regard it as intervening between this period and that when we *may* know when we are to go home, appears *an age*. Good-night.

Sunday, September 5th.

I feel so wretchedly, to-night, that were it not Sunday I do not think that I could say even a few words to you. We fancy that very important and interesting events are taking place in the City to-day. Heavy firing we think we heard, and continued, too, for some time. If this be so, Santa Anna must have been engaged in quelling some pronunciamiento. He is so shrewd that it is probable that he foresaw and was prepared. In that case if his Army prove faithful, he will place himself more firmly in power, in consequence of the riot. If his Army participated in the disaffection, he will certainly be hurled from his high, but usurped, position. To-morrow we shall know whether our speculations and imaginations are true or not, and I hope that I shall then feel well enough to write to you. May God keep you both in health and happiness.

Monday, September 6th.

Only a word or two to-night. For really I am so much out of spirits at this continuance of my indisposition, at the very time I may desire to have all my energies. The Mexicans are acting in bad faith to-day, and I learn that Genl. Scott has sent word to Santa Anna that unless an apology be sent to-morrow for the violation of the truce to-day, our batteries will open to-morrow at 12 M.

The troops in Ft. Chapultepec have been seen at work at its defences to-day, in clear violation of the Articles of the truce. All of our wounded and sick are now being moved to what is called the Palace, a building belonging, I think, to Genl. Santa Anna.

Chill and fever again this morning! Is this not *too* hard? I take a dose to-night which will, I hope, get everything right by Wednesday, and we shall scarcely have any heavy work before that day. Our troops lie, to-night, ready to move at a moment's warning. I *must* be in the next fight.

Tuesday, September 7th, three P.M.

We have been ready for the last three hours to move at a moment's warning. The truce was broken yesterday, by the Mexicans, and this morning, Genl. Santa Anna, I hear, wrote and sent a very impertinent "buncombe" letter to the Genl. Their troops, at all events, commenced moving out of the City early this morning, and are now drawn up in line of battle with their left resting on Ft. Chapultepec. Genl. Scott and Staff are engaged in reconnoitring his position, so that not many hours can elapse before we have another battle.

What Santa Anna expects to gain by the great loss of blood which must flow in such an event, I cannot conceive, unless it be that the numbers of the Mexicans are so greatly over the handful of men *our* Govt. has sent here as its Army, that he can well give us a few battles, five to one, and knows that in this way we must soon be annihilated.

So constantly has victory perched on our banners under every disadvantage and with every odds against us, that we may well hope and believe that God is fighting our battles with us, or rather for us.

Whilst midway of the last sentence, we were called out by the cry that "the Mexicans are coming," but soon finding that it was a false alarm, we returned to our quarters. I begin now to doubt whether we will have a fight to-night, or not. Perhaps we may make a night attack, perhaps the battle will be fought to-morrow.

SCENE AT THE BATTLE OF MOLINO DEL REY
From an engraving of the painting by Chappel

In Mexico

Should God spare my life, I will resume this letter the earliest moment after victory. That He may continue to guard and guide you in your path to Heaven I humbly pray.

MEXICO, September 22nd.

This day two weeks ago since I was wounded. Oh, how devotedly I should offer thanks to our Heavenly Father for His preservation of my life on that dreadful day. The papers will give you full details of our losses in killed and wounded. I will now, as I cannot write much at a time, confine my remarks to what will be most interesting to you.

Leaving our Quarters about half-past two A.M., 8th Sept., we, after being kept a long time in the streets of Tacubaya, reached our position in front of the building called the Foundry, and better known as "El Molino del Rey," our men were ordered to lie down on the road, so as to conceal themselves from the observation of the troops in Ft. Chapultepec. We remained there until a few discharges had been made by our Arty. when, just before sunrise, we were ordered to advance.

The firing of musketry and cannon was at this time very severe on our left. We approached and when within about two hundred yards of the Foundry, we were received with an awful shower of grape and musketry, the column was ordered to halt, and the men ordered to shelter themselves against the wall on our right, the angle here making a shoulder which partially protected our troops.

This rough sketch[1] may help me a little. The line at the right and top, marked "*a-a-a-*" is where the troops took shelter from the fire of the enemy, who

---
[1] A diagram was enclosed in letter.

lined the housetop in every part. When we had remained a short time there, two of Capt. Drum's guns were unlimbered and, seeing that there were few men at the first, which they were bringing up by hand, I, more for example's sake than anything else, assisted at it. This gun was placed in position, and commenced firing. I then stepped a few paces back, and observing that the men were slow in bringing the other gun forward, I took hold of the trail, which I left as soon as it was in position, and when I saw men enough at it to manage it.

I then hurried towards the Regt., which was then some paces in the rear, when I felt a severe blow against my right shoulder; it was like the blow from the ball in a leaded cane;—I supposed that it was a *spent ball* which had hit me, and fallen to the ground—another step and I felt a tingling pricking sensation in my left arm. I, without raising my hand or giving any intimation of being wounded, regained my Command, and on my remarking to some Officer that I believed I had been touched by a spent ball, was told that there was blood on my cloak. In a few minutes, I heard some one call out, "Come on, they are abandoning their battery." I stepped out and saw Lt. Prince, 4th Infy., in the road, waving his hand (the 4th and 6th Regts. Infy. were in front or advance of us). I immediately called out "Forward 3rd Arty.," and rushed forward. Lt. Prince was shot down while he was calling out. I found myself under the enclosure of the Foundry, the enemy still lining its walls.

My wound giving me much pain, had now rendered me a little less vigorous than I was, and I was joined by Lt. Andrews and Capt. Ayres and went forward. Mr. Andrews begged me to send for more men, as the

In Mexico

Mexicans were in too great force for us to enter the passageway marked (X), the enemy being in considerable numbers in the enclosure (d) and on the walls around it. Getting a half dozen men more, I went forward and entered the enclosure under a pretty galling fire. As I passed through the passageway, a ball grazed my right leg, grazing the bone outside about three inches below the knee.

We had tolerably warm work in retaining possession of this place, and in killing and driving the enemy from it. He made repeated attempts to dislodge us, but, thanks to God, did not succeed. In about two hours officers came in with re-enforcements, who ranked me, and then all the fighting, responsibility, and excitement being over, and my wound becoming stiff, I realized that I felt discomfort from my wound. A drink of spirits from a soldier's canteen revived me, but in a few minutes I fell.

In a half hour I was on my way to my quarters, Lt. Andrews kindly accompanying me. Dr. Harney soon came to see me and told me that the ball was in me but would do no harm. Without probing the wound, or allowing anything to be done to give me pain, he ordered a poultice of bread and milk, or water to be applied. I am now using the same kind. My wound is about three inches below the point of the shoulder, and the ball, Dr. Steiner (who probed the wound for me to-day) thinks, is under the knot of muscles under my arm. The hits on my left arm are from slugs or buckshot and though they leave a mark, are nothing. The Doctors say that I must have been shot by some Mexican above me; if so, it must have been as I faced to the left at the trail of the second gun and the man must have been on the wall at the angle "c."

On the 11th I was taken in my "old camp bed-cot," to Mixcoac where I was kindly received by Lt. Caldwell, U. S. Marines, and remained with him, Dr. Harney coming to see me two or three times each day, till the 18th when I came to this City, my cot being placed as it stands in an Ambulance.

I remained that night in Genl. Tornel's house, used as a Hospital for the Officers of the 1st Division, and the next day came to the Qrs. I now occupy,—a room in Genl. Valentia's house. My house mates are Major Wade, whose wound is doing well, Capt. Huger and his three Ordnance Subalterns.

The battle of the 13th of course I missed. My old cloak (which I wore on the 8th thinking I would have a chill that day, having had one on the 6th) bears the marks of service. Thanks be to Almighty God for my preservation; the fire was more severe than I ever thought it could be in battle. For a few moments I was apprehensive that we must either be cut down or driven back, but God gave us the victory. The enemy's forces more than quintupled ours. Poor Lt. Col. Graham fell, gallantly cheering his men on. I have written too much and will stop for to-day.

Thursday, September 23rd.

I find that my letter to you from Tacubaya which I endeavored to have sent by the Br. Courier, did not go. Most deeply do I regret this, as I fear the one which was taken two or three days ago has been captured by some of the guerrilla bands that infest every part of the road to Vera Cruz. The City has been quiet since I entered it. But an order of Genl. Scott's, published yesterday, informs us that there is a conspiracy headed by some cowardly officers and

THE BATTLE OF CHAPULTEPEC
From an engraving by J. Duthie after the painting by H. Billings

false priests to assassinate our brave little Army. The principal conspirator is said to be an Irish priest, named McNamara, who has been tampering with our soldiers, offering them lands in California if they desert, etc., etc. I hope, if the evidence is conclusive against him, that he will be hung.

Santa Anna, the night he fled, opened the prison doors, letting loose the scoundrels who were undergoing their just punishment for murder, robbery, and other crimes. These are some of the tools he designed to be used in this conspiracy. The Genl. enjoins vigilance on officers and men, and will doubtless take all possible means to detect and stifle this vile plot. I cannot but think that we are here to carry out some great scheme of Providence, and that God will interpose his powerful arm in our defence and protection. We hear that Genl. Patterson brings from Brazos about 4000 men. Having written as much as I ought, I will here stop.

Friday, 24th.

Dr. Steiner has changed my dressing, having given me a simple layer of lint, kept in place by thin strips of adhesive plaster. He says that the wound has a healthy appearance and that it is doing well.

To-day I have been shopping, intending to procure some engravings for you, representing the manners and customs of the Indians of the Country. I succeeded in getting only three, and fear that I will not be able to procure any more. I amuse myself walking a short distance down the street, looking at their stores, some of which excel, in the richness of their goods, anything I ever saw in the United States. But such prices! A man who furnishes his house here as many of them are furnished, must be rich indeed.

I saw Genl. Bravo's saddle to-day, the seat worked with gold and with much rich ornamental work about it: it cost the genteel sum of five hundred dollars. I have not visited the market or any of the public buildings, but hope in a week to be well enough to wear my coat, when I will take my time in examining the curiosities of the City. Good-night.

No. 20.   Mexico, October 1, 1847.

Thanks be to God, for so far having restored me to health as to enable me to resume my nightly conversations with my wife. Will the letters despatched by the Br. Minister's Express on the 28th ult. and the note sent this morning by private express reach you? I hope they, or at least one of them may, for I know the interest, the almost burning anxiety which you will feel, till you have it from my own hand that I am safe.

My wound is now nearly well; the new skin commenced forming over its edges yesterday. Yesterday, too, was the first day that I have been able to shave myself; the task was executed, I assure you, with a thankful heart, and almost boyish delight, but the day previous was not quite so delightful a day to me, as I had my old enemy, a chill, succeeded by a most burning and long continued fever. Under Dr. Steiner's prescriptions (he comes and dresses my wound daily), I took eleven pills yesterday and this morning, and I have missed the chill to-day. I presume that I shall have to take quinine for a long time.

This attack has delayed my moving to Genl. Scott's Quarters. I shall go to-morrow should nothing occur to prevent it.

To-day I sent for Sergt. Robinson, who was very ac-

In Mexico

tive in procuring additional men for us when we first entered the Foundry on the 8th Sept., and thanked him for his valuable services. He seemed highly gratified at what I said to him. On the 8th I recommended for promotion to a Corporalcy, one of the privates of "G" Co. whose conduct was reported to me as having been very gallant; Capt. Burke handsomely acceded to my recommendation, and he was appointed on the field of battle. My poor Company is cruelly cut up; I shall resume its command with melancholy feelings. Leaving Vera Cruz with nearly a hundred in its ranks, I shall now find its privates reduced by death and absentees in the hospitals, to less than thirty. I feel that I have written enough for to-night. Good-night.

Sunday, 3rd.

Yesterday, I moved to Genl. Hd. Qrs. where I am now very comfortably at home. Mr. Trist is the only fellow-liver with the Genl. Thinking yesterday, that, as I was coming here, I would spruce up a little, I had my suspenders put on, and wore them all day. Last night I suffered for my folly, their pressure on the muscles just below the point of the shoulder giving me an uneasy stiffness and heaviness of my shoulder all night. Dr. Steiner says he never knew a similar wound to heal as well and rapidly as mine has. He says that had the ball penetrated perpendicularly at the point where it struck, I must certainly either have lost my life instantly, or that amputation must have been made at the shoulder joint. It was deflected from its course, turning down the arm, by the muscles. Every day's reflection convinces me more and more of the vastness of my obligation to God, for having preserved my life on that dark and most bloody day. Oh, that my gratitude may effect a salutary change in my cold and sinful heart.

To-day, I am wearing my old comfort, the morning gown, properly, with the right arm in its sleeve—the first day I have done so; I am still compelled to wear my night-shirts, as they only are sufficiently large for me to put on and off with any comfort, and to enable the Dr. to dress my wound. I have now been using simple salve on the lint four days. Dr. Steiner is very attentive. I am not sure whether I mentioned that my *valet* was wounded the same day I was. He was wounded in the breast, the ball grazing the breast bone, and passing horizontally out about three inches from the first hole where it entered. I have kept him with me, though, until I moved here, I have had another man with me, a young soldier, named Hart,[1] who has been exceedingly kind and attentive. I shall miss his services much, as he is much smarter and quicker than my firm friend Derr.

Yesterday at a quarter to eight A.M. we experienced the severest earthquake I ever felt. The house shook and undulated so *sea-like* as to make many persons sea-sick. The Mexicans threw themselves on their knees, and so remained till all was again still. Old Popocatepetl must have been thinking of paying us a prank, reminding us that his volcanic fires are not extinct. The gentleman, now Prussian Minister to Washington, found its fires active enough to throw stones nearly to the top of the crater, when he visited its edges some ten years ago.

Rumor states to-day that Genl. Taylor is marching

---

[1] Hart was taken down by my mother to Ft. Sumter, remained with my father, and hoisted the Flag after it was shot down.

towards San Luis Potosi. The Genl. discredits the report. Enough writing for to-day.

Monday, 4th.

Still doing well—rested well last night. *Not until yesterday did I learn that Genl. Scott had made application about the 19th or 21st of last November, for me to be appointed Asst. Adjt. Genl. with the rank of Major, to enable him to select me as Chief of his Staff;* my name was sent in with two others, Capts. De Hart and Vinton. As if to show him that his desires and rights should both be disregarded, neither was appointed, and thus has the Genl. had thrown upon himself a vast quantity of labor which would have been confided to an experienced Staff Officer. Never before was a Genl. commanding an Army on the Field, he the highest Officer of the Army, refused, in any other service, the right of selection of his Chief of Staff. 'T is too contemptible. If the people of the United States do not see through, and visit with just indignation, the conduct pursued by the War Dept. towards Genl. S. ever since he left the United States, they are not fit to be ruled by, or to have honest men in office.

No news to-day from any point. Col. Hitchcock did me the honor to read to me last night, requesting my suggestion of any alteration that might occur to me, a proposed introduction to a number of letters, written in this City the night of the 20th Aug., and giving their comments on the operations of that day. The Colonel's introduction is, like everything from his pen, well written. If he decides upon its publication, I shall take care of a copy for *home.*

Genls. P. and W. have given the Genl. infinite distress, by inaccuracies in their reports, assuming to themselves the giving of Orders and the execution of Movements upon the field of battle, distinctly directed by the Genl. The selfish vanity of some men leads their memory entirely astray; vanity and ingratitude together have destroyed high merits in others. Good-evening.

Wednesday, 6th.

Genl. S. gave me a duty to execute last afternoon, which prevented my continuing my letter. I am to-day doing well. This morning Lt. Hamilton and I walked to the Museum courtyard, where we saw the justly celebrated equestrian statue of Charles IV. It is colossal, cast in bronze by a Mexican artist, named Tolsa. I admire neither the expression of the rider, nor the form of his horse, but the perfectness of so huge a casting is wonderful and the effect is very fine. I prefer it to *our* marble Washington by Greenough.

Brantz Myer's work, which I saw for the first time to-day, presents a very fair engraving of this statue, and gives a pretty good critique on the fat Mexican horse, evidently too fat for any other than a very slow and short ride. In the beauty and variety of the wax figures of the City, so highly praised by foreigners, I am thus far, much disappointed. At Puebla I could have formed a better and more interesting collection. But when, or how I am to get them home, are questions which, not being able to answer as yet, keep me from making such purchases.

Last night, for appearance' sake, being in a parlor through which Mr. Trist and his visitors have to pass, I indulged in sheets, with which I have just provided myself. The declaration will appear strange, but 't is true; so long have I been accustomed to our common

In Mexico

camp bed covering, that it was a sacrifice of comfort to appearance. We know nothing certain about Santa Anna. He will probably, if he has not already done so, leave Col. Childs and go towards the Coast; if so, you will hear of him before we do. The Mexicans who bring reports are such consummate liars that if they tell the truth, 't is by mistake.

Night before last, we were visited by another earthquake, indeed by two, 't is said a slight one before ten, and a tolerably severe one a quarter before twelve. I dreamt, or thought in my sleep, that there was one, but it did not awaken me.

The so much talked of rainy season is said to be nearly over; soon after the heavens brighten in the fall, the *vomito* takes its departure, and then come the Northers. I hope that the Northers will bring us heavy arrivals of troops at Vera Cruz, open the communication with the United States and give us letters.

Here the Genl. came in, and asked me to join him in a walk. I have been with him fifteen minutes and left him to finish his walk. The pressure of the cloak upon my shoulder prevents my wearing it a longer time with any comfort. I have purchased a very light sword, which I carry as a cane and as a means of defence. My old sword is too heavy for me now to use. To-morrow, a gentleman leaves this city for Puebla. He may go further; if so, I will ask a favor of him— one letter will not be much additional to his baggage. Enough for to-day.

Thursday, 7th.

The gentleman messenger has gone, I believe, but I did not succeed in sending a line. News reached the City last evening, that Santa Anna left Puebla on the morning of the 2nd on his way south; whether he looks for prey or safety, no one knows. Many of his troops had deserted at Puebla and those still pretending to stand by their colors are said to be rather rabble than soldier-like in their conduct.

To-day we hear that detachments from Vera Cruz are en route, that one is on the southern road at Orizaba. 'T is a pity that the other two (three are said to be marching up) had not united. It would be unfortunate were either detachment to meet with the slightest reverse; it would be magnified into an immense victory, and might fan the flame of military ardor which all good friends of peace and order in Mexico hope may soon be extinguished.

The condition of the Mexican officers, taken prisoners by us, is truly lamentable. Many of them, some of rank as high as Lt. Colonels, have told our officers that they were without money, and could obtain not a cent from their countrymen. They have been in many cases assisted by their enemies. Some apprehensions are entertained about the safety of the letters sent by the last express. If my letters by him *are* intercepted, I think I may despond of getting a line to you.

I hope that in your next letter you will tell me when Father proposes to take up his line of march homewards. I am half inclined to change the direction of all letters I may send after the 20th of this month, so as to place those that may reach the United States after the 10th of Nov. in the Camden Post Office. I feel anxious to hear how you have passed the summer; what a crowd of news my heart yearns for! About your kind and excellent Grandmother's health, I feel great anxiety. I can scarcely think after the severe attacks she had just prior to my last news from her, she can have survived through the summer. She is, however, blessed with a glorious constitution, and may have recovered to live many years longer.

Who will dare to read the decisions and will of God, under whose displeasure the strong man falls in a moment, whilst, at His good will, the invalid is raised to health and a happy long life? The shades of evening are rapidly darkening my paper, and as I have already written as much as I ought to, I shall close with a God bless you.

Friday, October 8th.

This day one month ago, came off the foully murderous tragedy of "El Molino del Rey," a day, an event I can never forget. Praised be God that I live to remember His mercy alone preserved me; may it prove to be for a good end! The rainy season, now that we are "revelling in the Halls," seems to have begun anew, as we have had rain daily for nearly a week. Most fortunate was it for our poor soldiers that it did not pay us daily visits whilst in march for, and operating against this City and its dependencies.

I have heard one or two newspaper slips read to-day from *home* papers. The *Sun* of New York is abusive, vulgarly abusive of Genl. S. These slips belong to an Editor of a Mexican paper. I will try and get a perusal of them. A rumor is current in the City that Genl. Santa Anna's guard of Cavalry is rapidly deserting, that he directed or had four of them shot, and that their companions mutinied, and that he narrowly escaped. Mrs. Santa Anna has gone, 't is said, to Orizaba. If the above rumor be true, the sooner his Excellency, "El bien merito," leaves the Country the better. The people have no sympathy with him, and his only dependence is the Army.

I did not mention the duty Genl. S. gave me the other day; 't is to collect and arrange all the information I can, relative to the Zodiacal or Calendrical Stone of the Ancient Mexicans. He thinks somewhat of taking it to Washington, if the Mexicans do not make peace with us.

Though my wound, the Dr. assures me, is healing very well, I recover so very slowly that I begin to fear that a long time will elapse before I can have the good use of my shoulder. A little feeling of heaviness or pain about the shoulder always indicates when the muscles have had exercise enough. I cannot but obey the warning; therefore now my adieu.

Saturday, 9th.

A captain from Santa Anna's Army reported to the Inspector Genl. of our Army, this morning, that he, Genl. S. A., went to El Piñal from Puebla, with 5000 men; that he commenced fortifying there, but, that on learning that Genl. Patterson was on his way up with 3500 men, he abandoned that position, informed the Officers that he was going to Oajaca, and offered all who desired them, passports. This man says that so many applied for them, that Santa Anna soon declined giving any; that the Army is without pay, and entirely disorganized, 700 men having deserted since they left Puebla. This Captain shewed his passport, and says that he left the Army on last Monday, 5th inst. How much of this is true time will shew. I believe no Mexican story. All these public men seem to make a virtue of lying, in all statements having any bearing upon us.

Our wounded are generally doing well. I fear that

In Mexico

we shall lose three Lieuts.: Shackelford and Daniels, 2nd Arty., and Lieut. Bacon, 6th Infy. All three are very low, and but slight hopes are entertained of their recovery. Genl. S. is still engaged upon his report of the battles of the 12th and 13th September. He was delayed by waiting for the Division Reports, and is compelled to write a lengthy report, in order to set transactions in a true light, which are misrepresented in some two of the Division Reports. The affair of the 8th, more deadly and requiring more nerve than almost any portion of the other battles, is not dwelt upon, because 't is an affair that, though reflecting high credit on the troops, if truly criticised will not do as much for the Milty. reputation of a certain Commander and some of his Staff. That Commander is not Genl. Scott. We hear nothing from Queretaro, the seat of the nominal Mexican Govt. Enough. Good-evening.

Monday, 11th.

Report says to-day, that over three thousand American soldiers have arrived at Puebla, and that the Mexican troops abandoned, thereupon, that City. I presume that they (our troops) will not come any farther, as there are now as many troops here as will be necessary; the Army that has *won*, can surely *keep* the City. I am delighted to hear of the approach of reenforcements, as I look to them for letters, and also as being the means of, ere long, opening, and keeping open, the road to Vera Cruz. With the troops *en route* may be expected some Officers who have been on the recruiting service. Many of the wounded have hoped to be ordered home in their places. I fear that most of them will be disappointed, as from an expression used by the Genl. a day or two since, I think he will send very few, if any, home.

I read to-day, with infinite disgust, Genl. Worth's report of the battle of Molino del Rey; he mingles, in a single paragraph, the names of Officers who distinguished themselves greatly by gallantry and zeal, and those who were not remarked for more than an ordinary discharge of their duty. In the *3rd* he mentions every Officer on the field but one, and to my knowledge, he deserved to be named *equally* as much as two who were. He makes Lt. Col. Duncan his hero; the Division do not, in this case, confirm his decree—not that Duncan was not brave, but, as he had charge of the Arty., we know that a longer continuance of its fires that morning, before the advance of the Infy., would have saved many valuable lives.

Our force on the 8th including everybody engaged, was 3251 against a Mexican force Genl. Worth reports at 14,000. We lost, *killed* 116, including 9 Officers; *wounded* 665 (49 Officers included); *missing* 18, total of losses 799!! being very near *one* man out of every *four*. May I not call that a murderous affair? On the 19th and 20th Aug. our force engaged was 8497, of whom 137 (14 officers included) were *killed;* 877 (62 officers included) *wounded,* and 38 were *missing;* a total of 1052. On the 12, 13, and 14th September 7180 were engaged: *killed* 130 (including 10 officers), and *wounded* 703 (68 officers included), and *missing* 29: making a *total of 862.* Grand total in killed, wounded, and missing since we reached this basin 2713!!

Tuesday, October 12th.

On looking at an old chart (1762) of the coast, from Pensacola, East and West, for many miles, I find some remarkable differences in the spelling of several of the places, etc., showing how much we have modernized the original names: San Miguel de Panzacola, Movila, Pascagula, B. S. Luis, Pontchartvin, La Baliza, Misissippi—the latter may have been spelt incorrectly on the chart.

Yesterday's report about the arrival of troops at or very near Puebla is believed here. A member of the Mexican Congress, now on his way to Queretaro, says that he wants us to annihilate their Army, that this being done, the friends of *good government* will be able to establish and maintain that great desideratum. If they cannot keep the Army down now they may as well abandon all idea of Republican Government. I am too much fatigued to write more. Adieu.

Saturday, October 16th.

As the Spy Company goes down this evening with despatches, I thought of sending this letter by it, but am in doubt, even as I write, whether to do so or not. As this one has no special news, but embraces a great portion of the time since I was wounded, I think I will trust it. The Genl. sends a copy of his reports by this express—he sent another 4 days ago. I find that, though Col. Garland and Capt. Burke mention my conduct on the 8th Sept. in terms very complimentary, and too flattering, my friend Col. Belton does not name me in his report. I know the man *too well*, and he thinks by his petty malice he can punish me for it. Thank God, the testimony of a good conscience and the approbation of my brother officers, witness to my bearing, more than make amends for his silence.

My arm is improving slowly in strength. I hope

that in a week or ten days I will be well enough to return to duty. Lts. Shackelford, 2nd Arty., and Bacon, 6th Infy., with Asst. Surgeon Roberts (of Georgia) were buried two mornings since. Lt. Daniels, 2nd Arty., is very much reduced, but hopes are entertained for his recovery. I am now wearing an old mixed cotton coat I purchased at Tampico. My uniform presses too heavily on my shoulder; I found, much to my delight on the 13th inst., that I could wear this coat; up to that time I had worn my dressing-gown. I have not seen Major Wade for several days, but hear that he is doing well. Col. Burnett, N. Y. Regt., came to see Genl. Scott to-day. His case is a most wonderful one; shot through the leg, he had the *lockjaw* for nearly three weeks.

I may as well say a word or two about this great City, in the appearance of which I have been greatly disappointed. Its Cathedral, market, and the general effect of the appearance of the houses as you pass through the streets, all compare unfavorably with their similars in the "City of the Angels." Perhaps, as I am still too much of an invalid to walk much about the City, I should not express an opinion till I see the whole of it. I will give another opinion without hesitation, adverse to this, if I am hereafter better pleased with the City than I am now.

We know not whether Duncan is with the troops said to have reached Puebla, or not. They will probably remain there, as we have as many here as we want.

That our Heavenly Father will ever continue to guard and guide you is the earnest prayer of your own husband, and with all His blessings, I hope He will soon enable us to thank Him for restoring me to my beloved family.

MEXICO CITY LOOKING SOUTHWEST FROM THE CATHEDRAL

In Mexico

No. 21. MEXICO, October 14th.

Casa del El Señor Loreti Vivanca de Moran, Calle Espirito Santo. Such I find to be the title of the owner of the house in which I now write. Spanish and Mexican houses have been so frequently described, indeed you may see some of their style of building in New Orleans, that I shall say but a few words about this. It has two courts; steps leading a few feet from the wall to your right, lead you by an entresol, reserved for the servants, to the second or upper story where the rooms for the family are; directly in front as you reach the last step, you see the door of a little antechamber, which you approach through an open balcony, having on your right a double row of geraniums, roses, lilies, hydrangias, violets, etc., in large and handsome painted earthen pots, the upper row projecting above the top of the iron railing of the balcony. On your left, the wall is covered with canvas, handsomely painted to represent niches, containing vases filled with beautiful flowers, having in the background views of country and city. The antechamber, has on your left a neat bookcase, of inlaid wood, and in different places around the wall you find a half dozen cases of glass filled with birds (prepared) of Mexico.

Passing through this room you enter, through a double glass door, the parlor, a room about 36 by 16 feet; the walls and ceilings are very tastefully painted. In front of you stands against the wall a long mirror with gilded frame, on your left is a long piano. The walls are hung with handsome French engravings; from the centre of the ceiling hangs a huge bronze chandelier, and of course a French clock is to be found on a side stand.

But if you are fatigued, I advise you to be seated

upon one of the three luxuriant straw-colored sofas with blue silk stripes, now as well as the room full of chairs so carefully covered with their linen *chemises*. Two large double glass doors lead on to the little platform which runs the length of this room with its iron balustrade, and enables you to have a view of this City of immense wealth, and indescribable misery and poverty.

A door in the middle of the right hand wall (as you enter) leads into the Genl.'s bedroom, which, as it has no Mexican furniture in it except chairs, tables, and a glass doored armoire, I will not describe. This room has two doors, one in the same wall as the door through which you enter, and to your right leads into an exceedingly comfortable room for bathing, washing, etc. The door near this one and on its left, leads into Mr. Trist's room, next to which is the room I occupy, which I must try to draw.[1]

Friday, 15th.

I was called off to join the Genl. in a walk and finished my house talk to-day. I thought after commencing that I would describe with greater minuteness than I at first deemed necessary; it has so many conveniences, that I may say more at some other time—closing now, as it is about our time for walking, by saying that all the walls of the rooms are covered with canvas painted very neatly above and below, and that all the sofas and chairs in my room have on their covers of brown linen. I omitted mentioning that the curtains, very large and full, in the parlor are beautifully and heavily worked with thread lace; they are white, and have a blue top piece, with gilded head piece. Good-evening.

[1] A sketch was enclosed in letter.

In Mexico

Sunday, October 17th.

Yesterday I wrote a little in No. 20, despatched by our robber band. I pray that that letter may reach you; it will show you that you have no cause for uneasiness, as I tell you there of my daily improvement. I have just returned from a stroll, and am so much fatigued that I shall now close. To-day I have thanked God for His preservation; may He long continue to bless us with the light of His countenance and soon restore me to you.

Monday, 18th.

I have this moment heard that a gentleman, Mr. Sandoff, starts for Vera Cruz to-morrow morning, and that he will take a few letters. I shall, therefore, hastily finish this letter. I was interrupted here by a conversation which occurred between Genl. Scott and a wounded Capt., one who has lost his right arm. The Capt. desired to know whether there was a chance of his being permitted to leave the Country. The Genl. laid down the principle he intends pursuing, without deviation, he says, for friend or foe—*viz.:* to permit no Officer to leave the Army unless an Army Surgeon (in whom he has confidence) shall certify that the Officer will not be fit for service for three months. This decision is, though, entirely proper, as we have very few Officers present with the Companies.

God grant that ere very long something may bring us to a peace. But this hope is almost entirely removed by what was told Genl. S. a few days since, by a member of Congress (the second one who advanced this opinion) that there was a very respectable party in this Country opposed to our leaving this Country. They fear, that as soon as we leave their unfortunate

Country, the Military will again usurp all authority and curse them, as hitherto, with their arbitrary and unjust acts. Now although this is very flattering to us, as Soldiers and Christians, still it presents a gloomy picture of the future to us.

When will the friends of good order and civil government feel themselves sufficiently strong to walk without our sustaining help in the cause of self-government? Not until the yeomanry—the voters—are sufficiently educated and informed to understand and practise their rights, and so debased are they that it must take years—many long years—before this result, so necessary and desirable, can be effected. The *home question* then bears upon the soul—are we to be kept here as guardians of a people who acknowledge themselves incompetent of self-government?

Genl. Scott, you will see, has submitted to the consideration of the Govt. three propositions, one of which he thinks the Govt. must adopt. As you will soon see this in print, I will now merely state that two of the plans keep us in the Country till Mexico sues for peace, and that the third places our Army on the line of boundary selected by our Govt.

The man who took down two letters for you last month has returned, and I thus know that they reached Vera Cruz in safety. You may know how delighted I am at this; I think, as the gentleman who takes this is a Mexican, with whom our people will not have any questioning, other than perhaps to see his passport (rather *safe guard* from Genl. S.), that this will soon reach you. News from below informs us that a large mail must be at Puebla. When we shall get our letters here is exceedingly doubtful, as Genl. Scott says nothing about sending down for it. What would I not give for your letters; not a line from you of a later date than the 24th June. And how many things have occurred since, of which you regularly informed me.

Indeed, indeed, my wife, though I write no more about resigning—if I can get out of this Country, I cannot return to the Army whilst this administration holds the reins of power. The news of every appointment shows us their prosecution of a plan to insult and break down the spirits of our Regular Army Officers, many of whom have applied for promotion in new regiments and their respectful requests have been scornfully treated with silent contempt. Thank God my pride has not received THAT blow from them! The troops now en route have been ordered to garrison some new posts intermediate between this place and Vera Cruz. Genl. Patterson is permitted to select Puebla as his Hd. Qrs., but many think as the command there will not be equal to his rank, that he prefers to come to this place.

The papers received by the Br. Consul show that you have heard of our entrance into the City. But I fear that you have not heard of my lucky escape and that your fears represented things in the worst light. You have by this time received assurances under my own hand, which must have set your heart at rest. How signally, how kindly have I been guarded; let us never forget to thank God, day and night, for His constant protection of our little flock. My heart, my confidence in Him, whispers to me that your letters, so long and ardently expected and hoped for, will show that His care has been for you.

I have been scribbling as hurriedly as possible ever since this letter (I mean to-day's portion) was commenced, as the young gentleman who volunteered to have it taken went hurriedly off to ascertain when the letters must be sent and I have been momentarily expecting his return. I hope that he may not have become so much interested in a dinner party as to make him forget my poor letter. It would be almost an unpardonable offence. I must now close, however, as it is the General's walking time, and the shades of evening, now setting in, show that I have but a few minutes more of daylight; the twilight is here, so near the equator, very short. May God continue to guard you and keep our hearts filled with religious thankfulness and gratitude for all His mercies and goodness to us.

No. 22. Espiritu Santo, Mexico,
Wednesday, October 20, 1847.

No. 21 was hurriedly finished and despatched yesterday morning by Mr. Linder, a gentleman, friend of one of the young gentlemen of the General's Staff, who went down in company with the Br. Minister. That letter is, I suppose, certain of reaching Vera Cruz safely, and I hope that my wife will soon receive it. I almost regret not having directed it to Jeffersonton, as a long passage would, perhaps, place it there about the time of your return. Here there seems to be no other change in season than what is produced by the rain.

I stepped this morning into the house just left by the Br. Minister to see how his articles sold at auction. I find the people here as big fools as they are with us, paying more for things than they could buy them for in stores. I thought of buying two little pieces of plate, but they soon jumped over my limit. Most of the purchasers were foreigners, English and French.

In Mexico

No news to-day from the seat of Govt. Santa Anna has, finding he could gain no laurels on the road, started on his return to the seat of Genl. Govt. and issued an edict, *pronouncing* against Peña y Peña on whom his resignation threw the robes of office, and reassuming the office of President. This is certainly the most inconsistent and servile people in the world; they allow that man to play upon them as he pleases.

Until they feel more of the spirit of freedom, and even of manhood, than they do now, they are only fit to be governed by tyrants. I very much fear that the impossibility of forming and maintaining a good, stable Govt. will keep us here for an indefinite time. I however never allow myself to despair, as I have ever found things finally (and frequently sooner than I had hoped) to be as I hoped and desired. Poor Capt. McKenzie, 2nd Arty., was buried this afternoon; he had an attack of the pleurisy, I think, and persisted in doctoring himself.

Friday, October 22nd.

Genl. Scott last night decided that a train of wagons were to go to Vera Cruz, leaving this place in five or six days. Oh, that I could go with it—but under the circumstances in which we are here, that would, I suppose, be entirely out of the question. It would be unkind in me to make an application after the strong manner in which the Genl. has laid down his principles relative to Officers leaving the Country.

To-day I have been out with Derr, trying to make up a little box. I have purchased several trifles which I thought might amuse you, but I could have pleased myself much better at Puebla. I hope to find something for you, but at present, in consequence of the long continuance of our War and blockade, their stock of foreign goods is very much reduced, and of domestic articles the Mexicans produce none of any value. Derr is a most honest and warmly attached man. His wound is, I am glad to say, entirely well.

Many of the cases of Officers, whose limbs have been amputated, have not taken so favorable a turn within a few days as their previous condition warranted us in hoping for. I scribble away, but my heart is in my mouth. I can think of nothing but the train that is going down and of the hearts that will be gladdened by the return of friends and relatives, in some cases husbands and fathers. My time may come sooner than I dare *hope*. God grant it. But I almost despair.

Some one will go whom you will see and they will tell you all about me. Do not despond, my wife. We shall, I hope, soon meet again, never more to be separated; I am "tired of War's Alarms," and disgusted the more and more perfectly as I hear of the appointments made at Washington over us. The Army will soon not be, it hardly is now, a place for gentlemen. Enough for to-day. *Bonsoir*.

Sunday, October 24th.

Can it be that *I* shall be the bearer of this letter? I will not even yet indulge the delightful thought. Lt. Lay told me this morning that Genl. Scott had directed his Acting Adjt. Genl. to order me to the United States. *I have not applied.* The Genl. has, in his many conversations with me, spoken so warmly about everybody's wanting to go home, that I made up my mind to remain here. Dr. Steiner told me yesterday morning, in the presence of Lt. Hamilton, that I ought to go to the United States; that it would be much longer than three months before my arm would be well, and that I would not be fit for duty. Lt. H. mentioned this conversation to the Genl. who told Lt. H. to say to me that if I wished it, I should go. This morning Dr. Steiner told me that he would give me a certificate, that I would not be fit for duty in three months. But I have not even hinted to the Genl. that I desired to go, except in general remarks before the publication of his order. I am therefore rejoiced that, if I go, it will be from no application of my own.

A strange incident has just occurred. The Genl. had just taken his seat in his bedroom on returning from church, when a Mexican entered it with a confused air, and asked in French and in a loud tone if he was Genl. Scott. The Genl. immediately sprang up, approached him, and asked him in a bold tone how he dared enter his bedroom. The man became intimidated and the Genl. ordered him out. It appears from his questionings of the guard below, that he was seeking Genl. Smith, who struck one of his companions for rudely, and in a blackguard's manner, blocking the sidewalk as the Genl. and his friends went to, or returned from church, this afternoon.

But am I so soon to see my own beloved? God grant that this so great happiness may be in store for me. I will indulge a little in the hope. Good-day.

No. 22. Mexico, October 27, 1847.

Dearest Wife,

Words cannot express the gratitude to God I enjoy in saying to you that to-morrow I leave Mexico to rejoin you. This little note will be sent by the Br. Courier, and though he leaves a day after we do, he will reach Vera Cruz a week or ten days before us. A large train of wagons go down, and our march will necessarily be slow. Major Wade and Lt. Welsh also leave this Country. Genl. Scott most kindly ordered me out without my making an application. He wishes me to commence duties on the recruiting service as soon as I am sufficiently well to do so. You must not expect me until about the 20th of November, as I may be detained some days in Vera Cruz, and then have a tedious passage to New Orleans. Remember the tedious trip I made from Tampa Bay to Tampico.

I was anxious to take Derr with me, but fear that I will not be permitted to do so. He had set his heart on it, but he has so far recovered that he cannot go out with the invalids. My arm, or rather my shoulder, is still very stiff and unmanageable, but a little home nursing with quiet will, by the blessing of God, bring everything right again. The newspapers will, I think it quite probable, announce our coming, as two Generals go out—Generals Quitman and Shields—and other friends will certainly herald their approach. They are both brave and honorable men. Genl. Pillow's inordinate vanity has so inflated him as to disgust everybody. I must not omit mention of your old friends—Lts. Judd and Thomas (the smaller) go to Vera Cruz on their way to join Genl. Taylor's Army, as the Compy. to which they belong is there. Lt. Brown remains here—he is very well and deservedly a favorite with all who know him.

October 28th.

The Express of the Br. Minister is now in Mr. Trist's room, having come for the letters. I must therefore close. The roads are so muddy that we cannot leave

for two or three days. That God may bless you, is the earnest prayer of your own devoted
ROBERT ANDERSON.

CITY OF MEXICO,
October 24, 1847.

I certify on honor, that Captain Robert Anderson of the 3rd Artillery has been under my professional charge for the last month, from a gun-shot wound in the right shoulder, received at the battle of Molino del Rey, and that, in my opinion, he will not recover the use of his right arm (it being now completely disabled) for at least two or three months to come.

(signed) H. H. STEINER,
Asst. Surgeon, U. S. A.